GONE *for a* SOJER BOY

GONE *for a* SOJER BOY

The revealing Letters and Diaries of Union Soldiers in the Civil War as they endure the Siege of Charleston S.C., the Virginia Campaigns of Petersburg and Richmond, and Captivity in Andersonville Prison

NEAL E. WIXSON, EDITOR

iUniverse, Inc.
Bloomington

Gone for a Sojer Boy
The revealing Letters and Diaries of Union Soldiers in the Civil War as they endure the Siege of Charleston S.C., the Virginia Campaigns of Petersburg and Richmond, and Captivity in Andersonville Prison

Cover photograph courtesy of the Buffalo and Erie County Historical Society, Buffalo, New York

iUniverse books may be ordered through booksellers or by contacting:

iUniverse
1663 Liberty Drive
Bloomington, IN 47403
www.iuniverse.com
1-800-Authors (1-800-288-4677)

ISBN: 978-1-4502-6773-1 (sc)
ISBN: 978-1-4502-6774-8 (ebk)

Printed in the United States of America

iUniverse rev. date: 12/06/2010

Table of Contents

MAPS

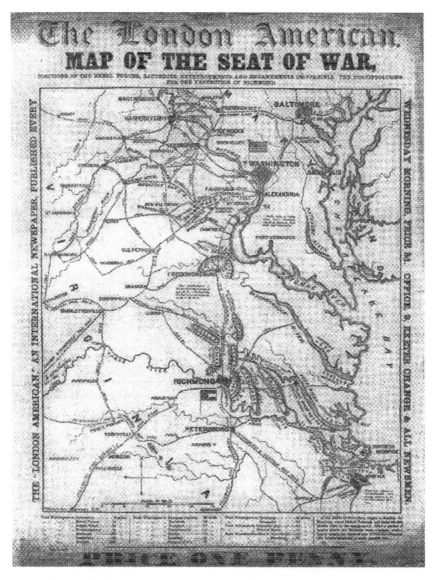

Map of the Seat of War, Waters & Son, The London American, 1861

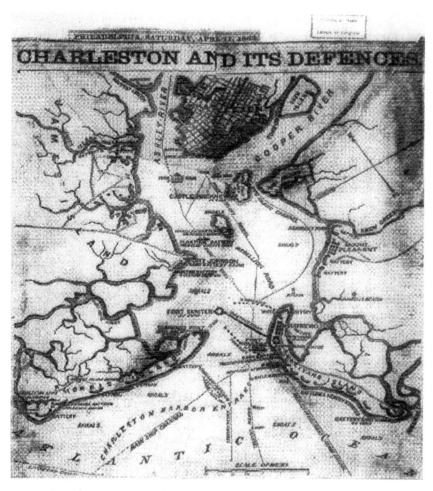

Charleston and its Defenses, Philadelphia Inquirer, April 11, 1863

EDWARD COOK LETTER DATED JULY 19, 1863

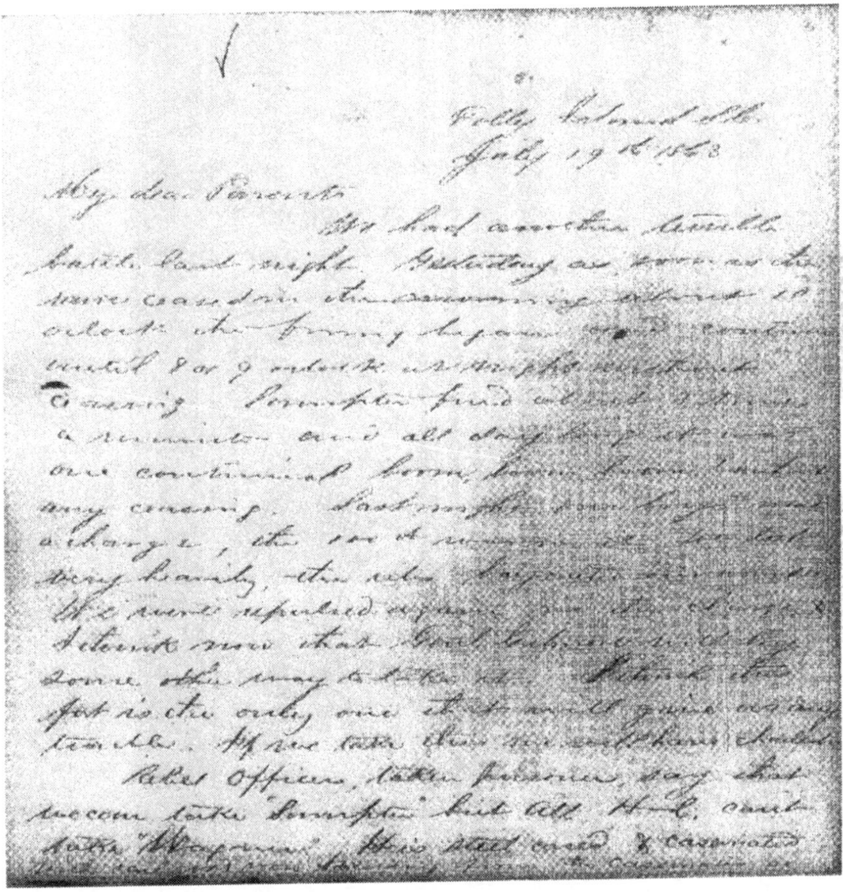
Folly Island S.C.
July 19th 1863

My dear Parents

We had another terrible battle last night. Yesterday as soon as the [illegible] the morning at about 10 o'clock the firing began and continued until 8 or 9 o'clock at night without ceasing. Sumpter fired about 3 times a minute and all day long it was one continual boom, boom, boom without any ceasing. Last night our troops made a charge, the [illegible] were cut very heavily, the [illegible]. We were repulsed again in the charge & I think now that Genl [illegible] will try some other way to take it. I think this fort is the only one that will give us any trouble. If we take this we will have Charleston.

Rebel Officers taken prisoners say that we can take "Sumpter" but all H—l can't take "Wagner". It is [illegible] & casemated [illegible] that it is perfectly Bomb proof.

I think we will take within a fortnight
our hold is terrible. One regiment lost all
their field officers all the line officers
but five. Our Major was wounded,
Cols. Strong & Seymour were
wounded. What do the people north think
of the attack on Charleston? do they expect
it? I have not heard direct from
the 100th but if I hear anything about
Lees. Clark I will write you.

I am in great haste. I never worked
so hard in my life as I am doing now
and have done for the last month or
more. I do not want anything but
but you. News is very scarce
a dollar was offered today for a single
coppies of the N.Y. Herald & the it
and even then those that had them would
not sell. They sell in camp for 25 cents
and here 2 dollars would hardly buy one.

Sam will write to me soon. I send all the
news. his stand and as well liked by his quartermaster
The buffalo told me yesterday it is he was going to
their George and pay him 25 or 30 cents street pay
Your affectionate Edward

X

PICTURES

PREFACE

⁓

During the Civil War, my great-grandfather Thomas Maharg served in Company H of the 100th Regiment of the New York State Volunteers. His Civil War souvenirs started me on a quest to learn more about his service and, in turn, him as a person. It was an odyssey that stretched over five years of extensive research, reviewing letters, diaries, and notes housed anywhere from California to New York State. He was a so-called common soldier, but along with his comrades, he had an uncommon experience that lasted over three years.

The culmination of this search led to my book *Echoes from the Boys of Company H*. It focuses on the lives of a few soldiers in Company H of the 100th Regiment, New York State Volunteers. It traces these men from enlistment to death and relates their experiences as soldiers in camp, battle, and prison. It is a story about young men who evolve from idealistic, adventure-seeking individuals into seasoned soldiers. Eventually they become heroes who after the war continue the camaraderie established through shared times serving the Union.

The primary "echoes" were from the letters of Edward Cook and Alfred Lyth. Edward Cook was born in Buffalo, New York, in 1839. After he enlisted, he served as a clerk in the Quartermasters Department from February, 1863, to December, 1864, and was promoted to first lieutenant and then to captain in February, 1865, before he mustered out. Alfred Lyth was born in York, England, in 1844. He enlisted in August, 1862. He contracted typhoid fever in July, 1863, and was hospitalized until December of that year. After his return to his company, he was captured in May, 1864, and imprisoned in Andersonville until December of 1864. He remained in Camp Parole in Maryland until he later rejoined his company in Richmond, Virginia, before being mustered out.

Other "echoes" are from the letters, diaries, or journals of Thomas Maharg, George Barnum, and Edwin Nichols. Thomas Maharg was born in Buffalo, New York, in 1842 and enlisted into service as a private at nineteen. He was promoted to commissary sergeant in January, 1865, before being mustered out. A letter is included from his brother John advising him of the death of their father; however, George Barnum had already told Thomas of this sad loss. George Barnum was born in Buffalo, New York, in 1843. He enlisted as a private and was rapidly promoted to sergeant in 1863, second lieutenant in February, 1864, and first lieutenant in May, 1864. Edwin Nichols enlisted as a private, was promoted to sergeant in July, 1863, and to captain in December, 1864.

The book is based on unpublished letters, diaries, and notes written by these young soldiers. Through these sources, they are able to tell their own stories. They comment on everything from camp life and games, food, medical and dental care, women, religion, and politics to marches, dress drills, and fighting. Their initial exciting "expedition" and camp life turn into the horrors of adapting to battles, executions, and lost comrades. The soldiers eventually seem to be more and more unmoved by disease, hunger, death, and tragedy and relate these events almost with the objectivity of a reporter. Though written by different authors, the letters illustrate little disparity in relating common experiences. They reflect upon the observations of a limited number of comrades of essentially the same events. These events are reported differently only in the sense of the individual writer's personal interest and assessment of their importance to their reader. The letters offer a unique window into each author's mind and character. In a way, they silently express the isolation and loneliness that each man feels.

As I wrote *Echoes* I began to explore the attitudinal changes that these "common" soldiers experienced during their service. Imagine leaving Buffalo for the first time, exploring New York City, Philadelphia, and Washington, D.C., and then arriving on "secession soil." They only had heard about the South and slaves through books and minstrel shows. It must have been like entering a foreign country. These young men had never been away from home, and their writing skills, though taught in normal school, had not been fully utilized. Their perspectives of death, religion, and politics had been developed in the Victorian culture and in the home. Hence, once again using their letters and diaries, I have authored this new book to explore these changes that came about in the "boys" during the course of the Civil War. *Gone for a Sojer Boy* reviews the camp life of these soldiers and their battles as well as the evolution of their thoughts about important aspects of a soldier's life: namely, death, politics, and religion. I also have included a section devoted to Alfred Lyth's experiences at Andersonville Prison, Georgia, which presented him with new and life changing challenges. The title, *Gone for a Sojer Boy*, is based upon references to the song "Johnny Gone for a Soldier" contained in Edward Cook's letter to his father dated November 4, 1862, and his letter to his parents and relatives dated March 9, 1863.

The letter and diaries are only minimally edited so that their content and character remain intact. Some words that are offensive by today's standards remain in the transcribed letters. Writing style are varied with Alfred Lyth's long, run-on sentences punctuated only by commas being the most difficult to read.

The letters and diaries were probably written with quill pens which increasingly smudge as the nib of the quill wears down. Every quarter, the soldiers were able to acquire twelve new quills and ink from the army as part of their stationery ration. This would not be a huge supply for a prolific letter writer. Thus, some words in the original letters are totally illegible for transcription.

I am extremely grateful to the following for their assistance and support so readily given as well as access to their collections and permission to use materials where appropriate: The Library of Congress: Geography and Map Division, the Manuscript Division, and the Photography Division; Cynthia Conides, former Executive Director, and Cynthia Van Ness, Director of Archives and Library, both of the Buffalo and Erie County Historical Society, Buffalo, New York; and the Buffalo and Erie County Public Library, Buffalo, New York. Most especially, gratitude is expressed to Edward C. Fields, Supervisor, Information Services, Department of Special Collections, Davidson Library, University of California, Santa Barbara, California, for permitting access to Edward Cook's wonderful letters which can now be shared with the world.

Words cannot adequately express my appreciation to my mentor Jeff Toalson who is a noted author of Civil War books. He responded with interest to my many questions about my projects and gave me words of encouragement. David Barnum provided the personal notes about his great-grandfather George Barnum. John Lyth has contacted me and expressed his deep appreciation for uncovering the letters and journals of his great-grandfather Alfred Lyth. Both men share a strong bond with me as great-grandsons of three of the "boys" of Company H. They, too, are fellow perpetual members of the 100th Regiment Veterans Association.

Special recognition and appreciation is also given to my daughter, Lindsey P. Wixson, who labored tirelessly for over two years transcribing copies of the original letters of Edward Cook and Alfred Lyth and to my wife, Donna R. Wixson, who read those transcribed copies in minute detail and gave me many suggestions for improvement to the book.

I thank the families who had the foresight to preserve the letters, diaries, and records of these soldiers by donating them to the historical societies and libraries where they remain. Their eloquent words have truly brought me a new depth of understanding of my great-grandfather that had been missing in earlier years as well as a powerful sense of gratitude for the sacrifices made by all who fought during the Civil War.

LEADING LETTER AND DIARY WRITERS

George Barnum was born in 1840 and was 20 when he enlisted in the 100th Regiment, Company H. His father, George, was a grocer born in Connecticut and living in Buffalo, New York, when George enlisted. The elder George and his wife, Ellen, had five children:

George, age 18, clerk
Kate, age 15
Alexander, age, 13
Margaret, age 9
Alice, age 7

George Clark was born in 1836 and was 24 when he enlisted in the 100th Regiment, Company H. In the 1860 census, he was shown to be living with the Newton Stoddard family. Amongst the Stoddard family's three children, George Stoddard also enlisted in the 100th Regiment, Company H. They were occasionally referred to as the "two Georges" in some of the letters.

Edward Cook was born in 1839 and was 22 when he enlisted in the 100th Regiment, Company H. His father, Lyman, was a carpenter born in England and living in Buffalo, New York, when Edward enlisted. Lyman and his wife, Mary, had four children:

At the time of the 1860 census, the children included:

> Edward, 21, bookkeeper
> Mary, 19
> Elizabeth (Eliza), 17
> Lora (Laura, Lillie, Lucy, Lilie), 13

Alfred Lyth was born in 1844 in England and was 18 when he enlisted in the 100th Regiment, Company H. His father, John, was a potter born in England and living in Buffalo, New York, when Alfred enlisted. John and his wife, Mary, had five children.

At the time of the 1860 Census, the children included:

> Alfred, age 16
> Francis, age 3
> John, age 14
> Mary, age 12
> William, age 9

Thomas Maharg was born in 1842 and was 19 when he enlisted in the 100th Regiment. His father, John, was a drayman born in Ireland and living in Buffalo, New York, when Thomas enlisted. John and his wife, Sara, had six children.

At the time of the 1860 census, the children included:

> Thomas, age 16
> Nancy, age 19

John, age 17
Mary, age 14
Charles, age 8
Frank, age 6

Edward Nichols was an orphan born in England. He enlisted in the 100th Regiment, Company H in 1862. He does not show up in the 1860 Census as living in Buffalo, New York.

INTRODUCTION

In 1861, Edward Cook, Alfred Lyth, and Thomas Maharg had just graduated from normal school and had started their new jobs. They got together with their friends, the "boys," to talk about the war and the events swirling around them.

In school, they had learned about the economic and social differences between the North and the South. For the most part, the South was an agrarian economy dependent upon cheap labor, namely slavery, which was based upon the plantation system, an antiquated social order of stratified wealth. The northern economy was established more upon an industrial, urban model which welcomed people of different cultures and classes to work together to produce goods.

Likewise, the "boys" had studied the Constitution and states rights' issues as to whether states could vote to accept or not accept a federal act. The fight between slave and non-slave state proponents raged, and with the eminent expansion of the country and ultimate admittance of new states to the Union, the balance was a pressing issue. The abolitionist movement continued to grow, and the slavery issue was being discussed in newspapers, books, and plays. The election of Lincoln and the belief that he was anti-slavery and in favor of northern interests forced several states at that point to secede from the Union.

The "boys" were more fully made aware of many of these issues through the development of communication vehicles. Increasingly mass circulations of newspapers, both national and local, began in the 1850s. They provided much more information about events on a timely basis and were eagerly read. In the late 1850s, the North's *Frank Leslie's Illustrated* newspaper and *Harper's Weekly* as well as the South's *Southern Illustrated News* were introduced, and their circulation significantly increased.

American culture was vibrant, and entertainment venues flourished. P.T. Barnum embodied the essence of showmanship and achieved fame and fortune with his museum of oddities in New York City. Pseudoscience was popular as well. Phrenology linked one's character to the shape of and bumps on a person's skull. Stage entertainment also thrived, and a night at the theater included a play, musical interludes, magic tricks, or pantomime. Melodramas were popular as well as oratory with its speeches, poetry readings, and lectures.

The minstrel show entertained the audience with comedy, music, dance, and novelty acts. Stephen Foster songs were very popular. The image of the South as the "land of cotton" was established through the song "Dixie" written by Daniel D. Emmett. Blackface humor presented blacks in a denigrating manner, and actors portraying blacks wore makeup and spoke in dialects.

Prior to 1860, popular writers created the South's image as one of aristocratic planters, beautiful southern belles, poor white trash, and faithful slaves. However, some authors of the day began to write from a different perspective. Initially serialized in the newspaper, Harriett Beecher Stowe's *Uncle Tom's Cabin*, a novel, portrayed the evils of slavery and attempted to shatter the myth that slavery was a benevolent, paternalistic institution. It drew critics from both the pro-slavery and abolitionist camps. The story found its way into stage productions which spread across the country, most notably in minstrel shows that incorporated the characters and themes into their shows. Her book sold more copies than any other preceding American piece of literature and became a lightning rod for social and political commentary. Stowe also created a version of her novel for dramatic readings. In 1856, she then wrote *Dred: A Tale of the Treat Dismal Swamp*. She used this book to attempt to silence her critics and strengthen her anti-slavery position. She advocated emancipation of and education for the blacks.

In the 1850s, America's ethnic and racial minorities also began to publish novels, poems, histories, and autobiographies. Frederick Douglas, in his book *My Bondage and My Freedom*, wrote about the hardships and cruelties experienced in his life as a slave. Many Sunday sermons began to focus upon the immorality of slavery.

Frederic Law Olmstead's journals provided greater detail as to the southern culture. As he toured the south, his narrative of his travels as contained in *The Cotton Kingdom* cited slavery not as a moral issue but rather as an economic one. The unequal distribution of wealth in which economic activities were concentrated at the plantation level did not produce overall good roads, bridges, strong cities, or infrastructure that benefitted the entire population. Other businesses such as banks or wholesalers of produce and goods were normally owned by a major landowner in a given county. They did not necessarily bring education and entertainment to residents in general such as would be provided by libraries, museums, and theaters. Southern towns were lacking in public institutions and public buildings since most business was transacted at the plantation level. The invention of Eli Whitney's cotton gin resulted in the elimination of the laborious and time-consuming task of extracting seeds from the cotton and increased the demand for slaves to raise short-staple cotton instead. Furthermore, Olmstead argued that growing cotton ruined the land and caused the abandonment of plantations at times in favor of moving to richer soil in new areas. He felt that managing slaves through threats and punishments resulted in slaves as well as poor, white manual laborers becoming lazy, indolent, and careless.

As the "boys" pondered these issues, they must have wondered just how a single nation could succeed with such divergent cultures. They were just boys who had been raised in Buffalo, New York, and had not ventured out of their city as of yet. They wanted to join the Union Army before the war was over. They were raised in the Victorian time when one's duty was a binding moral obligation. Patriotism and nationalism were highly important. Glory, honor, courage, and sacrifice were not abstract thoughts. Even romanticism was important in this sentimental age. There was genuine concern that their country as they knew it would change if the Union lost the war. Their northern view held that slavery had degraded southern society and destroyed democracy in the South by creating an elite class of wealthy land owners. The Confederacy had to be destroyed not only to save the Union but to preserve the foundations of the nation.

Recruitment for the 100th Volunteers had been going on since September 2, 1861. The initial companies in the regiment left the state on March 10, 1862, and sustained heavy losses in their first battle, The Seven Days Battle. Their regiment's aggregate casualty count was 176 men, and they needed volunteers to fill the ranks desperately.

An excerpt from Lt. Col. Charles Walbridge's speech at the first reunion of the new Veteran's Association following the war describes the initial service of the 100th Regiment:

"We arrived at Washington ... and were conducted to our camp ground. Tents were issued, and we were speedily instructed in the modus operandi of pitching them. Here our first tribulation with the commissary department began, for instead of bread, rations

were issued of flour, which in an uncooked state was of no earthly use to us and of coffee unburned, and ungrounded.

One evening in the latter part of March, we broke camp with the rest of our division, marched down through the city, crossed the Potomac over the 'long bridge' and arrived in the outskirts of Alexandria about ten o'clock on a clear, cold night. We were halted by the roadside, stacked arms, and dismissed, with intimation that we could make ourselves comfortable by lying around loose, anywhere in the vicinity. This is memorable because it was our first bivouac, and that, too, at a very inclement time of the year, and under peculiarly trying circumstances, many of us having neither overcoats or blankets, having indiscreetly left them to come with the baggage. We'll, we got through that night and the next, somehow, and the third day marched to the wharf and embarked with the rest of your brigade on the monster steamship *Constitution* … Arrived at Newport News, we were quickly established in camp at the peach orchard, or Camp Scott, as it was officially designated, and our campaign on the peninsula was begun.

After a few days' sojourn, we advanced to Warwick Court House, and on this march realized the burden of knapsack, overcoat, blanket, arms haversack and forty rounds of ammunition, when marching under a Southern sun, and we then, for this first time, witnessed the sight of poor fellows stopping by the roadside overcome by the heat. Opening their knapsacks and throwing their trinkets and even clothing right and left, they were willing to do anything to lighten their unaccustomed load.

We were without tents; those we had formerly used having been left with all the extra baggage. It was some days before shelter tents were received and in the meantime we made little booths, in which we weathered several severe rainstorms. Provisions were in very scant supply, owing to the great difficulty of transporting them through the deep mud and wretched roads.

. . . after [General] Magrauder had delayed us for a whole month, when at last our big siege guns were mounted and all preparations were made to assault his line, he took 'French leave' one night, and in the morning the fortifications in front of us were evacuated. We were quickly in pursuit but by some blunder which I never heard explained, our regiment, and I believe our whole division, marched without overcoats, blankets or knapsacks, and with only one day's rations. We supposed we were sent out for a reconnaissance, and that we would return to camp at night just as we had from similar expeditions before. This careless blunder on the part of some cost an immense and needless amount of suffering.

The next day was the battle of Williamsburg, where the enemy under Longstreet and Magruder made a determined effort to still further delay the advance of our army. The 100th lay in the woods until late in the afternoon, although we were within distinct sound of the firing all day. There were thousands of troops like us close at hand.

It was now dusk and we were formed in line of battle and remained there till morning. The suffering of that night will ever be remembered by all who were there. We were without overcoats or blankets, had eaten no proper food all day and now as the cold night set in became chilled through and through. Not a spark of fire was allowed along the whole line; many of the men were seized with severe pains, and as they were brought by the stretcher corps and laid in a row along the edge of the woods, where the surgeons could do but little to relieve them, their groans and agony added to their discomfort and suffering of the rest of us. It was such experiences as these that soon filled the hospitals with sick and disabled soldiers, and death was already busy gathering in his harvest.

Well, the longest night has an ending, and the morning came at last. We found as we had turned the enemy's flank, he had evacuated his whole line of works, not to make another stand until the defenses of Richmond were reached. We therefore had nothing to do but to build great fires, lie down and rest in the warm sunshine, and wait for welcome rations which soon arrived. I shall always remember gratefully that lovely morning and the comfort it brought us...

All the morning they have been getting their troops into position and now their solid columns and long lines speedily emerged from the dense woods which skirted the battle field, and with screeching shells and rattle of musketry, the ball opened; This was the first general battle between the Army of the Potomac and the brave foes, the Army of Northern Virginia; neither side appreciated as yet the value of rifle pits, and we stood there squarely facing the coming storm.

Our fellows were dropping rapidly, but no attempt was made to reinforce our line, all the effort of our Commanders being to establish a second line while we held our ground in front. As they pressed us hard, with the hope of staying them yet a little longer, the order was given us to charge. This charge has always seemed to us a most desperate expedient. There was then, however, no thought of holding back, or of questioning the propriety of the order, but away we went, clambering over logs and stumps of the slashing in our front, until the fire of the enemy was so intense that no troops could breast such a storm of lead. It was in this advance and the subsequent withdrawal that we met with our heaviest losses. Soon the order came to fall back, and I can now in memory see [General] Naglee as he rode along the rear of the line, swinging his hat, and shouting "Retreat!" "Retreat!" As we passed to the rear there was no hurry, and no panic... Thus the 100th regiment received its baptism of fire. After that eventful afternoon, we felt that we were no longer green troops, but veterans.

In August the final abandonment of the peninsula was decided upon, and the 100ᵗʰ took up its line of March with the rest of the army for Fortress Monroe. The heat was intense, and we were almost choked with dust but we at least reached our goal, when, instead of embarking with the bulk of the army to go to the aid of General Pope, we were sent to Gloucester Point on the York river, directly opposite historic village of Yorktown."[1]

On July 1 1862, President Lincoln issued a call into service for an additional 300,000 men. He indicated that the new troops must be enrolled and activated without delay so as "to bring this unnecessary and injurious civil war to a speedy and satisfactory conclusion."

The "boys" school principal was putting together a company in the 100ᵗʰ Regiment and it was time for them to make a commitment. Whether this commitment arose from the spirit of patriotism or the spirit of adventure, we will never know. The "boys" then made a pact to enlist and return the next evening to report on joining the Union army.

The "boys" returned the following night, and their adventure was ready to begin. Edward Cook, Albert Lyth, Thomas Maharg, George Barnum, Edwin Nichols and others were now a part of Company H in the New York State Volunteers 100ᵗʰ Regiment. Their service in the regiment would last for over three years and include such locations of Gloucester Point, Virginia; the Coastal Carolinas; St. Helena Island, Coles Island, Morris Island, South Carolina; Petersburg, Virginia; and the areas around Richmond, Virginia.

Their feelings, reactions, values and beliefs will be poured into numerous letters to home. However, to give us a greater sense of their experiences, the songs that they sang to encourage their enlistment and encompass their beliefs as to why they were fighting are also included. Songs rallied the troops, expressed their loneliness and homesickness or just passed the time. They made marches easier and camp life tolerable. They prepared the soldiers for battle and celebrated victory. Together, the letters, diaries, and songs will give the reader a sense of their service.

PART I

CAMP LIFE

Chapter 1

We are coming, Father Abra'am, three hundred thousand

Words by James Sloan Gibbons (1862)
Music by Luther Orlando Emerson

We are coming, Father Abra'am, three hundred thousand more
From Mississippi's winding stream and from New England's shore;
We leave our plows and workshops our wives and children dear,
With hearts too full for utterance, with but a silent tear;
We dare not look behind us, but steadfastly before—

Chorus
We are coming, we are coming,
Our Union to restore;
We are coming, Father Abra'am with three hundred thousand more,
We are coming Father Abra'am with three hundred thousand more.

2.
If you look across the hill tops that meet the northern sky,
Long moving lines of rising dust your vision may descry;
And now the wind, an instant, tears the cloudy veil aside,
And floats aloft our spangled flag in glory and in pride'
And bayonets in the sunlight gleam, and bands brave music pour—

Chorus

3.
If you look all up our valleys, where the growing harvest shine,
You may see our sturdy farmer boys fast forming into line;
And children from their mother's knees are pulling at the weeds,
And learning how to reap and sow, against their country's needs;
And a farewell group stands weeping at every cottage door—

Chorus

4.
You have called us and we're coming, by Richmond's bloody tide'
To lay us down for freedom's sake, our brother's bone beside;
Or from foul treason's savage group, to wrench the murderous blade,
And in the face of foreign foes its fragments to parade;
Six hundred thousand loyal men and true have gone before—

Letter from Private E. Cook to his Parents

Albany Barracks Albany, New York Sept 18/62

Dear Parents

There is a phrenologist up on the top bunk telling a man his character it is quite laughable; you can see by my writing that I am giving more attention to what he says than I am to the letter. He is just telling a man that he would make a good mechanic particularly a tailor I was up on top of the Capitol today and wrote my name on the dome. I saw the way [weigh] lock where they weigh canal boats + had a good time generally. All the boys are in good spirits.

Letter from Private E. Cook to his Parents

Camp Elsworth, New York City Sunday Sept 21/62

Dear Parents

I speak of the beauty of Central Park but it far exceeds any description I had ever seen. It is about 4 or 6 miles from the foot of Broadway and across one hundred acres. The best way to reach it is to take the Broadway and 6th Avenue cars and they take the visitor direct to the park

Carriages are always standing at the terminus of the streetcars; and for 1 Dollar they will carry a person all over the ground. It takes about 1 hour to ride through all of the park. I cannot describe the scene as it deserves. It is nature beautified. The park is laid in a part of the city that would be almost useless for anything else; the ground is very uneven and stony and in many places the huge rocks extend several feet above the surface of the ground and the ground around the vacinity of the dirty gray rocks is so neat and arranged as to make the very rock its self appear picturesque + beautiful. The park as yet has no fence around it but it soon will have; the streets of the city run through it but they in no manner interfere with it as they are all lowered below the average level of the park. The park its self is on high ground and the street of the park run over those of the city.

You can see by this that the park does not in any way interrupt the trafic on the streets although the streets of the city run directly through the park and are crossed by the park streets. They have a beautiful artificial lake in the park which is used for rowing in summer + skating in the winter. I saw in the park a tree planted by the Prince of Wales and another planted by one of the Dukes who accompanied him; that which was planted by the prince did not flourish very well and the top was cut off so that it is now a little low English oak. The pond is alive with beautiful white swans and in the park is a very large cage full of beautiful deer. You can well imagine that the park must be large to allow of a place being partitioned off large enough to allow a quantity of deer to run in. The cage that contains them is a high wire fence painted Green and you can scarcely notice it until you get almost to it so that a little way off the deer appear to be running at large. The park also contains several other animals and a number of birds in large cages. It is one of the loveliest places I ever visited and I would advise any person that comes to New York not to leave the city until they have visited Central Park. The park contains 100 acres; there is about 6 miles of carriage way in it, and it takes about an hour to drive through it and after a person has rode through the park and found out all the places of interest, he wants to leave the carriage and start through it again on foot and spend an hour at each of the places of interest in the park. After we had been through the park we took the 6th Avenue cars and rode down to Broadway, got out of the cars and walked up broadway as far as Barnum Museum where I saw so many things that it is impossible to tell you all or even to recollect them. There were wax figures + figures not of wax; live fishes + dead fishes; animals stuffed + animals for stuffing – everything in fact that it is possible to imagine but the most pleasing thing that I saw was his happy family of animals. In one cage were contained cats + rats woodchucks, raccoons, monkeys and baboons, chickens, owls and I don't know what there was not.

Your Loving Son
E.L. Cook, Acting Sergeant
100th Regt N.Y.S.V.

Ed: In 1853, after much debate, Central Park, over 800 acres, was authorized to be acquired by eminent domain by the New York State Legislature. It contained swamps and bluffs that were undesirable for development and was envisioned to be an attractive setting for carriage rides and a respite for New Yorkers from the saloons and crowded housing in the city. Wealthy merchants and landowners had admired the public grounds in London and Paris and hoped to develop a public park of similar reputation. In 1857, Frederick Law Olmstead's and Clark Vaux's plans for landscape design were accepted. It was first opened for public use in 1859 with skating ponds, carriage drives, and walking trails. By 1865, Central Park received more than seven million visitors a year.

Letter from Private E. Cook to his Parents

Washington Barracks, Washington D.C. Sept 20/62

Well dear Parents, here we are at last in Washington ready almost to fight and will be entirely ready as soon as we get our uniforms + rifles.

Our march through the streets of Albany was a lively affair. There was a large squad ahead of us but our boys were the one that attracted all the attention. Indeed where ever we go we seem to be the favorites among the other soldiers. We marched down one of the principal street of Albany and all of the girls (I was going to say good looking girls but there are no good looking girls in Albany) came out + bid us goodby and threw us a kiss. I said goodby so many times that I was almost hoarse; threw so many kisses that my lip is sore and turned round so many times that it almost made my back ache.

[E Cook]

Ed: The community receptions were well received by the soldiers who felt that the citizens appreciated their defense of the country. The soldiers felt as if they were treated as heroes. However, as the war progressed, the sight of soldiers in the North became more commonplace, and the soldiers began to complain about the lack of respect that they received and the lack of recognition from the citizens while on furloughs home. They became increasingly aware of the social and monetary advancement of those who did not serve and remained with their families back home.

Letter from Private A. Lyth to his Folks

10am Barracks Washington DC

Dear Folks

My last letter that I wrote you was from Jersey city I cannot tell weather you received it or not as I did not post it myself we took the cars from Jersey city through to Philadelphia where we arrived about 5 oclock P.M. I shall never forget the reception the citizens of that city gave us from the depot where we landed to the Soldiers Rest which is over a mile and a half the streets where lined on both sides with young ladys welcoming us to Philadelphia the little boys would run along with us and carry our knapsacks while the ladies would grasp our hands and shake them saying welcome to Philadelphia hope we shall see you again we got our suppers at the Soldiers Rest then we fell into ranks and marched through the city to another depot the biding us goodby and shaking hands with us as before.

[A. Lyth]

"Discipline and training"

Ed: The small prewar peacetime army had mushroomed into Union and Confederate armies totaling nearly a million men now. The volunteers considered themselves civilians temporarily in uniform. Their hope was to do their duty as quickly as possible so they could return to their homes and families.

In most volunteer regiments the men elected their company officers, few of whom had combat experience. Infantry training, mainly from the manual of arms, consisted of closed-order drill with a little bayonet and target practice when time permitted. Officers saw drill as an essential means to inculcate unit cohesion and the habit of unquestioned obedience. This was easier said than done in an army of independent minded citizen volunteers who had elected many of their officers. American white males were the most individualistic, democratic people on earth. Authority, discipline and obedience were new concepts to them.

"Private George Barnum, Personal Notes"

"The Colonel of the regiment had been killed up at Fair Oaks and the regiment was in a rather disorganized condition being composed mainly of clerks and farmer boys and having officers that were not very strict.

They seemed to do pretty much as they liked through the influence of the Buffalo Board of Trade they secured the services of Colonel Dandy who was at that time the Chief quarter master on General McClellan's staff and a West Point man. Our tents were put up most anywhere and I remember the first thing the Colonel did when he arrived at the regiment was to have every tent taken down. He then laid out a regular city of ten streets and every tent in line on every street. He had the ground thoroughly policed and cleaned up.

I remember the first night we went out on dress parade. The Colonel started in at one end of the regiment. My company was in the center, the color company. Soon I noticed that a lot of men were leaving the ranks and going back to their tents and could not imagine what was the trouble. When the Colonel came along some of the men had a dress coat on, some a sack coat, some had caps and some soft hats, some had shoes and some not, some had their brasses and their equipment brightened and others not. When the appearance of a man did not satisfy him, he gave him 10 minutes to go back to his tent and come back again dressed properly."[2]

Letter from Private A. Lyth to his Brother

Gloucester Point, Va Sat Sept 27 1862

Dear Brother

I am expecting a letter from you every day as father said in his letter that you was going to write to me next so having nothing to occupy my time at present I thought I write you a few lines and hope they will find you well a it leaves me at present I have pretty good times here we do not have to drill so much now as we had at first when we came here we go down to the river and catch fish + oysters and cook them I have met a few boys that I knew in Buffalo, and they tell me a good many stories of the battles they have been into The river is a first rate place to bathe in I have been in swiming twice since I have been here I was out on picket with our company on Wednesday and I had a pretty good time we have to go on at 8 oclock in the morning and stop until 9 oclock next morning there are 3 of us stationed on a post and sometimes 4 or 5 and we take turns watching for any signs of the Rebels and if we should happen to hear or see anything unusal we wake up our companions and alarm the other posts and if it should happen to be rebels a coming we should fire our guns and run back in to the woods on to the reserve which is stationed a piece back into the woods which are all cut down and make it very difficult for anybody to pass through there only being a small foot path which one can pass through at a time then when the alarm is given the regiments turn out in line of battle and then if we should be attacked we should all march in to the fort which is a very large and strongly fortified 11 oclock night before last there was an alarm given that we were attacked by the rebels and we were all called out in line of battle and a company of volunteers deployed on to the picket line to see what the matter was and bring in the pickets but it was a false alarm some say it was a fellow saw a couple or so of mules in the pasture and though they were rebel cavelry and a good many other storys as to how it originated but however it turned out to be nothing we are at present encamped on a large common outside of the fort but we are going to have all new tents in a day or two and move inside of the fort and are likely to remain there sometime. I was very glad to here you got along very well since I left home. I have to leave my writing at present and go with my company to fire at the target.I have just got back from shooting at the target and only 9 of us hit it out of 40 of us.

Your Loving Brother
Alfred Lyth

"In the beautiful autumn weather, we soon regained health and strength; our ranks were filled with new comrades, many of whom were old schoolmates and friends from home, and therefore, doublely welcome. Under our accomplished commander, we made rapid progress in drill, and we doubtless all recall with pleasure those beautiful October days and nights on picket, on the front or along the banks of Sarah's creek. Verily those tours were more like *picnic* than picket duty. In December we made that raid to Gloucester Court House, driving out the squadron of Confederate cavalry which made that village its headquarters, and how the rebel chickens and turkeys did suffer. It was one of the very few occasions on which the 100th distinguished itself in that species of warfare." [3]

Letter from Private E. Cook to his Parents

Gloucester Point Va. Sept. 28th 1862

Dear Parents

… I mailed a letter to you from Fortress Monroe on Friday day before yesterday. I had not been returned to the boat many minutes, after going to the post office, before we received orders to proceed to Suffolk opposite Norfolk in Va and before we had time to cast off the ropes + let the boat loose another order came out as the first order and again in a few minutes came a 3d order telling us to proceed to Yorktown. This is the way that business is done in the Army; there seems to be no certainty or decision in anything relating to Army Matters. We sailed from the Fortress about 1 oclock P.M. of Friday + arrived at Yorktown about 8 o'clock P.M. of the same day. Our ride up the York river was very pleasant, the water is salt and I sat for an hour or two watching the different kinds of sea fish that we passed on our way up. There is a kind of thing here that they call the sea nettle, when it touches you it stings like a nettle and it is nothing more than a kind of thick transparent colorless jelly and yet it has life + breathes in the water. In the evening whenever the water is disturbed it is all alive with spots of light or phosphoresant fire. It looks splendid in the evening, I can tell you…From Yorktown we crossed the river to Gloucester Point, which is exactly opposite Yorktown, and remained on board the boat until morning thus making 3 nights that we were aboard of the nasty dirty lousey boat. We marched from the boat up the hill about ½ a mile + found ourselves within the lines of our regiment. You cannot guess how pleased we are to be with our regiment after being on the road so many days. We had to tent with some of the other boys last night but I suppose our tents will be here today so we can put it up by night.

We all went outside the first line yesterday after dinner and got some oysters to eat about 3 dozen raw and if we had time I might have eat dozen more. They are very cheap here at present I am going out on the river a little ways tomorrow and get some more. They are very plenty up the river about ½ a mile above our camp and all we have to do is to pull off our clothes + wade in after them. We have not had 1 unpleasant day since we left Buffalo. Some of the days are very hot + sultry but the majority are quite pleasant. The days pass by very quickly but it seems an age almost since we left Buffalo. I have not been homesick since we left Buffalo. I would not return now if I could. We have had some pretty hard fare since we left but are very comfortably situated now. On board the boat we had hard crackers + water the first day and the crackers had both bugs + maggots in them but we did not care for that as we were pretty hungry. We split open the crackers knocked the worms off + eat them with a relish. We had not slept more than one night with our clothes off and that was on board the boat down the Hudson. None of us are lousey as yet but the boys here tell us that we soon will be in spite of our selves. Yesterday I took a salt water bath for the first time in my life. I enjoyed it first rate. There are lots of salt water fish here if I only had hooks + lines to catch them with. I have sent you a letter asking for some things and I wish father would put a fishline in + 1 or 2 hooks. You might send them in a letter for that matter if you like. That cotton cloth you gave me will come in first rate for cleaning my musket, but woolen cloth is better + I don't care if you send me a few scraps of old woolen cloth with the other things.

Tuesday Sept. 30th 1862

Our tent has been pitched low and we have been sleeping on the ground heretofore but today we took it down and moved it over onto its west side of the skirt and built a bed in it so that now we have a nice shade in front of tent in the afternoon and can sleep on our bedstead without catching the cramp in our legs. The tent is pitched over a frame 2 feet high so we have just so much more room to stand up, the frame also is our bedstead. Our bedcords are staves and our bedding is made of leaves. We sleep now very nicely, indeed we find it quite as comfortable as a feather bed almost.

Our company came in about 2 oclock. All the company was inspected this morning. Their arms, knapsacks, tents, streets + everything were all carefully examined by all of the field officers. Everyone is wondering what it is. I think likely they are testing the range on guns down on the rip raps at Fortress Monroe. This evening I took a delightful bath in the river by moonlight. The moon was so bright tonight that I finished a letter by moonlight that I had commensed this afternoon to one of my girls, and did not have time to finish before dress parade. The evenings are lovely, bright and starlight every night; we have not had one unpleasant day since we started.

They have some of the strangest games here that I ever witnessed. One of them is for one man to step in the middle of a ring and cover his face in his cap and scoop down then the other boys step up one at a time, and sometimes more, and give him an awful kick in the stern part of his body; and when he guesses the name of any one that kicks him that one takes his place in the ring and the same kind of an operation is gone through with that one. It is laughable to see the sport.

Wednesday Oct. 1st 1862

This A.M. G. Stoddard + I went off on the beach of the river about a mile to collect a lot of boards to wall up the sides of our tent from the ground to the bed frame + to lay a floor in front of our bed. The tent is rather a rough looking place + would make you laugh somewhat to see it. The floor puts me in mind of the old floor that we used to have in the shed at the old house before we had the kitchen built on. We learned to day that the firing yesterday was from Newport News about 9 miles above Fortress Monroe on the James River. They were testing the guns on one of the new Gunboats. We could hear the noise distinctly as if it were only a mile from us.

Thursday Oct. 2nd 1862

Some one of our boys unintentionally leaned against the front pole of our tent this morning + misplaced it and in a few minutes our tent came tumbling down over our heads and occasioned considerable merriment among the boys. It did not take many seconds for us to put it up again. We all of us had to strip naked again this morning and be examined by the doctors since we enlisted. We have not yet received our clothing or knapsacks + Guns but expect them every day. We are going to move our camp in a day or 2 about a quarter of a mile farther up the river + extend our picket line one mile farther to the front. I guess George S. will make a good picture + send it home. Neither of us have yet heard from home but expect a letter in a day or two. Both the boys are well again now and are able to do duty. G. Clark has had the bloody Dysentery. He looks very thin + ematiated in the face but will soon pick up again. Somehow or other sickness does not seem to reduce a man as it does up north but if you are away down sick one day you are all right the next day. I should like to stay here a long time. If you want any machine needles to sew with you can get them of C.S. Pierce at his residence on Seneca Street. I don't know the number but you can find out by looking in the Directory. It is on the north side of Seneca between Michigan + Ellicott pretty near Michigan. Father knows him; he used to keep a lumber yard. Give our love to Grandma and tell her to think of us often. Ask Eliza if she ever looks in the Almanac to see if the stars are going to shine. Tell Laura to write to me and give my love to Ellen S. – when she sees her. Send as many papers as you can + write often. Let Eliza tell all the young girls of my acquaintance that I will be home one of the days + take care of those that are not used well now. Has Aunt Eliza Gone?

Friday Oct 3rd, 1862

Lieut. Walbridge while we were out in the field drilling this afternoon pointed it out to us as an old house that was built before the Revolution and was used by the British Col. Tarleton as a hospital. At present it is a pile of bricks and 3 great high old fashioned chimneys. We had a good supper to night of sweet potatoes baked in the ashes. Our company is going out on picket Sunday. I am going out there to trade off some of our spare rations such as bread, pork, sugar + salt. We get more bread + pork than we can use and we have now [INK SPILL] about 2 lbs. of sugar that we have not used in Buffalo I [INK SPILL] 2 cents per pound. The rebels here will pay almost any [INK SPILL]. A little handful of salt will readily bring 25 cents; and they would much sooner take either sugar or salt in exchange for their pies, apples + potatoes than to have the money. We are not allowed to sell them these articles but Uncle Sam will not let us steal of them so we have to steal a march on him to do a little smuggling once in a while. I have been eating a big handful of sugar so you may know my sweet tooth does not suffer much. I caught a louse on my clothes a day or two ago and it set me looking all over for some more but I did not find any. They are great big things and the boys out here call them – "Government Lice" you can always tell them from the common vermin because they have "U.S." in great big letters branded on their backs. I saw a Buffalo Paper last night dated Saturday Sept 27/62 which said that our regiment was going to Fortress Monroe but we have received no order to that effect; on the contrary our Lieut. Colonel told some of the boys we were going to remain here all winter. As soon as any change is ordered I will inform you.

The company that went out last evening came in this morning without having met with any particular incident. We learned that their object in going was to capture a rebel mail from Richmond but they did not obtain it. Capt. has been under arrest ever since we came here and a day or two ago he was court martialed upon a charge of riotous conduct, drunkenness, using profane language, disobedience of orders, mutinous expressions and several other charges. He was tried and plead not guilty. The verdict was not guilty and his sword was returned to him today and he appeared on dress parade this evening for the first time since we came here. It seems that he was in a tent with some other officers and remained until after 12 oclock at night drinking and making a good deal of noise and disturbing the camp. The commanding officer sent to him 3 times to have him cease and the company of officers to disperce; he refused twice and one sent back a very abusive answer to the Colonel. The 3^d time the order was accompanied by a guard with orders to pull down the tent over his head if he did not comply; and the company broke up. All these charges were read before the whole regiment at dress parade together with the language that he used against McClellen + our Colonel. He was present and heard it all – how he must have felt, if he has any manhood about him, thus to have made known, in his presence, to the common soldiers, his loaferish actions + expressions. Our time is our own from Dress Parade to 9 oclock and in that interval we can do

Yorktown, Virgina. Landing Opposite Gloucester (1861-1869)

just what we have a mind to. We are soldiers now and in good earnest. Tomorrow we will be put on duty and held liable to be called on for guards and picket duty and anything else that comes along. The only part of soldier life that I dread is guard duty but I shall have to do it now. We have had first-rate times so far but now then comes the tug of war. I hear the drum beating for the afternoon Battallion Drill so I must stop for the present. All but five of the recruits in our company have been taken out of what we call the awkward squad and placed in the company to drill with them. This speaks pretty well for our ability to learn although some of us had drilled before which in part accounts for it. Our company is going out on picket again Friday and I am going to take my writing materials with me and I will write you a letter while on picket duty. The two Georges [Stoddard and Clark] have gone fishing this evening and I am all alone. The moon is at the full and not a cloud is to be seen. I wish you could have looked in upon our company a few minutes ago as I stood over a camp fire roasting sweet potatoes in the ashes; there were about a dozen sitting + standing around the fire and I warrant that not one of them gave a single thought to the dear ones at home. The time flew swiftly by and the laugh went merrily around as each one made some witty remark or careless expression. We seem to feel just as secure here in our cotton tent with the front entirely open and the back only partly closed as we did in our own beds at home. We have roll call at 9 o'clock + we cannot retire until that hour or if we do we have to turn out again and answer to our names. The evenings passed slowly at first but now they slip by almost before we are aware of it and tattoo sounds as soon as we are ready for it.

Our squad began to drill this morning and drilled 2 or 3 times during the day. We have to turn out at 5 oclock in the morning and answer to roll call; immediately after roll call we have to clean up the ground in and around the tents + sweep the streets in front of our tents. This takes only about 20 minutes, then we go down to the river and perform our ablution in the spring water and by the time we return our breakfast is ready for us. Breakfast consists of roasted pea water (called coffee) and dry bread or hard tack; the bread is very unwholesome + gives me the heart burn every time I eat. I don't know what I should do if I did not have that bottle of bitters. After breakfast we drill from 7 to 8 and again from 10 to 11. At 12 we have dinner which consists generally of bean soup and bread and most generally some kind of meat once in a while we have onions and today we are going to have potatoes for the first time 2 weeks; they are rotten but we don't care for that so long as they are potatoes, sometimes we get dried apple sauce but it is so wormy + they are so careless in cooking it that I do not like to eat it; from 1 to 2 again we have drill + from 4 to 5. At 5 we all have to turn to dress parade when the whole Regt is drawn up into line and the Adjutant reads to us such orders as the Colonel had for the next day. After dinner we always go down to the river and wash our tin cups + plates (we only wash dishes once a day). After dress parade comes supper which like the breakfast consists of Pea Coffee + bread. This is the government food but so far we have lived better than the government allows. We have bought cheese to eat with our bread and mackerel so that we have quite a relish. We can buy sweet potatoes for $1⁰⁰ per bushel + oysters for 20 cents per quart. We are going to buy the potatoes as soon as we can get out to the picket line and then we will live rich for a short time I can tell you.

Saturday Oct. 4th 1862

Our squad of new recruits drilled in the company with muskets for the first time this morning. We must have made pretty good advancement in order to be put in company drill so soon when we have been in the camp only one week to day, and did not commence the squad drill until last Monday. This afternoon I went down to a little kind of a brook and washed some of my things consisting of one pair of drawers, one undershirt one overshirt, 1 pair of stockings + one handkerchief.

The boys say they are going to hire their washing done at 6 cents a piece but I think I can wash my own things well enough for me as long as I have plenty of water + soap. A sixpence saved is sixpence earned. I think you would have laughed to have seen me yesterday with nothing on but my hat pants + boots stooping over that pool of water and rubbing away in good earnest at that washing. I did it pretty well considering that the water was none of the cleanest and my soap not over abundant, as well as being a greenhorn at the business myself. The things are hanging across the ridge pole of my tent this evening drying in the bright moonlight.

Friday morning Oct. 10th 1862

It is raining this morning but not very hard. We have had breakfast and cleaned up our tent and all of us are now engaged in writing. The soil here is rather sandy, so a slight rain does not make the ground muddy. It is wet outside but our cotton covering protects us thoroughly and we are as dry and comfortable in here as you can imagine. When it stops raining we are going to put down a new floor in front of our bed. All we have at present is a lot of small pieces of wood of many sizes and shapes put together as well as different-shaped pieces will admit of being placed. I said in one of my letters it reminded me of old floors that we used to have in the old kitchen on the alley. Yesterday we found 4 nice pieces of board that will make us a first rate floor in front of our bed and we have enough to fill out to the front of our tent. We got a cracker lot the other day and made us a nice little cupboard so as to keep our victuals clean. Our tin cups and plates are all kept bright + clean and I tell you our tent inside looks as slick + comfortable as the chamber in the "City of Buffalo" – all but the looking glass over head. The rain is almost stopped and I think it is going to clear up and we will have a nice day of it yet.

I am very glad indeed to tell you that we received our muskets, clothing, knapsacks, haversacks + canteens this day. Our muskets are the Enfield Rifle of English manufacture and considered the best in the field. Our knapsacks are of black oilcloth and our haversacks are of the same. The haversack is for carrying rations when on a march. The inside of them, that is the lining, can be taken out + washed when dirty. Our canteens are of good black tin + hold 3 pints of water. Our clothing consists of 1 pair of shoes, 2 pair of socks woollen, 1 pair of pants, 1 pair of drawers, 2 shirts – white woollen, 1 jacket, 1 frock coat – dark blue, 1 overcoat cape – light blue + 1 cap. I did not draw the cap, socks, drawers or shirts as those I now have are preferable to the government articles. We are also entitled to a blanket but as I bought one in Alexandria I did not draw any here though the government blanket is the best that can be bought and costs the least money.

[Ed Cook]

Ed: In his October 3, 1862, letter, Edward Cook refers "to steal a march." It means to outwit or to take advantage of someone.

Letter from Private E. Cook to his Parents

Picket in front of Camp at Gloucester Point Oct. 19th 1862

My Dear parents

Last Sunday was a most tedious day for me. It rained all day + night and I was first unfortunate enough to be appointed on guard. The rules are that guards shall be on duty two hours and off four, that is they shall stand 2 hours out every six in the 24 making 8 hours standing duty. During the rest of the time they are to remain in the guard house and can go to sleep if they choose. The guard house is nothing more than a tent and is used as a prison for those who are remiss in their duty and as such persons are generally the lazy + Louzy of the regiment, the guard house is always the filthyest place in the army and no soldier will remain in it if he can help it. So in pleasant weather the guard always sleeps out of doors and in rainy weather he stands up and takes it. I obtained permission to go to my tent from 1 until 4 in the night and as guards are not allowed to remove their clothing or accoutrements I had to lay down in my wet things. I slept for 2 hours and only dreaded to go out the more. The next day was cold but it did not rain. I had an awful head ache and a most tedious pain through the hips. The old soldiers said I was going to have the camp fever but it did not alarm me very much as I knew it was nothing but a cold. It is customary for the guard on the second day often after he goes on to act as Camp Police.

Monday Morning Oct. 20th 1862

I left off my story last night at Yorktown, which place I visited Tuesday Oct. 19/62. There was one or 2 things that I saw there that I wished to speak to you about. One of them was the chimneys. Every Southerner seems to have a particular hatred of chimneys, and so strong is that hatred that they turn their chimneys out of doors. It looks so odd to go along and see sticking out and up at the back end of the house a long chimney. It looks as if the chimney was built first and then the house added on.

Did I ever tell you what constitutes a village in this country? It is 1 courthouse 1 shop + 2 dwelling houses with a black smith shop in front of one of them. Only the C.H. + shop are absolutely indispensable; the dwelling houses are not necessary.

[E Cook]

Letter from Private E. Cook to his Parents and Relatives

Camp at Gloucester Point, Va Sunday Nov. 2/62

My Dear Parents + Relatives

Our colonel is getting so unreasonably strict that all the boys are getting down on him. He is trying to introduce his regular army rules into our volunteer regiment + he will find out one of these days that it is not going to give the best kind of satisfaction. My leg still continues very stiff + painful but I think it is now getting better. I have been up only once since last evening + that was to make me a fresh bread + water poultice. I went to the doctor yesterday morning + he excused me from duty.

This morning I did not go + so he came to my tent to see me; he told me to keep on poulticing it + it would come around all right in a few days. One of the boys in our company received a box from home night before last. It contained 2 Pillows and everything else from bologney sausages to rich fruit cake. He gave me a large piece of cake and I can tell you it did relish nice. I think I shall send for some things in a week or two. His box was only four days in coming through. I cannot see why it is that my things do not come. I am afraid that Mr. Burson made some mistake in directing it.

I went down to the river yesterday to wash some dirty clothes that have been laying around for 3 or 4 days. I had not been down there more than 10 minutes before one of our company came running down to tell us that the long roll was beating and the regiment was out under arms. I immediately snatched up my bundle left my kettles of water on the fire and commenced hobbling up to the camp. The rest of the boys far outstripped me in the race and when I got to camp the line was dismissed and the companies were returning to their quarters. Those that were down to the river supposed as much as could be that the rebels were coming. I could not march but I knew if the regiment stood still + fired that I could shoot as fast as anyone. The alarm was a false one + was ordered by the Colonel in order to teach the soldiers not to stray so far away from camp as to be out of hearing of the drum. You would have laughed I think to have seen Ed with his stiff knee hobbling along with a stick in one hand and a washboard + bundle of dirty clothes in the other. The faster I tried to go the slower I went. Several of our men were very much excited. One fellow came into my tent and commenced fumbling among one of the boys traps. He did not know where he was or what he was doing until we told him 2 or 3 times that he was in the wrong tent and then he looked around with a kind of vacant stare + tumbled out again. Another fellow, a sailor who has been here only a short time, and has been spinning off his long yarns about his daring deeds + terrible adventures ever since he came, was cooking oysters when the roll sounded. The boys said he was so scared that he turned white + so excited that he stewed his oysters twice without knowing it. There are many laughable incidents every time a regiment is ordered out, if a person is only present to witness them. After the scare was over I went down to the river again + washed my clothes. I washed them in hot water. I had a tub + washboard so I got them pretty clean. The washboard was made out of a pine board with creases cut in it. I think when I return I shall have to hire out to do washing + darning.

I had my fortune told yesterday as I was lying in my tent by one of the old soldiers. He believed everything he told me as fully as if it had already come to pass. It took him about an hour to project my horoscope before he could commence to read my fortune. He foretold the future by a regular mathematical calculation based upon a system logarithms and governed by the signs of the zodiac. He paid some Judge $15 to learn him the science + he places implicit confidence in the rule. He can only foretell from the 1st of Jany to the 31st of Dec. or one year at a time and then he has to form a new scale of figures for the next year. He said I should be in or near some little battle before long, I am to be lucky in gaming until the 20th of this month: I am going to receive some money. I am to receive no wounds or injuries and am going have an office in the regiment of some kind or other.

[E. Cook]

Letter from Private E. Cook to his Father

Camp at Gloucester Point Va. Nov. 4/62

Dear Sir

Your very welcome notes of the 28th came duly to hand. In the completest sense do we now realize that as cool water is to a thirsty man so is good news from a far country? A letter from a friend at home is more welcome than the richest meal that wealth could offer. It would do the heart of any one good to witness the avidity with which the poor soldier grasps his letter as his name is called. Picture a group of 7 in a common tent. Four of the group are playing a game of euchre to quicken the slow moving steps of the coming hour of nine; two are looking on, learning to profit by the misplays of those engaged in the game; the 7th and last is writing (by the unsteady light produced by a piece of cotton cloth burning in a dish of salt pork grease) to his parents perhaps or some dear friend at home. Another group is gathered around the dying embers of the cooks fire watching the pictures that are playing among the coals. One is telling a long + highly interesting yarn about his adventures at sea, to a listening crowd of non-believers; three others are fighting over again the great 7 Day battle at Fair Oaks and again are in full retreat down the peninsula and involuntarily look over their shoulder as if they expected to see a body of rebel cavalry in full persuit; one other is saying I wish I was in Brockways place and on my way home (Brockway has just received a discharge.) Another says yes I would give him one hundred dollars and my back pay for his papers. Another has just dropped some sweet potatoes in the ashes and stands watching them with an eager look wishing they were done for his mouth is watering for the sweet morsel, others are thinking of home and talking of fond ones not here while the last is trying to read the latest letter from the 100th in the daily Express of Buffalo: But Hark! The voice of "Pete came squeaking down the street. "This way boys if you want to get your mail" In an instant the "cards" are dashed aside, the "pen" is dropped, the "yarn" is broken, and the "fighting" stopped, "Brockway's discharge" forgotten, "sweet potatoes" left to burn while the "thoughts of home + fond ones" for a moment take a turn, and "letters <u>from</u> the hundredth", half read, are put away, while letters <u>for</u> the regiment hold undisputed sway. At the word letter the men in their tents come crawling out like sand crabs out of the muck. I have often laughed to see some soldier cooped up in a little shelter tent come crawling out in the morning at reveille on his hands + knees and when fairly out rise up + still up gradually until he is expanded into a good long 6 ft. man, and you wonder how in the world such a little place can contain so much flesh + bone. What do you think of 3 of us living in a little wedge shape tent 10 ft. long 6 ft. wide + notquite 5 feet high. Think of it to live + move + have our beings in such a place as this. **Never go for a "sojer" boy.**

[Ed Cook]

Ed: Mail call was the highlight of the day for a soldier. If he received a letter, his spirits soared. Soldiers often expressed concern if their families were not writing enough. The letters from home represented the emotional tie to one's family and their way of life. Should the Confederacy win the war, the southern economy would spread to the North and destroy democracy.

Chapter 2

⟋⟍

Johnny's Gone for a Soldier

To the tune of the Irish song "Shule Arron" dating back to the 17th Century
Lyrics by Septimus Winner

1.Hear I sit on Buttermilk Hill
Who can blame me, cryin' my fill
And ev'ry tear would turn a mill,
Johnny has gone for a soldier.

2. Me, oh my, I loved him so,
Broke my heart to see him go
And only time will heal my woe,
Johnny has gone for a soldier.

3. I'll sell my rod, I'll sell my reel,
Likewise, I'll sell my spinning wheel,
Johnny has gone for a soldier.

4. I'll dye my dress, I'll dye it red,
And through the street I'll beg for bread,
For the lad I love from me has fled,
Johnny has gone for a soldier.

Letter from Private E. Cook to his Parents

Gloucester Point, Va Monday, Nov. 24th 1862

Dear Parents

We have been busy to day putting bunks in our tent. When we have things all fixed up right in our tent I will send you a plan of it and you can compare it with the plan that Uncle David sent you. We commenced altering our tent about a week ago but what with rainey weather and going on forageing expeditions + Picket we had been delayed in our work

27

until today but now we are fairly at it again I think we will soon have it finished up. We amused our selves this evening with playing a game we call proverbs and find it very entertaining and perhaps a little instructional as it is a kind of mental disapline. It is played like this: one of the company steps outside the tent and while he is away the rest of the company chose a proverb, either religious or otherwise, and assign the words of the proverb in their proper order to the different members of the company as they sit in a circle around the stove. For instance we take the proverb "Wisdom is better than Riches" a proverb of 5 words: - the 1st word is given to the 1st man of the circle: the 2d word to the 2d man + so on. The person outside is then called in and steps up to the 1st man of the circle + asks him a question, and the answer to the question must contain the 1st word of the proverb. He then goes to the second man + asks him some question and the answer to the question must contain the 2d word of the proverb + the answer to the 3d question must contain the 3d word of the proverb + so on; and from all the answers the man must guess the proverb which is often very difficult + requires much memory to recollect all the answers. As we have voted that neither the questions or the answers shall contain any thing that is not immoral we enjoy the game very much.

[Ed Cook]

Letter from Private E. Cook to his Parents

Gloucester Point, Va.Nov. 29th 1862 Saturday

Dear Parents

We were on picket today. When we started from our tents about half past seven in the morning the weather looked rather dubious and we all thought we were going to have a wet and miserable day of it; but in a short time the clouds cleared up, the sun came out and we had a most lovely day. I had a very pleasant time reading my testament aloud to those that were on post with me and copying a letter that I had written to [ ] the day before but which was blotted so that I was ashamed to send it + so copied it over on picket. We passed the night quietly + comfortably. I stood guard only 2 ½ hours during the night but I did not sleep an hour. We were on the centre, the same line we occupied last time. When we returned from picket and went out to discharge our pieces we found our boys that were left in camp had put up a nice new target. I was the first one that shot and I plumbed the target quite nicely. After fireing our pieces we were allowed about half an hour to get ourselves ready for inspection + review. We had not time to pack our knapsacks properly and when the Colonel came to our company and saw how the knapsacks were packed he said "Oh hell! I dont want to inspect that company" and passed us by without more than a passing glance. Inspection over we were given about a quarter of an hour to rest ourselves, eat our dinner and then turn out for Brigade drill. Brigadier General Naglee drilled us for about 3 hours. We had 5 Regts. on the ground our regt., the 104th Penn. and the 11 Maine + 98th + 56th N.Y. from Yorktown across the river. We went through a great number of movements and did them up just as well as they are generally performed. But this is great Sunday work is it not? I must not stop to moralise however for if I do I shall never finish this letter.

[E. Cook]

Letter from Private E. Cook to his Parents

Gloucester Point, Va Tuesday Dec. 2^{d} 1862

Dear Parents

I went down to the river this morning at 8 o'clock and took a bath in salt water after having first taken a good wash in spring water. It made me feel first rate. The water however was pretty cold as also the sand I stood on to wash + dress after bathing I boiled some water and washed 2 shirts, 1 pair of stockings, one towel + a handkerchief and returned to camp just in time to fall in with the boys for company drill about 10 oclock A.M. At 1 oclock the boys company fell in again for target shooting. I guess they intend to make a regt. of sharpshooters of us. We fired 5 rounds of cartridge. It was rather cold in the afternoon and a wind was blowing. Forty nine shots hit the target My shooting was not of the first class but I hit the target 2 or 3 times out of 5 and could have done better if my hands had been warm enough to hold the gun steady. The 2 Georges [Stoddard and Clark] + myself generally as good any of them and better than the majority. The shooting occupied us about 2 hours and when we came in the Lieut. told us to fall out without arms except want belt + bayonet to attend the [ ] of some soldier that was to be buried from the hospital. The order was to have the regiment in line at 3 ½ oclock but for some reason or other it did not form until 5 oclock so that we buried the soldier by moonlight.

When we were on Brigade drill last Sunday we had a brass band that came across the river. It played part of the time when we were marching and the music sounded perfectly delicious. It seemed as though we could march for ever if the music would only continue playing. We were tired before we commenced the drill having slept none the night before on picket but the moment the brass band struck up all thoughts of tediousness, weariness + fatigue were gone in a moment. It reminded us of Old Buffalo to hear that music and made us think of many home scenes that once gave us much pleasure. I wish I could hear Lillie playing on the Piano for a few moments. Music will sound extremely sweet to us when first we hear it after our return if a return awaits us

Nobody knows the hardships of the soldiers life except the soldier himself for no soldier writes home all the hardships that he has to endure. I have seen the time that I would be glad to sleep in a barn at [

] but we are over those times I hope. We are comfortably situated now and I hope we will continue so.

I am very much pleased with the map you sent me and prefer it even to the one that George has. It is a map on which I can trace the route taken by either army as the information is acquired by the various telegraphs that reach us. Our Lieut wished me to let the map remain in his tent and I have done so. He says it is the best map he has ever seen. Those Cigars are just old comfort. Where did you buy them? The three cent ones are about as good as those that cost 5 cents. At least there is not 2 cent difference in them + in case you ever send me any more I would about as lief have the 3 cent ones. I do not smoke much only when I feel kinder lonesome. Everybody in camp smokes and next time I have anything sent to me I am going to have some smoking tobacco put in the box and have you buy me a nice little [ ] pipe. I do not want a large pipe for I do not like to smoke much tobacco at a time. I wish you would inquire the price of a nice little pipe + pipe stem of sweet briar or witch hazel wood. I really believe that smoking in camp is beneficial. It seems to destroy all bad odors that sometimes are floating around. You sent me quite a number of things that I did not expect. That Pillow is delicious and the comforter is most acceptable but if we go on a march I must throw it away. The can of jelly is a luxury and those peaches are just outstanding. That Liniment has cured one man in my tent of the Rheumatism so it has paid for itself already. The catsup is the best I ever tasted. I guess you made it different from what you used to for I did not like catsup in Buffalo. Tell [ ] I am very, very much obliged to him for the bitters he sent me. I had the heartburn day before yesterday so that I could not eat and I took a little of the bitters and it cured me right off. I think this is excellent and if the other was better than this it must have been good indeed. The raspberry vinegar I have not yet touched but I know what it is. I am going to keep it for sickness. The sleeping cap is just "old comfort" That Molassas candy is quite a novelty but it is an excellent pastime to get it out of the can. It grows less very slowly. The bread, unfermented, had to go the rounds of the tent the first night. I finished the second loaf the last time I was on picket. Next time I want you to send me a little [ ] box. The Envelopes are first class and I am much pleased with them. I hate to use them until I have disposed of the others that you sent me. Two of the boys in my tent received boxes the other night and both of them contained fruit cake but it did not begin to come up to the one that Mary sent me. One of the boys eat so much that he made himself sick. High living does not agree with us in camp

[E Cook]

Ed: Edward writes of the hardship of a soldier's life, and all he has done to date is drill and camp. Campaigns, marches and battle are all in his future. Then he will know the true meaning of the hardships of a soldier's life.

Ed: Letters were the most important thing in the soldiers' lives, but number two on their list were the boxes received from home. As you can see in the letters, it was a great occasion to receive a box which contained assorted items from cakes to jams to clothing and even feather pillows. Each box was opened and inspected at regimental headquarters to make sure that no liquor was in the box. As the war progresses, the folks at home will know which types of items to send and which items are not appropriate for an army on the move.

Ed: Most towns and cities in American had brass bands for parades, picnics, and political rallies. Bands were useful in recruiting citizen soldiers. By the closing of the months of 1861, the federal government could no longer afford the luxury of having volunteer bands. Regimental bands were abolished in the summer of 1862, but some regiments were able to retain their bands by re-listing the men as combatants. In addition to playing for dress parades, reviews, funerals and executions, band musicians also served as stretcher bearers. They also played to entertain the troops. Their patriotic music built morale.

Letter from Private E Cook to his Parents

Gloucester Point, Va Thursday Dec. 4th 1862

Dear Parents

Hello! It has been a warm + pleasant day. The regiment was called out again this afternoon to attend another funeral. It was that of a man who died in camp. He had been sick for some time but was getting well. He had received a discharge + was waiting for his papers to come so that he could go home. The night before he died he was out to the color line talking to the guard and appeared all right when he went to bed but when the boys in his tent awoke in the morning they found him dead. It was too bad and seems worse because he was on the point of going home + was probably expected by his friends.

[E Cook]

Letter from Private A. Lyth to his Father

Gloucester Point Va Dec 1st 1862

Dear Father

Tom Maharg got a box a little before Thanksgiving and I tell you we had a good time of it on thanksgiving day we had 3 large mince pies to beef toungs and Jellies + preserves + cake to any amount of Tomato catsup and various other things to numerous to mention. you need not be afraid of me not receiving the box you send me if we should move for the box will always follow the Regiment no matter where it goes to but I guess we are going to stay here awhile longer if not till the war is over of course this place has to be held as long as the army goes to Richmond the road they are going now but if they should send an army by the way of Yorktown and up the peninsula then we should stand a chance of seeing Richmond then they would not need any troops to be left at Yorktown or this Point I send my love to you all

Your Son
Alfred Lyth

Letter from Private E. Cook to his Parents

Gloucester Point, Va Thursday Dec. 11/62

Dear Parents

We were up bright + early this morning. Everything promises a fine day for marching. It was cold last night and the ground is frozen which is quite an item in marching on this sandy soil. We were in line about 6 oclock but did not begin our march until 7 ½ oclock. We started with 4 Regts of Infantry 4 comprised of cavalry + 4 pieces of artillery. 3 of the Infantry Regts + the cavalry companies were from the other side of the river. We marched today to Gloucester C.H. a distance of 15 miles and arrived there about 3 o'clock.

We had just got our tents pitched and our fires made and were on the point of cooking our supper when Genl Naglee Arrived at the camp and ordered us to pass through the town + camp on the other side, so we struck tents again and marched about a ¼ of a mile. It was dark when we broke up camp, and darker still when we pitched tents the second time. We camped in a cornfield where the corn had been cut + put in stacks preparatory to husking but I can tell you that there were very few stacks of corn left in 10 minutes after we stacked arms. I had a nice warm bed that night although the night was cold and the ground was covered with hoar frost in the morning. We had nothing but shelter tents but I slept very warm. My feet were not cold once during the night. There is something grand and enticing in this campaigning – entering and plundering are enemy's country – camping + sleeping soundly + sweetly in the very midst of danger – placing our lives in the hands of our Guards and Pickets and feeling safe + secure in their watchfulness and care. It is dangerous, it is tedious, it causes aching bones and tired limbs but somehow I love it and wished for a battle.

[E Cook]

Letter from Private E. Cook to his Parents

Gloucester Point, Va Friday December 19th, 1862

Dear Parents

When we left Camp I carried only my rubber blanket, my woollen blanket + lining + a pair of stocking. If we had remained away our underclothes would have been sent to us but my pillow, comfator, butter +c would have been destroyed. If you get a war map you can find Gloucester Point exactly opposite Yorktown and Gloucester C.H. is exactly north of Gloucester Point so you can trace our march of Wednesday

There is an old secesh that lives close by the woods where we were chopping and it was said that he had threatened to shoot anyone who laid a hand on anything that he had or if we burnt his fence rails. So to fix his lordship wherever we could see a tree that would fall across the fence we felled it so it would fall across the fence he came out and was in a duce of a sweat and he was told to hold his tounge if he did not it would be the worse for him I should not like to be a drafted soldier The drafted Regiment here are everyone drafted from the drummers to the Lt Col in fact all the Officer are drafted and they know no more about drill than I did when I first enlisted and our officers have to drill them with the musket so that as the officers learn they learn the men and the drummers dont know how to play a single tune or beat a call last night they beat the long roll for to put out the lights When the right way is to give just three taps on the drum And the long roll is to call the Regiment out when they are attacked by the enemey and is not to be beat on any account except on such an occation and they will get their muskets and go out shooting after game and get arrested some came out to the picket lines and they asked us if we had to take our guns out on picket and they are the laughing stock of the volunteers My

Boots are giving way in the uppers and I am going to have new fronts put on which will cost me 50 cents which I wish you would send me as I have not got quite that amount

[E Cook]

Letter from Private E. Cook to his Parents

Camp at Gloucester Point Va Saturday Dec. 20th 1862

Dear Parents

The weather was very cold this day. We had a drill this morning but it was so cold they did not keep us out very long. The water froze in our wash dish – we <u>have</u> a wash dish. – Some of the old soldiers never use a wash dish; they take a mouth full of water from their canteen and then spit it into their hands and wash their face but <u>we</u> don't do so <u>we</u> paid 50 cents for a wash dish and we now enjoy the rich pleasure of a comfortable morning ablution without going away down to the spring. I was busy for 2 or 3 hours engaged in drawing the rations for our company and afterwards issueing them to the members. It is a tedious job and not a very desirable one for Sunday but soldiers are slaves or worse than slaves and must do as they are ordered. I might almost say there is no Sabbath in the Army so little respect is paid to the day. If during the week we are ordered to clean up during the whole forenoon in expectation of a Brigade drill 3 hours long in the afternoon you will hear the boys remarking to each other "It seems to me just like Sunday; don't it to you?

Gloucester Point, Va Tuesday Dec 23ᵈ 1862

Today has been very pleasant indeed. It was so warm that it was uncomfortable drilling both this a.m. and afternoon. I have been round in my shirt sleeves all day except when we were drilling. I did my washing today under difficulties. We cannot get at our washing so early in the morning as you can at home. We are call up at sunrise but I generally am up an hour or more before that time and have a good fire going in our stove before roll call. At roll call every man (except the sick) has to fall out and answer to his name. After roll call we sweep the street in front of our tent, fold our blankets and clean out the tent. Then comes our breakfast of greasy coffee + bread (Greasy because boiled in the same kettles that are used boiling fat pork + salt horse). By the time we have finished our breakfast it is nearly 8 o'clock. Then if we wish to do our washing we must go out and cut our wood (for we are not allowed to chop wood or make any noise before roll call) and travel down to the spring start our fire boil our water and go ahead. It is sometimes 9 o'clock before we get started: but this time there were three of us washed together. We hurried up things so that we had our breakfast finished, our wood chopped and our fire started before 8 o'clock. Drill generally takes place at 10½ o'clock but for some unaccountable reason the companies were called out this morning at 9½ o'clock and we did not have our washing quite finished but we had to leave off immediately and go up and fall in with the company or else go to the guard house. So we spilled out 2 kettles of boiling water that we just going to pour into our tub and snatched up our clothes (clean + dirty) took our kettles + washtub and started for camp on the double quick. We got there just before the roll was called and thus saved our bacon that time. After drill we went down to the spring again and started another fire and finished up our washing before we eat our dinner. After we did our washing we all stripped ourselves and went into the tub and had a gay old swim. What do you think of that taking a bath with open air on the 20th of December? Oh! this is the country for me and if they ever exterminate slavery in Virginia + I am alive + well after it is done I am coming down here to live. This afternoon was our day for Target Practice but instead of that we had to have one of those long and hated battalion drills. Somehow or other every time that it is our turn to go target shooting we have to have a battalion drill and get cheated out of our fun. I am afraid this lovely weather is but the forerunner of a heavy storm. Tomorrow is our picket day and I am hoping that it will not rain until after we return. It is just like spring weather so lovely that I cannot describe it.

Gloucester Point Va Twenty 4th of Dec. Day before Christmas.

Happy times there will be in Buffalo tonight + happier still tomorrow morning but there is no Christmas Eve for the poor soldier. My Christmas Eve will be spent in the open air, the stars twinkling laughingly and the new moon smiling down upon me. With my long gray coat closely buttoned up around me and my musket over my shoulder, Christmas Eve will find me walking my narrow "beat" looking towards the enemy + thinking of my home. It was indeed a happy hour and one that I shall ne'er regret for having spent it as I did. I was straining my gaze into the darkness before me and yet my thoughts were wandering off in a few different directions and dwelling upon a holier and a happier theme.

Thursday Evening

I am quite certain that we shall leave this camp in a very short time. I dread it for I shall have to leave so many comfortable things and valuable articles. I almost wish that you had not sent some of them but if I should have to leave them now I think I have received the value of them already in the comfort I have received from them already.

I destroyed all of my letters this evening. There was 30 or more of them and it was like pulling a tooth for each letter that I burned. I should have left them if I had thought there was any hope of our staying here. I had expected as much as could be that I should receive a letter from you to night but it did not come and I felt disappointed. I have not received a letter from you since last Saturday and it seems a very long time now that we are thinking of moving and do not know as we shall stay to see another mail come into our quarters. But if we move, the letters will follow the regiment so that if we do not receive them here we shall get them after we leave. This has not been a Merry Christmas to us for the knowledge that we are going to leave our nice comfortable winter quarters to go we know not where, has cast a kind of silent gloom over the minds + feelings of the soldiers that even the thought of the enjoyment that roams the hearts of the dear ones at the north on this anniversary of our Savior's Birth could not produce a happier state of feeling. Some few in our tent had calculated on having something a little extra for dinner today but this rumor has knocked it all in the head and about drove the thought of eating from our minds. If we have to move I will drop you a line just before we start. I hope we are not going to join the Army under the immediate command of Burnside. I would rather go to Carolina or even Texas than to form part of the Army opposite Fredericksburg. Is it not shameful the way our poor soldiers were slaughtered before the entrenchments on those heights near the city? I have almost lost confidence in Burnside. You do not hear all the news for I do not think the papers dare publish everything. You should read the letters that some of our boys receive from boys in Burnside's army. It is from them + from them only that you can get the facts of the engagement. But it is almost time for Roll call so I must close my letter and make my bed. Remember me in your prayers and bear in mind that where 2 or 3 shall ask any thing in the name of the Lord that he will give it unto them. Give my love to Grandma and all the children. Tell Sammy that I do not forget him because I do not always speak of him. Goodbye.

From Your Affectionate Son
Edward

Ed: Soldiers used the letters home to start campfires and also as toilet paper. Those who had saved letters would normally destroy them before a troop movement.

Ed: Edward refers to the December 12, 1862, Battle of Fredericksburg and the slaughter of Union troops. There were over 12,500 casualties, including the loss of two Union generals. The South called it a great victory over the invaders.

"After a rough passage we arrived at Morehead City, N.C., which we found was to be the rendezvous for a great expedition. After 1 week of delay we put to sea again, on the fine steamer New England, and the morning of January 31, 1863, a lovely morning, entered with the rest of the fleet the noble harbor of Port Royal. The sight, as the mist lifted and disclosed the beautiful surroundings and the great fleet, with colors flying and bands playing, steaming up the bay, were one never to be forgotten."[4]

Letter from Private E. Cook to his Parents

Moorhead City, N.C.Monday Jany 5th 1863

Dear Parents

We had quite a lively time this evening playing a game they call prison. Myself and another Corporal chose an equal number of men and then we take two points on opposite sides of the field and a few feet to the right or left of the points we select other points which we call the prisons; then each side tries to catch the men of the other side when they are off their point or home. And when they are caught they have to remain on the prison until some of their own side can come up and touch them and get them off. The side that catches the most men + keeps them from the other side is the victor. Just as the drum beat for roll call, my side had every man from the other side on our prison so my victory was complete.

[E Cook]

Letter from Private A. Lyth to his Father

Beaufort Harbor S.C. Jan 24th 1863

Dear Father

Day before yesterday I went up the masts of a brig that lay along side of our boat furnishing us with coal and counted the number of vessels steamers + gunboats anchored in this harbor there being 57 in all of which 10 or 11 are large steam transports loaded each with Regt of soldiers all day yesterday and to there is quite a fleet of steamers coming in to be load with soldiers to go with us and we have learned that there is a large fleet fitting up in New York either to go with us or follow us up I cannot tell for sure where we are going we still think that we are going to Willmington then to Charleston but that is a supposition this morning there was one of the boys fell overboard but he was soon got out of water after getting a ducking the weather is very fine I cannot tell when we shall sail as we learn we shall have to wait until the troops come down from Newbern and embark on board of the transports that came in yesterday. I send you all my love and give my best respects to the Neighbors.

From Your Affect Son
Alfred Lyth

Letter from Private E Cook to his Parents

Beaufort, S.C. Tuesday Jan'y 27th 1863

Rainy + dismal. There are was some 20 scooners started out of Beaufort belonging to our expedition just before the Steamers loaded with troops started and I tell you it looked splendid to see as many scooners all about the same size and with all their sails spread they were all loaded with the horses, provisions, ammunition +c then after they had all got out of the harbor the Steamers put out with the troops the vessels have not arrived here as yet. This morning Just outside of the harbor we met a large gunboat going out having the Passaic one of the Monitor Build of gun boats we passed close past her we had a fair view of her.

It was a splendid sight to see her cutting through the water as the sea had calmed through the night it was quite smothe she stood about a foot out of the water her deck was clear of everything and as smothe as a peice of glass only the turret and the crew were to be seen on deck as she past by us the whole Regt gave her three hearty cheers which were as heartly responded to by her crew. We are still on board of the boat and I cannot tell weather we are going to land here or not it is the opion of a great many that we are not going to land here. It is very pleasent and warm here today. We can see Fort Walker + Fort Beauregard from the boat as we lay in the harbor. I wish that mother would get some of that checked stuff and make me two shirts as the shirts they have here are very miserable things being both to short in the sleeves and body they are not near as good as the government shirts we drew at Albany. The men will not wear them when they can get others from home or buy some of the suttlers for which he charges like he does for everything else then I should like a pair of suspenders you can send these when you send my boots but don't send them until I send for them. I received the letter you speak of all of the children having sent me some small change and as I said in the answer to that letter it came in very handy I spent the last of it today. I will close this letter with my love to you all and hope to have another from you soon they say we shall receive all our back mail when we reach our destination were that is I cannot tell you probably Savanna. No more at present

From Your Affect Son
Alfred Lyth

Letter from QM Clerk E. Cook to his Parents

Q.M. Department H'd. Qrs. 2ᵈ Brig. Naglee's Div.

On board Steam Transport "{UNKNOWN WORD}"
anchor'd off Beaufort S.C.

Tuesday Feby 3ᵈ 1863

My Dear Parents

The two regiments on board this vessel disembarked this morning for a day or two while the boat hands clean the ship. It was a great joy to the boys to see their feet on land once more. It will give them an opportunity to clean themselves and wash their clothes if nothing more. Close by the landing is a cotton mill that runs 9 gins. All the hands employed are negroes – men + women – except the overseer who is white.

When reading of Whitney, the inventor of the cotton gin, I have many times desired to see the operation of one of these wonderful inventions and here unexpectedly the wish is gratified. The machines used in the factory here are of very simple construction. They are run by steam power and the work is performed by a roller around which is glued a leather strap running diagonally like a screw. As this revolves it pulls the cotton from the seed with great perfection. After witnessing the operations of the machines I went out on the beach with {UNKNOWN NAME} and had a hunt. I found one big one about 20 little young ones and 50 nits. I gave my clothes to the wash woman and told her if there was one on them when she returned them I wouldent pay her a red. These are the first I have found on my clothes since I enlisted, but this is the result of living on board of transports. In the afternoon I took a stroll around town. Those who have been here for some length of time say that when they first came here it was one of the loveliest places they ever saw; Every yard was filled with flowers and every street shaded with beautiful trees. Orange trees are common and Lemon trees abundant. The walks were all nicely kept and everything was loveliness, but now the fences are broken or destroyed entirely, the houses are torn and dilapidated, the flowers plants + fine shrubery are trodden down and they say it does not look like the same place. Still there are some beautiful residences here yet but there are no occupants for them except officers + niggers. You have seen orange + Lemon trees but they bear no comparison to those down here. I saw an orange tree today that was as high as a 2 ½ or 3 story house and a large and beautiful tree it was I tell you. They are about as common here as peach trees in Cleveland. Some flowers are in blossom here now. This afternoon I picked a full blown Dandelion. It was a beauty in my eyes for it made me think of home. This is the place which when taken contained only 1 white man. Dont you recollect the papers spoke of him. Well I saw him this afternoon and bought some peanuts in his store. His name is Allen. He is an elderly looking man of medium height, Greyish hair and wears spectacles. I have had quite a spree of it today. It was quite a novelty for us to be in a town of any size. Beaufort formerly contained about 2000 inhabitants. Very many of the houses that were formerly occupied by the residents as dwellings are now turned into stores + {UNKNOWN WORD} shops.

I bought my dinner to day in a small eating house. It consisted of Pork Steak, Pancakes + coffee. It is the first <u>meal</u> that I have had since I left home. There is a negro regiment here that was raised in this state. They went down the coast a few days ago in transports and had a fight. They say they fought well. As we came up the river yesterday we saw a small steamer that was captured from the rebels by a negro sometime last summer. She was fitted out at Charleston and was built with especial referance to speed. The negro that captured her was employed with several others as one of the boat hands. One night when the officers were ashore the negro got up steam and run her out. The rebels fired on her from the forts and sent boats out after her but she was too quick for them and the negro run her safely into this harbor. She is lying at this place now. The negro who captured her has just been pointed out to me in a little sail boat which he owns himself and takes great pride in sailing round the harbor. He is only half black and is quite intelligent looking.

There is a printing office at this place and they get off quite a respectable looking paper. One of the clerks gave me one of them and I will send it to you tomorrow to preserve until I return. Did you ever get that package of small sea shells that I sent home to you?

I think that I never told you that in the box that George Clark sent to Comstock when we left the "{UNKNOWN WORD}" there was a blanket, a pair of pant, a coat, a quilt, and one or two shirts that

Beaufort, S. C. View of Beaufort from the Wateerfront.
Fuller's House (1861) Timothy 0'Sullivan, Photographer

belonged to me. If you have not already received them you had better call on Mr. C. and inquire about them for they worth having.

Tuesday Feby 10/63

Went to Hilton Head again today and had the rations that I dun yesterday brought up on a schooner. The weather for the past two days has been warm and pleasant. The birds sing so sweetly in the warm mornings that it almost makes me love the sunny South to hear the joyful songs they warble from their little swelling throats.

Thursday Feby 19-63

I slept last evening in a cot at the "Port Royal House". I had a good soft bed and a pillow to lie my head on but I could not sleep much. I have got so used to lying outdoors and in a tent that it does not seem like home to sleep in a house. When I was on the transport I caught cold the first or second night that I slept in the cabin and I did not get rid of it entirely until I got on shore but I had not been here more than 4 or 5 days before all traces of it had left me.

I almost think that if I ever get safely to "B" again that I will be surprising you by ordering my bed made in the wood pile or on the housetop where I can get the air and keep from catching cold. I paid 25 cents for my bed last night before I laid my head on it and in the A.M. I wished I had it back again to buy my breakfast with for I felt a little hungry having had nothing to eat since yesterday noon. About nine oclock, as I was waiting on the wharf for the boat to come up and take my good on board, I saw a couple of hardtacks lying on the dirty ground which I eagerly snatched up and commenced to devour when a negro exclaimed "[ ]!" I knew what he meant but I walked hurridly on and had the tacks used up before the poor nigger could recover from the surprise which my refusal to obey his order had occasioned. After a while when the boat got ready (and she waited until she did get a <u>good</u> ready) she came alongside the pier nose end foremost and after they had put fifty horses on board of her I managed to get the boxes of clothing +c put onto her and off we started for the Island of St. Helena where we arrived just about dinner time and the first thing I did was to take a horse and ride up to camp and eat my supper for last night which consisted of "Baked Beans"; and my breakfast for this morning which consisted of Baked Beans + the two hard tacks I stole from the nigger; and my dinner for this noon which I think consisted of Baked Beans. These 3 meals being finished I again jumped onto my horse and started for the pier and arrived there just as the boat had managed to get into a good place where she could land the horses conveniently and with safety. I helped get the boxes on shore and load them in the wagon. There were 3 army wagon loads of them (13 large boxes) Well we got them to camp and before night we had them all distributed except a very few articles to the 100th Regt. That was considerable of a number of incidents for one day.

Tuesday Feby 24th 1863

Weather just warm enough to be pleasant and cool enough to be comfortable. 'Lovely' is the word that best describes it. There was a grand review this morning of all the troops on this Island by Genl Hunter. The parade was formed on a plantation about a mile to the rear of the camps. There were 5 Brigades of 18 regiments – over 10,000 men. It took upward of 2 hours for the troops to pass the colors or stand point of the General. I was up in a large tree and had a good view of all of the troops in the field. I saw Genl Hunter, Genl Seymour, Genl Terry, Gen Naglee (our present commander) + some others who I do not recollect. Seymour + Terry are on Hunters Staff. I do not like the military appearance of Gen Hunter. When he shuts his mouth, turns his head to one side and cocks up his eye to squint under one corner of his old French military hat, he reminds me for all the world of [ ]. He is bald on the top of his head and as he is quite an elderly man and has jet black hair I am inclined to think that he is vain enough to use hair dye.

The two Generals on his staff are both very insignificant looking men. Our general Naglee, who commands the troop on this island and who is only a Brigadier, is by far the most military + intelligent looking general that I have yet seen. He is about 45 years of age. His hair is sprinkled with gray and adds to his noble appearance. He is a small man and lightly built but has an iron frame. His eye is narrow and long and never at rest; its color is jet black and being sunken a little under the eye brows it gives him a very penetrating look. I think he knows more than Hunter could ever learn. He is loved by all of the soldiers although he never speaks to one of them, and it is very seldom that he ever addresses a remark to an officer of the Line. I never saw him laugh and only once have I ever seen a <u>large</u> smile on his countenance and then I was so surprised that I have not yet forgotten it. I should hate to be led into battle by Genl Hunter for I have no confidence in his ability but under Genl Naglee I should feel perfectly secure on that point. He is a general who will not send where <u>he</u> dare not go.

[E Cook]

Ed; The Passic was a Union monitor built for the Union Navy It was an ironclad warship with a revolving turret similar to the design on the U.S.S. Monitor.

Ed: Edward was promoted to a Quartermaster Clerk position probably because he was literate and could do some math.

Ed: Eli Whitney received a patent for his cotton gin in 1794. It was a machine that removed the seeds from cotton, formerly done by hand. A single cotton gin could clean up to 55 pounds of cotton a day. Prior to the gin, slave labor was primarily employed in growing rice and tobacco. By overcoming the obstacle of seed removal, cotton became a highly profitable crop for the Southern economy.

". . . we landed on the lovely island of St Helena, and soon were occupied with the ordinary routine of camp life. When at last all things were ready, and the advance on Charleston was commenced, the 100th, as usual, was selected to lead off, and once more we embarked on the briny deep."[5]

Letter from Private A. Lyth to his Parents and Relatives

St. Helena Island S.C. March 9, 1863

My dear Parents + Relatives

I have not rec'd a letter from you in a long time and I had made up my mind not to write to you again until I rec'd a letter from home but I find that I can not be so hard hearted for although it is very vexatious and provoking to have the mail brought into camp and see letters pass round to the other boys without receiving a single one myself, yet my natural feelings will not allow me to retaliate upon those who seemingly forget me. There have been some 3 or 4 mails brought to our camp within the past 2 or 3 weeks, but neither letter or paper did I receive by any of them. However I presume that I am just as much thought of as before and must attribute this apparent neglect to household duties and other unavoidable difficulties and obstacles that present themselves which are paramount to writing to **"The boy that's gone for a sojer"** and so I must overlook them and as I know you love to hear from me just as much as at any time heretofore I will withdraw my unfeeling resolution and send you another letter hoping thereby to set you a good example which I trust you will see fit to follow – So here goes!

Our Col issued an order to have this Regt supplied with blouces well of course we all have to take one which makes us all have an overcoat dress coat blouse and Jacket or roundabout so we call them now since we have got these blouses which by the way arevery comfortable things this summer time being very thin and light and the only thing that we can get to drill in with comfort we have no use for our Jackets and the first march we go on we will have to throw them away now pretty near every man in the Regt has a new jacket that he drew at Gloucester Point now some grumble very much at having to draw these but I and a good many more do not care so much but there are a good many who have familys to home to support hence they do not want to be buying clothes all the time now those Jackets cost $5.50 and have to be cast away. I dont care it takes half of pay I am bound to have desent clothes and look respectable I have draw a dollar or two of my account already and I it will take 6 or 7 dollars to clothe me the rest of my year out.

Mail's has come

[E Cook]

Friday March 20th Still cold and damp. This morning the Regt. rec'd orders to keep their knapsacks packed and hold themselves in readiness to march at a moments notice + in about an hour or less the boys were ready for a start. At sunset they rec'd the following order "Soldiers of the 100th your good name and discipline has at last reached the military authorities. You are to lead the **Advance on Charleston**.

[E Cook]

Port Royal Island, South Carolina, Coosay Ferry (1862)
Timothy O'Sullivan, Photographer

Hilton Head, S. C. Dock built by Federal Troops (April, 1872)
Timothy O'Sullivan, Photographer

Letter from Private A. Lyth to his Father and Mother

On Board of the Steamer Expounder
off Hilton Head S.C. Mar 24 1863

Dear Father + Mother

On sunday last we got orders to strike tent and pack Knapsacks and get ready to go aboard of the boat we got everything in readyness and gave away our bunks and other we could not go aboard untill the next morning we pitched our tents again and slept under them untill morning when we got a board of the steamship Expounder + went over to Hilton Head where we went ashore for the purpose of exchanging our guns for new ones which we did We gave in our Enfield and got the Austrian rifle they were made in this country although they are the Austrian style we do not like them so well as we did our old ones and I guess they are not as serviceable for from their appearance they look as if they had been got up in very cheap style. however they all being new guns they look pretty well we got aboard of the boat again and put out into the stream where we droped anchor. It is said that we shall put out early tomorrow morning. As far as I can learn we are going to Coal Island near Charleston. There are some gun boats going with us. You say you cannot see how all the negros should be punished for the wrong doings of a few. I and a good many more in the army are of the same opinion but there are a lot of the boys that hates the sight of the negros and they improve every opportunity they can get to abuse them It goes against them when orders are read that they are not allowed outside of the camp guard and the negros employed by the government are allowed to go where they please I have seen 2 or 3 of the Couriors articles about this Regt which they say they obtained from Soldiers letters from this Regt which speak of its spirit of demorilzation under its present Commander Col Dandy it is readily imagined where such sentiments come from no doubt from some unruly fellow who had been Court Martialed and five or ten dollars stoped off his pay. of course the officers some of them get drunk sometimes but they are put under arrest for it and have to suffer the consequences. one of the articals runs down our Col and does not senture Lt Col Otis or Major Nash but gives them praise now if our Col does ever happen to get too much he keeps in his tent which Col Otis + Maj Nash does not though Col Otis is the best hearted old man in the business and thinks a good deal of the boys and the boys think a good deal of him but Major Nash is the only officer in the Regt at the present who the most of the boys do not like he is a regular drunken bully who has been under arrest for a while back for getting drunk and pounding a couple of officers belonging to another Regt however enough of this now about the Chaplin the last mail we received but one there were 5 daily papers for George Barnum, when the mail was assorted at Brigade headquarters Ed Cook a fellow detailed from our Company for assisting in coping of orders and doing other writing saw these five papers for George and saw them put in the mail bag and sent over to the Regt for the Chaplin to assort out for the different Companies when the mail was distribeted Geo only got one paper. It turned out that the Chaplin had retained them to read. he made the excuse that some of the officers had took them to read. however he has not seen the end of the matter yet as some of the boys have swore to pay him for robbing the mail in that manner as a good many of the boys oft miss newspapers The Board of Trade had better have kept the Rev Mr. Linn in Buffalo. so no more at present and I hope these few lines will find you all in good health as it leaves me at present

From Your Affect Son
Alfred

"Cole's Island was soon reached, and from our camp on the wretched little sand-spit we looked of across the marshes to the deserted hamlet of Legarville, or across the Stono toward Kiowa, or over toward the island of Folly, and wondered what there was beyond."[6]

Letter from Private A. Lyth to the Folks at Home

about 4 miles from Charleston
Folly Island S.C. April 9th 63

Dear Folks at Home

I take this opportunity to write to you again as it is the first chance I have had to write since we left Coles Island I received last night 2 letters from you both containing a skein of thread and one six postage stamps also 3 harpers and 2 other papers the new york weekly times We left Coles Island on sunday night April 5th I am with the company again as we did not fetch those peices of Artillery with us but left them to protect Coles Island with another Regt. We embarked on leaving Coles Island on a large flat scow, somewhat larger than a canal boat and in quite a large number of small boats attached to the scow then as steamers hitched on to us to tow us out the harbor + across the river to follys Island we started out at about 12 oclock in the night I tell you it was a fine night to see the whole Regt in small boats all in tow of the steamer on that moonlight night we all loaded our guns and primed them as we expected that we should be fired into on landing we run as near the shore as we could with the boats but they being heavly loaded we had to jump out + and wade some 200 feet to the shore in wadind to the shore we got in places where the water was up to our hips but we got ashore all safe Admiral Comodore Dupont superintended the landing of the troops when we were landed the boats were sent back for more troops we deployed 2 Co as schrimmerishers across the Island and commenced the advance that night expecting every minute come upon some rebel forification which if we had I suppose we should have charged upon Our march was very slow as we had to feel our way we marched along the beach until about 12 oclock the next day when we had ourselves in the woods until night should come so that we could resume the march again we rested until 12 oclock at night and then we fell in and resumed the march along the sea shore which was very fatigueing until we came within ½ a mile to the furtherest extremity of the Island without encountering anything but some old deserted brest works when we came to a halt and the troops hid theirselves in the woods where the underbrush was very thick all this time we had to live on crackers and salt horse and pork + water as we durst not build fires to cook coffee we had just got settled down when our Co + 2 others had to go on picket our Co had the right which was at the furtherest extremity of the Island right on the river or creek which divides this Island from Morris Island we were posted behind bushes and cautioned not to show ourselves at the peril of our lives we had great scrambling through the bushes to get to our positions on picket at day break in the morning we could see the rebels runing around on the other side of the river very plain and could see the fort on the other side of the river with the guns mounted on it our forces lay right in under the guns of the fort and if the rebs had known our position they would certainly have shelled us which of course the result would have been very serious to us after day break in the morning we could see some of the Rebel come to the shore + shoot ducks and come within easy range of our guns I should liked to have tried my hand at them but we had strick orders not to fire if we had of course we might have expected the same from the rebels. we lay watching them all day but of course they found out of our presence but of course they could only see an odd man now + then and did not know of the close proximity of our forces occasionly in the afternoon. The men exposed theirselves but the rebels did not fire but the Gen and a couple of Cols and some other officers exposed theirselves and they got a couple of rifle bullets flying after them in double quick time but it did not hit any of them. along in the afternoon the ironsides crossed the bar + some of the monitors after her and made for Charleston harbor Fort [ ] emieadate opened upon them we could see the shell burst very plainly + see the water spurt up in the air when the shell + shot struck the water we could see the flag flying over fort

**Charleston Harbor, S.C. View from Fort Sumter Parapet
facing Morris Island (1865)**

Sumter + see every shot that was fired from where we were we should think that most all the fireing was done by the forts + land battries it is supposed by us that they just went into the harbor to find the range of the rebel guns get the range of the forts and hunt up the torpedoes. We thought once we could see one burst for there was an awful column of smoke rose in the air at once then a report above all the cannonadeing. The fireing ceased just before sunset after going it a great rate for about 3 hours. we stood picket all the next night again on account that they could not releive us as the rebels we on the watch all the while we could hear the railroad wistle in very distinct in Charleston and the drums of the various Rebels camps on James + Morrises Island + could see a Rebel Regt on drill we stayed on picket untill yesterday in the afternoon when the picket was drawn in we had to make our way to the Regt without being seen leaving one man to fire on the rebels if they attempted to cross the stream and then to retreat if they came across we had to crawl on our hand + knees through the wood + underbrush till we joined the Regt so that the rebels would not know that we had drawn our pickets in we joined the Regt and then we marched about ¾ of a mile back under the cover of the woods and then encamped in the woods we are allowed to build fires in the hollows where they are well protecked by brush + trees in the day time + cook coffee. There are quite a number of cannon planted in our front in case of an attack which is not very likely as the Rebels will wait for us to attack them in their fortifications which peice of business will be done by our gunboats on the final attack on Charleston the 2 turret monitor is sunk on the bar not a great ways from here I suppose before this reaches you will have an account of the whole affair in the newspapers so you will know more than I can tell you of the affair if our forces are succesful in this undertaking I shall very likely celebrate my birthday in the city of Charleston

[A Lyth]

Letter from Private A. Lyth to his Father and Mother

Folly Island, S. C. April 9, 1863

Dear Father + Mother

I think I do not miss many of the letters you write if any. There is some enemy to this Regt some wares who writes such disgraseful letters about us we have allway had the praise of being a good disciplined and cleanly looking Regt in speaking of Lice whoever wrote it it is a malicious falsehood of course in those 22 days that were aboard of the New England there were a great many lice amongst the soldiers + officers too as we lay almost stowed on top of one another. but as soon as we got ashore the whole Regt most went off to a little stream and stripped naked and washed all over and built fires + washed + boiled all their clothes and dried them the same so no more at present

From Your Affect Son
Alfred

Letter from Private A Lyth to his Father and Mother

Coles Island S.C. April 14 63

Dear Father + Mother

I received 3 letters from you on the 10th + three newspapers The Letters were dated Mar 23 + 26 + April 1 I was very glad to hear that you were all well as the last letter stated my health was never better than at the present We have left Folly Island and returned to our old camp on Coles Island and another Regt has taken our place on Follys Is On the night of the 9 + 10th a squad of rebels of about 100 or 150 in number came across from Morris Island and got in rear of our outposts that were set out there to watch signals and give the alarm if the Rebels came across at a certain point. They came on at about 12 oclock in the night and were approaching one of our posts when the man on guard who belong to our Co halted them 'Who comes There' 'Friends' Halt friends + give the counter sign. yes we will give you the counter sign you yankee s-n b-h upon whitch they emiately fired a volly right at him The other 2 men on post with him ran and got away but he was shot in the right shoulder then he to run when they fired again one ball hiting him in the heel passing through his heel and coming out of his ankle. The Rebels came up to him asked him what Regt he belonged to he told them the 100th N.Y. they asked him his name he told them it was Charles Sabin. they asked him how many forces we had on that Island he told them he did not know as we were the first Regt on and he had not been to the rear to see if there were any more Then he asked the officer what his name was and he said Col Howard They then left him finding he could not walk and he lay there 2 or 3 hours before he was picked up he was a first rate fellow and his loss is very much regreted in the Company. When they left him they past close past other posts but the men were hid in the grass and they did not see them only one of our company was hollering Corporal when the rebels heard him they said something when he said don't shoot. Oh no we wont shoot you come fall in + come along so they took him prisoner right within arms length of two other fellows that were hid in the grass. his name was John McDonal he was an old sailor The next night there was a stronger picket line thrown out and the next night a whole Regt went on picket and a 12 pounder howitzer which us that maned the brass peices at this Island had to take care of and a Co from our Regt to support us Our Col was up with us all night so was our doctor by the way I never told you that our Col was a Georgia man Though I guess there is not a better union man.

From your Affect Alfred

"Then we made the redoubtable conquest of Folly Island. We were drawn up in our company street on a starlit-night and solemnly warned of the dangerous duty which was before us. We embarked on that big scow and numerous smaller boats, were towed by a steamer as near as she could get to the Folly beach, jumped into the water waist deep, waded ashore and formed a line expecting that the woods in front of us would soon be alive with an opposing enemy. Burt no foe appeared and so we sat down on the sand and empted the water out of our shoes and prepared for the tedious march to the head of the island."[7]

Letter from Private A. Lyth to his Father and Mother

Folly Island S.C Tuesday April 21st 63

Dear Father + Mother

Our Regt has at last received its pay we received it last night + I have put $50 in the chaplins hands to deliver to {UNKNOWN NAME} as he is coming to Buffalo by order of the Col. There is a great many of the boys are sending their money by mail in preferance of sending it by him as they are afraid to trust him but I think that he will deliver it safe for his own interests + however I have let him have mine and hope he will deliver it safe I got $78 + 40 cts which leaves me $28.48 which I think I shall need for if I should happen to have the bad luck to be taken prisoner or wounded I shall need it a great many of the boys are keeping all theirs till after the coming conflict. I guess the final attack on Charleston will have commenced befor this reaches you I understand that Admiral Dupont has orders to take Charleston or sink the fleet we left Coles Island April 15th + landed again on this Island the same day we fetched our 2 pieces of Artillery with us + have them planted near the head Quarters + have our tent pitched in the woods near our peices so that we shall be on hand if the rebels show their noses. we have very easy times of it while the Regt has to go on picket every 3[d] day we are bothered by the mosquitos + nats a great deal + there is whole Regts of wood ticks + snakes the boys oft get a snake in their beds I was setting in one of the boys tents one afternoon having chat when all at once a snake about three + half feet long stuck his head from under the palmetto leaves that the bed was made of and commenced crawling out by degrees we let halfway out when we gave him a knock that settled.

May 20th 1863

Geo. Clark + I took a walk this afternoon and by the courtesy of the "Signal Officer" were permitted to ascend the "Lookout" and take a peep through the Telescope. We saw Sentinels walking in the Ramparts of Sumter + boatsmen rowing in the river. We could also look down into Charleston. There are 2 Rebel camps about 3 miles from Co"H" and I could distinctly see the "rebs" walking through the streets of their camp ground.

The woods on the island used to be full of snakes but the underbrush has been burned out and the dead snakes are lying thick as peas. There is any quantity of fire flies in the woods which the boys find quite useful +convenient. They (the boys) are not allowed to impose themselves or have any fires so when they are on guard at night they catch a fire fly and put him in their hats and the fly will give light enough to show the time on the face of a watch. There are also a great number of chammeleons in the woods. They look like a lizard but sometimes they are Green then yellow, brown and I dont know what other colors. Sharks are also quite numerous. Some of the soldiers killed one of the tiger sharks on the beach that weighed 380 pounds. It was left in a kind of basin when the tide went out. One of the boys, not knowing what it was, took hold of its tail when it immediately turned round and inflicted a serious bite on the arm or leg of this soldier.

A day or two ago the 3 or 4 rebel pickets + our pickets laid down their guns and each came to their own edge of the stream the rebels commences to black guard our fellows then they asked our fellow if they would trade coffee + sugar for tobacco or any thing they had they said they would give almost anything for a little salt and they asked if our boys would exchance newspapers They our men said they could not trade newspapers till they got premision from our officers but said they could let them have sugar + coffee when the rebels heard that they began to strip off to swim the stream for to make the exchange but our boys told them to float what they wanted to send across on little boats or board + they would do the same which they did I heard that they sent over a newpaper for a little salt

The day before we came on this Island this last time one of the 62^d Ohio boys shot one of their Captain he was officer of the day + he was making his round on the picket line in the night when on coming near the sentinals post the sentinal sung out who comes there Halt three times when receiveing no answer he fired and shot him dead. I hope these few lines will find you all well + in good health as it leaves me at present. My love to you all

From You Aff Son, Alfred

Ed: Northern soldiers described the southern soldiers narrowly with names such as Rebs, Johnnies, or Secessionists. They felt that many of the southerners professed Union sentiments. Friendly relations occurred between the Northern and Southern soldiers on the picket line. Trading of miscellaneous goods and newspapers was also common on the picket lines

Letter from QM Clerk E. Cook to his Father and Mother

Folly Island, S.C. Monday April 27th 1863

Dear Father and Mother

I do not see what put the idea in your heads that we could resign and go home. There is no way of getting out of the picnic expect through sickness, inability or death. I have serious thoughts about being mustered out of the 100th and joining one of the negro regiments for 5 years that are raising here in South Carolina. …

I go into the sea to have a bath every other day. The water is quite warm + it is glorious to go in when the tide is coming in full force + have a good racing of from the breakers or to go out beyond the breakers + let the tide wash you ashore. Everything is at the stand still here at the present time with the exception that there was another 2 or 3 Regts come on this Island.

[E. Cook]

Letter from Private A. Lyth to his Father and Mother

Follys Island S.C. May 9th 63

Dear Father + Mother

The mail arrived here yesterday and fetched me a couple of papers the Tribune {missing words} with the illustration of our Regt landing on Coles Island The picture is a very good resembleance + I acually think I can see myself there helping to get those peices of Artillery ashore I received no letter whatever by this mail + was very much disappointed as it is over two weeks since we received the last mail. Everything in this quarter as yet is at a standstill in the shape of an advance on Charleston but are very busy building fortifications + diging rifle pits making roads.. They have got a fine little fort built for our cannon + we are settled in it. We fired a few shell over into the wood on James Island the other day I have been put in charge of the ammunition and when the gun is in action I have to pass out the kind of ammunition the Leaut calls for + to cut the fuse of the shell we have very easy time as {missing words} drill one hour a day then the rest of the time is our own The other day we killed a large poisonous snake he was some five feet in length and as thick as a persons wrist in the thickest part of him we tied a string to him and hung him up in a palmetto tree in emblem of the Southern Confederacy Yesterday there was quite a phenomena occur on this Island in the afternoon a black cloud was observed rising in the west and it rose until it came directly over the point of this Island + about 60 or 70 rods from we were we are stationed when it began to desend rapidly in the shape of a waterspout but when it got very near to the ground it turned into a whirlwind then the waterspout burst into a mist + spray and began to ascend with greater rapidty than it came down then the whirlwind followed {missing words} and took the sand over a hundred feet high it crossed over on to the of Morris Island then worked off on to the ocean + carried the water a considerable distance into the air I wish you would send me a couple of watch keys in the first letter you write + you can send that brass watch chain if you think it will come in an envelope I have bought me a pretty goodwatch of one of the boys of another Regt that was pretty hard up and I have lost the cord + key that was attached to it while scrambling through the bushes the other day I must close now hoping these few lines will find you all in good health + spirits as it leaves me at present Give my love to William + Sarah Ann and let me know how they are getting along My love to you all

Your Affect Son Alfred

N.B. write soon let me know that you are alive

For how pleasant {missing words}	How pleasent tis to feel
Amid lifes changing scenes	The kind and fostering care
Some friend from whom the rays	Of those who seek our good
Of heavenly nature gleams	And who our sorrows share
From whom when weary hours	Then let us strive to be
To us are lingering near	A friend to all in need
The light of love can shine	That we from them may reap
To fill the Heart with cheer	The blessing of the deed

[A. Lyth]

Letter from QM Clerk E. Cook to Parents

Q. M. Dept. 1ˢᵗ Brig. {unknown} Div.
Beaufort S.C. May 23rd 1863

My dear Parents

I returned from Folly Island today only to learn that I have got to rejoin my regiment on Monday. Geo. Clark is now Orderly Sergeant which would have been my position if I had remained with the Company.

Co "H" has got the finest camp I ever saw. The tents are all trimmed with cedar boughs and present a splendid appearance. At the lower end of the street, where the Captains tent is, an arch is erected in which the letter "H" + {unknown} 100 are hanging. Their street is thoroughly cleaned every morning and look as neat as a new pin. The General passed through the other day and remarked that he did not see why all the companies could not have as fine a camp as Co "H". Wood ticks are countless. Geo. Stoddard pulled 10 or 12 off his body in one day.

View of Forts Wagner and Gregg on Morris Island, S. C. (1865)

Stinging Gnats fill the air and the only way the boys can live with them is to put a smoking brand inside their tent which drives away the gnats + mosquitoes at the expense of suffocation.

Letter from QM Clerk E. Cook to Parents

Q. M. Dept. 1ˢᵗ Brig. {unknown} Div.
Beaufort S.C. May 24ᵗʰ 1863

My dear Parents

I returned last evening from a visit to the 100ᵗʰ Reg't. on Folly Island and the first news I heard on my return was that all the detached men were ordered to report to their regiments. So tomorrow I must again join my company. I cannot say that I am sorry for it although if the order had not been received I think I should have remained where I am. If the regiment goes into a fight I want to be with it and try and earn another step in the line of promotion.

[ ] received notice on the 16ᵗʰ that he had been promoted to 2ᵈ Lieutenant and on the 17ᵗʰ we both started for the regiment. He to report for duty + I to make a visit. The boat did not leave Hilton Head until the next day and so we had to remain all night at the Port Royal house. I thought I was going to have a good nights rest but the flies troubled me so that I could not sleep and I had to get up in the middle of the night and put on my pants and shove the bottoms of them in my stockings to prevent being eat up entirely. The next day I left but {unknown name} had "Wet" his Commission so many times that things were rather messed up in his head and he got life. When I sailed from Folly Island he had

[E. Cook]

Letter from Private A. Lyth to his Brother

Folly Island S.C. May 25ᵗʰ 1863

Dear Brother

…We go into the sea every evening and have a bathe. By the way I must tell you of a little occurance that happened in our Regt a couple of week ago There has been a promotion of Company offices in our Regt and a couple of orderly Sergt have got Commisions. There is a kind of a simple fellow in Co. F. so some of the boys told him if he should try hard he might get a Commision So he said he would try if they would help him so as he could not write he got one of them to write him out a recommend and they all were to sign it which they all did They read it to him when they got through and read it thus. Since I enlisted in this army I have done my duty as a soldier I have never been in the guard house seldom on the doctors list never been court martialed and thus they read on giving such a glowing description of himself that he was sure of getting his commision but the document read quite the contraery stating Since I enlisted in this army I have never done my duty as a soldier should do I have been in the guard house a great many times and Court martialed some 6 or 7 times I often play up sick and go to the doctors to get excused from duty and thus it ran on giving him the worst kind of a caracter so they told him to take the paper and show it to the Captain The captain some how or other having heard of the affair took the paper when he presented it to him and read it without a smile and told him to take it to the doctor and let him see it then to go to the AdJuntant then to the Col well he went to the doctor in high spirits as the Capt had said nothing against it when the doctor read it he hunted him out of his tent double quick but not caring for the doctor much he went to the adjutant after the adjutant had read it he smiled and told it was all right he then went to the Col the Col took the paper and read it and then he handed it back to him and told him to go to his camp away he went back and the Capt asked him what the Col said he told him the adjutant told him it was all right and when the Col read it he had said nothing against it well said the captain you'll get your commision he went and told all the boys he was going to get his commision and that he would remember the services they had rendered him in helping to get it and he treated them to 12 dollars worth of wine he met the orderly sergent of his company who had Just been promoted and said oh...you can put on style with your shoulder straps but maybe in a week I can play as much of that as you can now that is a very good one but John if the Joke 4 or 5 and myself have on hand at present don't beat it I'm a dutchman when it is complete I will let you know of it

From Your Affect Brother Alfred

Letter from Private A. Lyth to his Father and Mother

Folly Island South Carolina June 9th 1863

Dear Father and Mother

I received your kind letter of May 25th also 2 Harpers Weekly's and 2 Weekly times I was very glad to hear that you were all well and in good health as it leaves me at present There has been orders read off that the troops of this department are all to be furnished with straw hats which will be furnished to us soon and the order also states that the men are to no fatigue work and as little other duty as possible through the day That the men should be furnished with fishing material and that they should fish in the morn and evening for the good of their health The order also states that every soldier should cover his tent with brush that is green limbs of trees and so forth and that every soldier must strike his tent twice a week and air it and all his clothing. All the tents in our detachment have our tents so fixed so we can take them down and put them up again in 3 minute We all have an abor of green bush built over them and another built in front in

71

which we pass the warm hours of the day either reading or writing playing cards or passing the time away somehow at our leasure Just as I was writing the last sentence small green snake fell out of a tree Just over my tent it fell on the tent then slid down to the ground near my feet were I soon put an end to him. Take things on the whole we should get along very well on this Island if it was not for the mosquitoes I tell you it makes a person open his eyes when a half a dozen come buzzing him when he has laid down to sleep each one carrying a brick under his wing to sharpen his bill with and I think it would astonish you to see a couple of them take hold of a large black snake and carry him off to feed their young ones

[A. Lyth]

Letter from Private A. Lyth to his Parents

Folly Island, S.C June 10th, 1863

Dear Mother and Father

It is rumored that all the troops on this Island except a Reg't or two are going to join the Potomac army and that a Brigade of negro troops are going to take their place here It is said that our Regt is a going to stay on account of it being the healthiest on the Island They are now issueing orders that solders shall do no duty whatever except picket duty only in the cool of the evening They will have no drill and they will only have dress parade in the cool of the evening I wish you could only see our Regt some time as they turn out for dress parade every man has his belts and shoes so that you might see yourself in them and each man has two pair of white gloves so he has to turn out with a clean pair on all such occations and they must be clean and neat in all respects and they are the largest Regt on the Island I tell you it looks splendid. Our Col is getting very strick though. We are pretty well fortified on this Island and now they are busy mounting seige peices on the fortifications The principal ones are those that are bearing on the Rebel fortifications on Morris Island. But the rebels are not idle all this time. I was down to the point of this Island the other day and see the rebels are mounting peices on the point of Morris Island bearing on this Island.

The day before yesterday a black snake came into my tent and commenced eating some crackers that I had soaking in a cup some half a dozen of us got sticks to kill him but he run up a tree and down another one before we knew where he was we had just killed 2 snakes simlar to him the day before.

[A Lyth]

Letter from Private A. Lyth to his Sister

Folly Island S.C. June 27th 63

Dear Sister

I received your kind letter of June 11th and was very glad to hear that you were all well and in good health as it leaves me at present Just as I received your letter last night the orders were going round to every Regt and battery on this Island for to get prepared for the attack and be ready on a moment's notice to open on the rebels No soldier is allowed to roam around the Island as we used to do as there are guards posted all over the Island to arrest all they find without a pass. I have a pass that will pass me anywhere on the island so you see I have a good chance to see what is going on. The attack will not begin untill the morning of the 4 of July so you see when all the peacefull citizens of Buffalo are woke from their nights rest by the noise of your cannons in the park. The soldiers in the vicinity of Charleston will be tumbleing out of their bunks and grasping their arm tightening their belts eager for the fight and victor.

[A Lyth]

Letter from Private A. Lyth to his Sister

Folly Island S.C. June 27th 63

Dear Sister

Yesterday every man in our Regt all drew a new india rubber blanket and new hats. The kind of hats we drew are those tall drab plug broad rim hats and when the Regt got them on we looked like a Regt of farmers though they are an excellent thing in this hot country Then we drew mosquitoes bars. these bars are 7 ½ feet long a little over 2 feet broad and 3 feet high they are wove like braze about as close as a sand sive now we fix these over our bunks and get in let down the front curin then we are in a cage out of the musquitoes reach but still if you get under your bars in the evening you can see them come and light on your bars and stick their bills out at you. The Regt has draw all new A tents so the soldiers wont have to carry our shelter tents any more the teams will carry the tents here after all that our musquitoes bars weigh when rolled up to put in the knapsack is 3 ounces

[A Lyth]

Chapter 3

Just Before the Battle, Mother

George H. Root (1862)

Just before the battle, mother,
I am thinking most of you,
While upon the field we're watching
With the enemy in view.
Comrades brave are 'round me lying,
Filled with the thoughts of home and God.
For well they know that on the morrow,
Some will sleep beneath the sod.

Chorus
Farewell, mother, you may never
Press me to your breast again;
But, Oh, you'll not forget me, mother;
If I'm numbered with the slain.

On, I long to see you, mother,
And the loving ones at home.
But I'll never leave the banner
Till in honor I can come
Tell all the traitors all around you,
That the cruel words we know,
In every battle kill our soldiers
By the help they give the foe

Chorus

Hark! I hear the bugles sounding,
'Tis the signal for the fight.
Now may God protect us, mother,
As He ever does the right.
Hear "The Battle Cry of Freedom,"
How it swells upon the air,
Oh yes, we'll rally 'round the standard
Or we'll perish nobly there

Chorus

"Pre-battle"

Ed: Many "rookie" soldiers eagerly awaited battles so that they could demonstrate their courage and bravery and defeat the enemy. In addition, it tested them and allowed them to come to grips with their own mortality. Patriotism and sense of duty strengthened their resolve before battle. Many soldiers, knowing of the randomness of injury or death, approached it with a sense of fatalism: their outcome was beyond their control. At this point, the "boys" were untried soldiers with a naive conception of what battle was like.

Letter from Private A. Lyth to his Father and Mother

Folly Island S.C. July 10th 63

Dear Father + Mother

I take this oppertunity of writing you these few lines not knowing when they will leave here as the operations against Charleston commenced this morning The batteries on this Island opened as 5 oclock this morning against the rebel batteries on the point of Morris I. after between 2 + 3 hours Bombarding The rebels guns were nearly silenced Gen Strong crossed folly river with his brigade and some negro troops and worked himself into the rear of the rebel batteries and captured all the rebs before the reingforcements that were coming up could reach them Our part of Regt was in the fight Our peices remain in their old position I belive there was quite a number wounded some very badly They established the hospital near were our peices are I am about well now though I am a little weak as yet I hope these few lines will find you all in good health

I should have wrote more particulars but you will see them in the papers. I send my love to you all

From Your Affect
Son Alfred

"Battle"

Ed: Civil war soldiers relied on the line. They stood next to each other, shoulder to shoulder, inspiring strength and support. If the line was broken, their collective strength dissipated, and the soldiers became more concerned with their own survival rather than defeating their common enemy. As a gap in the line opened due to death or injury, the officers exhorted the troops to close the gap.

Many soldiers in the civil war looked forward to battle in order to prove their courage. Religion, patriotism, and a sense of duty prepared them for this ultimate test. Granted, they were apprehensive and focused on their vulnerability and mortality. The randomness of death or injury was known and the sense of fatalism helped him cope with the apparent dangers. Their values and society's norms that were taught at home and in school sustained them in this trying time. Courage and character, together with a strong belief as to the cause, carried them into battle. Soldiers were encouraged when they saw long line of Union soldiers as far as they could see.

Once the battle commenced, the soldiers became disoriented and confused with the blinding smoke, loud noise, and lack of visibility. In night battles, such as Fort Wagner, muzzle flashes and exploding shells added to the chaos. In addition, they could hear the crying of the wounded soldiers. Officers standing or sitting on horseback behind the soldiers saw even less.

The battle tactic of shoulder-to-shoulder lines forming an unbroken chain across the field fortified those in the battle. They gave each other strength, shared the same chance of death or injury, and supported each other through these awful experiences. Lines were closed as gaps appeared. Despite the line, each discovered his own character and limits. In their first battle, often described as "seeing the elephant," the soldiers' thoughts moved from patriotism and glory to survival. When the line broke down, the chaotic nature of the battle increased. Soldiers were not trained in exchanging blows with muskets, fists, bayonets, or swords. Immediately after the battle, noncombatants and medical personnel tended to the wounded. The noise of the wounded faded, and they joined the silence of the dead. Remains were hastily interred, and all too often after a hard rain, the remains would reappear.

Subsequent to the battle, roll call was held and names were called for the record. Silence after a name gave the soldiers a repeated and painful reminder of the cost of the battle. The deaths of their comrades gave the soldiers further reason to fight. However, once soldiers had "seen the elephant," they were not eager to see it again.

The black soldiers, members of the 54th regiment from Massachusetts that had fought in the Battle of Fort Wagner had demonstrated their willingness to fight and ability to fight. While skeptical at first, the soldiers felt that the blacks should be able to join the fight for their freedom.

Sergeant Edwin Nichols Diary

Sunday – July 19 - We joined the regiment about noon and formed line of battle on the beach. About the same time the monitors and ironsides moved up and opened on Wagner, and continued blazing away until after sundown. Then commenced the horrid strife as to who should be master of Fort Wagner. The first brigade, commanded by General Strong, and headed by the 54th Massachusetts colored regiment led the attack and was repulsed with great slaughter. The second brigade followed and was also repulsed. The 7th N. H. was a little in advance of our regiment and succeeded in getting very near the fort, and a few men got inside, but could not stand the fearful fire they were exposed to, and those that were not cut down, retreated.

Our regiment marched in line of battle and kept a good line until they got near the fort, in spite of the gaps that were constantly made in its ranks; but the men closed up, and on they went without wavering or taking any notice of their comrades falling around them. It was now dark and the rebels were pouring murderous fire of grape and canister shot and shell from every gun they could bring to bear on us, besides musketry and hand-grenades. No tongue can tell or pen describe that terrible scene

Some of our men got inside the fort and held part of it for some time, in spite of musketry, hand-grenades and everything else the rebels could bring against us. Had reinforcements come up at this time the fort would have been ours, but none came, and those that were not killed or wounded made their way out again as best they could. As I crossed the moat on my way out again, it appeared to be full of dead and wounded soldiers, with no help for them; as it was certain death to any man who attempted to rescue them. At this time the groans of the wounded and dying were fearful to hear and were enough to appall the bravest amongst us.

A second time the regiment formed, or rather the remains of it, and marched back again; but before we got near the fort the orders were countermanded – all was lost.

We had seven companies in the fight and all the officers that are present now are the colonel, two captains and one lieutenant. Company C lost 32, killed, wounded or missing, but there is scarcely a man in the company but what was shot, through some part of his clothes, Yesterday there was not a better, or finer, or larger regiment in the department; today it would make a man's heart ache to look upon it. Today our men are burying the dead and caring for the wounded.

Tuesday, 21st – We had a dress parade last evening and all the officers we could muster were Col. Dandy, Capt. Evert, now acting adjutant, Capt. Bailey, and Lieut. Howell. It was a hard site to look upon and caused quite a sensation amongst the spectators, as well."[8]

"Unfortunately for us, the assault on Wagner was deferred until daybreak the next morning, by which the enemy as well as ourselves, were prepared for the struggle. Though our brave fellows reached the work, crossed the ditch, and even scaled the parapet, they could not maintain their footing and were driven back with severe loss, having their killed and wounded in the hands of the enemy. Then there was a week's delay, during which the iron-clads daily poured their shot into the fort, and we could see the great showers of each and dust displaced as the shell struck the work, while the garrison remained practically unharmed within the massive bomb-proofs. During this week of waiting, more troops had been landed, more guns put in position, and all preparations were made for another and desperate attempt to take the fort.

My comrades, let us in fancy transport ourselves this afternoon from these pleasant groves to that sandy island on the coast of South Carolina. Not a solitary tree shades us from the scorching heat, while the white sand reflects the sunlight with dazzling brightness. As we cast our gaze around the horizon and recall the scene that once was so familiar to us, in our rear lie the woods of Folly Island, across the marshes we see Secessionville in the distance, then the dark woods over on Black Island, then more marshes like a giant prairie, with Fort Sumter silent and sullen rising beyond them. On

Morris Island, S. C. Artillery Unit July, 1863 Haas & Peale Phtographers

Morris Island, S. C. Artillery Unit July 1863 Haas & Peale photographers

our right is the blue ocean with the blockading squadron in the offing, and the ironclads closer in shore. Since early morning the land batteries and the fleet have been hammering away at Wagner until at last the guns of the fort are silenced. All day you have been lying with other troops along the beach below the Beacon House, waiting for the decision of the Commanding General, and at last the order comes shall be stormed after dark.

How can we describe the horrors of a night attack, when friends as well as foes are concealed from view, or only revealed by the flashes of the guns; when it is almost impossible to convey orders, or to bring up re-inforcements, and when those who succeed in reaching the parapet, find themselves unsupported and alone. Just as the assault was made, a tremendous thunderstorm commenced, and the flashes of lightning and the roar of heaven's artillery added to the terrors of the scene. General Strong's brigade formed the first line, and went in gallantly, but Strong himself was soon mortally wounded, the gallant your Colonel Shaw of the 54th Massachusetts was killed, many others had fallen, and soon the whole line was driven back. Putnam's brigade, to which the 100th belongs, pressed forward through the storm of fire and through the flying fugitives of the first line, with a stern determination to carry the fort in spite of all obstacles.

You reach the other ditch, cross it beneath the plunging fire from the crest and commence the struggle for the parapet; a foothold is gained on one corner and messengers are dispatched from re-inforcements, but Colonel Putnam, like scores of others, is killed within the fort and the enemy pour out of the bomb-proofs, and have the advantage in their familiarity with the place, while you have, as it were, to feel your way in the dark, that all your sacrifice proves in vain, and the word is passed to fall back. Retreating under such circumstances is almost as fatal as advancing, and many a poor fellow fell during the retreat. The 100th lost heavily in this fearful night attack." [9]

Letter from Private E. Cook to Parents

Folly Island, S.C. July 19ᵗʰ 1863

My dear Parents

We had another terrible battle last night. Yesterday as soon as the rain ceased in the morning about 10 o'clock the firing began and continued until 8 or 9 oclock at night without ceasing. Sumter fired about 3 times a minute and all day long it was one continual boom, boom, and boom without any ceasing. Last night our boys made a charge, the 100ᵗʰ was in it. We lost very heavily, the rebs bayoneted out wounded. We were repulsed again in the charge. I think now that Genl. Gilmore will try some other way to take it. I think this fort is the only one that will give us any trouble. If we take this we will have Charleston.

Rebel Officers, taken prisoners, say that we can take "Sumter" but all H-l cant take "Wagner". It is steel cased + casemated with railroad iron {unknown} from the casemates so that it is perfectly Bombproof.

I think we will take within a fortnight our loss is terrible. Our regiment lost all their field officers all the hire offices but five. Our Major was wounded. Genls. Strong + Seymour were wounded. What do the people north think of the attack on Charleston? Did they expect it? I have not heard direct from the 100ᵗʰ but if I hear anything about Geo. Clark I will write to you.

I am in great haste. I never worked so hard in my life as I am doing now and have done for the last month or more. I do not write to anybody but you. News is very scarce. A Dollar was offered to day for a single copies of the N.Y. Herald of the 15th and even then those that had them would not sell. They sell in N.Y. for 2 cents and here

2 dollars would hardly buy one. I am well. Write to me soon + send all the news. Geo. Stoddard is well liked by his Quartermaster. The Captain told me yesterday that he was going to keep George and pay him 25 or 40 cents extra pay.

Your Aff Son
Edward

"Post-Battle"

Ed: All soldiers, including ones in this battle, experienced the risk of what is now called "friendly fire." Lack of training led to many unintended deaths. Hand to hand combat using fists or bayonets was not taught nor trained, and that is precisely what occurred in a major part of this battle. The firing of muskets was all around them. The cries of the dying and wounded pierced the night. Officers lost control of their regiments, and the struggle for survival prevailed. After a major battle, northern regiments had roll call. It was difficult to bear to hear the called names to which there was no response.

Letter from Private A. Lyth to his Folks at Home

Hilton Head Hospital
July 21st 63

Dear Folks at Home

I was taken pretty bad with the diorea when I was on Folly Island and they put me a board of the Hospital boat were I was 4 or 5 days then they fetched us to the Hospital here I have about got over the diorea and am gaining strength pretty fast Our Regt has been in a fight and is nearly cut to peices you will have seen the account in the papers before this reaches you A good many of the wounded came down on the boat that I came on I must close now excuse my short letter.

From Your Loving Son, Alfred

Letter from QM Clerk E. Cook to his Parents

Office [ ] Folly Island S.C.

My dear parents

I suppose you feel rather lonesome I am not in good health, nor have I been for several days. The heat is oppressive and causes a headache each day. We have considerable wind but as this island is white sand the wind becomes so heated in passing over it that when it reaches us it is oppressive instead of luxurious. We have lightning every night but little rain + thunder. When it does thunder it sounds as if everything was going to pieces. The lightning is grand and very different from the lightning we have up north. I am stationed now with Capt. Walbridge at the north end of Folly Island S.C. and right opposite Morris Island. I can have a plain + close view of every shot + shell that is fired by either side. There has been but little firing within the last 3 or 4 days. I should not wonder if the rebs were preparing for some kind of a move to cut us off. In the meantime our men are working hard every night with a few hundred yards of "Wagner" and within short rifle range of the sharp shooters. I guess some of our men are killed every day but the work goes on steadily + surely + all the rebs can do won't stop or impede our progress. If we can't batter down the hellish Iron hung institution we will dig under it and blow it into dust.

I fear that there is but little or no hope that we shall ever see George Clark again. Nothing has yet been heard from him. I have written to his brother for instructions in regard to the disposal of his effects. Dr. Howell wants me to come back to the company and be orderly sergeant. What would you advise me to do about it. I do not think I shall get my extra duty pay in the Q.M. Dept. for that has been stopped by an act of Congress and I am now working again for $10 # per month and patriotism.

I do not have to work as hard as I used to last month and in June, nor am I able to do it even if I had to. My head troubles me so that even in writing this letter page + a half I have had to knock off 2 or 3 times. Except the heat I am doing first rate. I am so fat that I think you would hardly know me. The sand is very fine and seems to sift right through a persons clothes and makes him feel nasty + dirty all the time. Oh won't I be glad when I can get back into old Buff and get off this dirty soldiers toggery and put on a nice clean shirt of pure white cotton and sleep between cotton sheets and have a chance to bathe in fresh water. I am sick of this salt water bathing. It is well enough in cool weather, but in these hot days it acts on the perspiration of the body just as water does on oil – It don't mix; and when we come out of the water instead of feeling nice + clean we feel just as if we had been in an oil can. Our Batteries will be ready to open on Sumter in about a week. I will write you all the news just as fast as possible. I think it is very likely that when our batteries are ready to open they will fire right over "Wagner" and try breach "Sumter".

I am strongly inclined to believe that within 10 days from this time there will be no rebels on Sumter. Our Batteries + floating batteries are almost finished and there will be but little delay in getting them to work after they are finished. Write to me as often as you can and tell me what the buffalo people say of the 100th Regt. in the last fight. Some of Co "H" boys were inside fort "Wagner" for nearly an hour but they were not supported and finally had to back out again.

Edward L. Cook

Letter from Private T. Maharg to Private A. Lyth

Morris Isl. July 26

Friend Al

Jim {unknown name} received your letter yesterday + I had the pleasure of reading it. We have had a pretty hard fight here lately it was on the evading of the 18th that we charged on fort Wagner & was drove back after holding it about two hours. All I believe we would have taken the fort if it had been daylight as it was it was so dark that our men shot one another our Regt fired a volly into the 48th and the 67th fired 3 vollys into us killing & wounding a great many.

All our Col. is a [ ] the last time I seen him in the fight he was in the line of file closers back of the flag he told us to keep as near the flag as we could. The 9th M was the Regt. a head of us and when they got about ¼ mile from the fort they broke and run through our lines which was enough to make any Regt. brake but ours did not flinch but went on loosing men at every step the first that fell was {unknown word} & John Allen and then Tom Wharton To was on my left + Townsend was on my right – they are both gone. Geo Clark I guess is killed for we have not heard anything from him Lient Runkill is killed + a great many more. There was 22 killed wounded & missing in our Camp. Major Nash was wounded and our Adjutant is missing Roby Henderson is wounded in the foot I seen him when he was shot. All they talk of opening again tomorrow the rebles keep up a brisk canonading on our pickets and there is more or less hurt every day we have been on picket twice the first time Camp I had 7 men wounded and the last time there was five our Camp done the scrimmishing last time + we went within 10 yards of the Rebles picket it was so dark we could not see them but one of our boys coughed + bang went a musket right at his nose but did not hurt him Give my respects to all the boys there and tell them to wright soon.

Yours For Ever Tom Maharg

Ed: "Friendly fire" as it is now termed did occur and there was no real interest to investigate it after the battle. It was survival, pure and simple.

Letter from QM Clerk E. Cook to his Parents

Folly Island S.C. July 29th 1863

My dear Parents

The weather is decidedly warm, but we do not feel the heat very much because we are on the beach of the ocean and generally have a cool sea breeze blowing all day.

I am afraid Geo. Clark is either a prisoner or else something worse. No trace can be found of him: he was wounded + left on the field. I have inquired of everybody that knew him but no one saw anything of him after he fell. <u>One</u> of the trio has gone; who shall the next be. The Lieut. of our company wants me to come back to the company and be orderly sergeant, but I have refused to go unless the boys of the company express the wish to have me that position. I told him I would come back as a corporal if he thought it was for the good of the company but I would not overstep any of the other noncommissioned officers. He replied that he did not want me back unless I came as orderly sergt. I do not know what steps he will take in the matter but I think I shall have to return to my company before many days. I shall try my best to have

Geo. Stoddard remain where he is. He is getting almost as fat as I am on high living.

We expect an attack from the rebs on this end of the Island every night. It is the only hope of the rebs attack us here and move up. They could do it to for we have no troops down here and our men are working now to get things in readiness but it will take us some little time get prepared for an attack. The officer commanding our river battery, and the only battery that commands the river both ways and the only battery that could be used against an attacking party, says that if the rebs should come down on us now, we could do nothing to oppose them but would have to desert this end of the island and 10 large guns, and retreat to Morris Island.

Give my love to all and tell them to write.

Good Bye in Haste
Your Aff. Son
Edward L. Cook
Co H. 100 N.Y.V.

"It seems to me that there can be no more severe test of the pluck and endurance of troops than such a long siege as that of Wagner. During the fifty days of its continuance the 100th rarely went on a tour of duty without the occurrence of more or less causalities, and as they returned to camp, instead to the satisfaction which men feel after a battle is over, there is nothing to look forward to but the certainty of going to the front again in three days, with the uncertainty as to who would be the next victim."[10]

Letter from Private A. Lyth to his Brother

Ward F.
General Hospital
Hilton Head Aug 6th 63

Dear Brother

I have seen fellows that run around all day long who look to have got their strength ask the doctor if they could go back to their Regts and he would say no you had better stay here a little longer than go back to your Regt and be taken sick again right off. I tell you when a soldier is stricken down with sickness and he is laid upon his sick bed then he wishes himself at that home he has left. Oh! how he wishes he could be amongst the kind friends he has left he thinks of his and what care she would take of him if he were but at home I know those were my thoughts as I lay sick in bed in the hospital and I have heard a good many say the same. Give my love to Sarah Ann + William + the Children My love to you all

From Your Loving Brother Alfred Lyth

Ed. While battles represented high adventure and excitement, sickness was not something that was contemplated upon enlistment. Nor was the reality of camp life with long stretches of inactivity and boredom. Severe illnesses, some of which resulted in death, together with the unsanitary camps and poor food caused fever, pain, and persistent fatigue. It seemed to take its toll on the invincibility of youth. Little did the soldiers in Company H imagine that sickness would kill more men between 1861 and 1865 than battle injuries. Diarrhea and dysentery were the primary cause of death in the war.

Letter from QM Clerk E. Cook to his Parents

Quartermasters Office Monday Morning Aug. 7th 1863

Dear Parents

Hurrah! Forts Wagner + Gregg are ours. The rebs skeddaddled last night leaving their dead unburied in the fort. They say the stench of dead bodies was so great that our boys could not stay in the fort. Our firing was so rapid + hot that they could not bury their dead. We were going to charge on the works this morning but before we could see to move the rebs had evacuated + we found an empty fort. We lost no man Except those killed by torpedoes buried in the earth and only a few in that manner.

[E Cook]

Letter from Private A. Lyth in the Hospital to his Parents

Ward F General Hospital Hilton Head S. C. August 14th, 1863

Dear Parents

Today it is quite cool we have a nice breeze off the ocean and the themometer is only 83 degrees in the shade Melons in this part of the country are all about gone there are a few tomatoes that the negroes peddel around and you can buy them very cheap of them when I buy five cents worth I have enough for three meals and I can get plenty of vinegar + plenty sugar to fix them up as they are both used on the table in the dining room where I go to get my meals When this place was taken by our forces all the rebels and planters cleared out double quick and you should have see them run as the negroes say they left household property and

Negros behind in their haste to get away so the Negros what staid settled down on their massas plantation and raise produce for to keep themselves on in the winter time and raise a great quantity of stuff which they sell to the soldiers they are begining to dig sweet potatoes for imeaditate use but they generally leave them in the ground untill the latter part of September or the month of October. Peaches are begining to get ripe

[A Lyth]

Letter from Private T. Maharg to Private A. Lyth

Hundredth Regt Camp
on Morris Isl Sep 2/63

Friend Al

I read your letter directed to John Warham + I was sory to hear that you ware taken sick again but I hope it will not last long + I hope to see you back soon Al John Warham was killed on the night of the 31 while on picket in the trenches he was on post + a shell came from Wagner + bursted right over him tareing him dreadfuly he never knew what struck him Al the Regt is having some hard times now we have the advance + have to go on picket every third night besides camp guard All there is not a time our Regt went up in the trenches but we have lost from 10 to 12 killed + wounded Stives was wonded in the foot the same night Warham was killed + has gone off somewhere. Dave White was slighlty wounded in the sholdier but he is with the company not fit for duty. I got a Slight touch of a shell on the lip but it is all right now but it was enough to let me taste how a little more would feal. Al we are now not more than 95 yards from fort Wagner when we go on picket.

From Your Friend+ Tentmate, Tom

Letter from QM Clerk E. Cook to his Parents

Folly Island S.C. Sept. 10/63

My dear parents

I have about an inch of candle left after having finished my work this evening and its light shall be devoted to your use. More than a year has now passed since I joined the volunteers. It does not seem so long does it? But when I think of the many things that have transpired in that short space of time then it seems as though I had been a long time away from my dear old home a very long while. One think, within that time 2 or 3 of my girls have got married and I don't know how many more are contemplating the same act so that by the time I return there will be none of them left for me. But never mind "Ed" + I have got a plan of our own. And I will it to you if you won't tell anybody. I have got a country girl picked out that none of you know anything about and when I return Ed + I are going to marry her – perhaps – and take father's land warrant and go out and locate it and turn cozy old farmers in short order. Will you come out and visit us once in a while? I would tell you the girls name but I do not know it myself although I know that there is such a girl.

Sept 11/63 <u>Evening</u>

I think our land forces are now going to have a short resting spell. I don't think though that Genl. Gilmore will keep them idle very long. This is the most unhealthy month in the South and he may perhaps keep them inactive until next month but no longer. It is my opinion also that only a small force of men and artillery will be kept on Morris Island. If the Ironclads do not soon succeed in reducing the long line of batteries on Sullivan Island, I think our general will take the job into his own hands, and by some move, get possession of the Island with his land forces. We have just heard the news that {unknown} has obtained possession of Chattanooga but the news is so good that we do not believe it. We do believe however that "Wagner" + "Gregg" are ours and Sumter soon will be. Several deserters came into our lines today from James Island S.C. They say that there is very much dissatisfaction among the rebel troops and that they are quarreling and fighting + murdering among themselves. The Georgia + North Carolina troops are calling to go home and protect themselves from {unknown}'s army who is threatening to invade their state with a large army. But Beauregard has them fixed for he has got the Georgia boys on James Island and the North Carolina troops on Sullivan's Island and the South Carolina troops garrisoning Charleston + {unknown}. So there is no chance for them to escape. Still every few days some of the most venturesome will swim the rivers + wade + crawl through the intervening swamps and come into our lines. Those that came last report that the conviction among the Officers and men of the rebel troops is that the City of Charleston must fall before long.

Their conviction is most certainly right, and no one among our troops has ever entertained the first doubt since we took Morris Island, that the fate of Charleston was as surely declared as though it had been written in letters of fire upon the vault of heaven. One of the greatest pieces of strategy + engineering that has proved successful, during this war (or in any war) was the taking of the lower end Morris Island. When we were strongest the Enemy thought we were weekest. While we were daily receiving reinforcements of troops, ordnance + ammunition, they thought we were evacuating. While we were building our sand batteries opposite and within pistol shot of their high sand hill batteries and while we had a large force to sustain the working party, they thought we had but a small picket posted along the beach and bank; and so confident were they that this supposition of theirs was correct and that we were evacuating that it was their intention to have attacked us the night that we opened on them but something prevented them. Right under the mouths of their guns we planted our mortars + erected our cannon, and to use their own language "<u>Stole from them Morris Island</u>.". The only drawback, the only

mismove that has been made by Gilmore on this campaigne was the false
+ fatal one of attacking by Storm the hell-hole "Wagner" on the night of
July 18/63. Everything else has worked beautifully except our little 200
pounder "Swamp Angel" which is a too much inclined to hide herself in
the mud when our folks make her speak.

Sept 16th

Yesterday it commenced to cloud up and today it is raining I am doing
well as usal and I may have to go back to my Regt soon how as they are
sending some away every day now, and they are going to send a lot of the
wounded north in a few days. I begin to think it is time that I was back
again to the Regt and that I had been here long enough. The duty is not
so heavy in the Reg't now as it was before the fall of fort Wagner and
I may have to go back to my Regt soon how as they are sending some
away every day now, and they are going to send a lot of the wounded
north in a few days. I begin to think it is time that I was back again to
the Regt and that I had been here long enough. The duty is not so heavy
in the Reg't now as it was before the fall of fort Wagner and I think Gen
Gillmore is giving the boys a bit of a resting spell untill the navy fetches
fort Moultre and other batteries so that by our troops may take peacefull
possesion of the city and the sooner that comes to pass I think the better
as it is fully expected that the fall of Charleston will be a death blow to
the rebelion and I sincerly hope it may all the rebel prisoners that have
been brought here that belong to North Carolina Tennesee Regts are
strong against the rebels and will take the oath of alleigence and even
some of the South Carolina Georgia Alabama and Mississippi Regts will
take the oath sooner than go back to the confederacy,

Speaking of those dirty soldiers – you must recollect that a soldier cannot
dig ditches and do soldiers fatigue work and keep their clothes clean. And
besides if those soldiers had new shoes + pants they were in their knapsacks
waiting to be put on when they drew near their cherished homes.

95

I am dirty now, dirty pants, dirty blouse and old cap. I almost believe not know me if you should see me. I never carry any extra clothes in my knapsack except shirts + stockings. I draw a pair of pants + wear them right straight along weekdays + Sundays until they are worn out + unfit for service, or unpassable on an inspection. Dirt is the soldiers badge of honor, for parlor soldiers who live in nice clean barracks and do Garrison duty on forts &c that can keep themselves looking clean It is as impossible for a soldier in the field, who has to skirmish & picket, to keep himself clean as it is for a pig in an irishman's shanty to appear like a lady in a drawing room. The Rebs think that dirt is their best friend for it protects them, as at Wagner, from assaults. Gillmore too is a friend to dirt. He gave the following toast immediately after the fall of Wagner in the presence of a number of officers of rank & his personal staff. "Spades are Trumps" Wagner + Gregg are ours and Sumter to a mass {unknown} bricks and mortar.

[E Cook]

Letter from QM Clerk E. Cook to his Parents

Office H.H. Q.M.
North End Folly Island S.C. Oct. 2/63

My dear Parents

I received a letter & three papers from Eliza yesterday. I have got just time enough to send you a line or two and no more. I have got Geo Clark's things packed in a box ready to send to Mr. Comstock. In the box is a segar box containing some old letters and a few little trinkets belonging to me. I have rec'd 2 months pay and will send you 15 or 20 dollars in my next letter. Dont fail to open the box I send to Mr. Comstock + take out the segar box belonging to me. I am in first rate health and feeling well. The weather lately has been cool but not uncomfortably so. I go out oystering every 2 or 3 days and get about 3 bushels to a time. They grow in great quantities in these rivers and are a very good flavor. Two men could gather a boat load in 2 hours.

[E Cook]

Ed: George Clark was presumed to be killed in the assault on Fort Wagner. Edward is sending his personal belongings home.

Letter from QM Clerk E. Cook to his Parents and Sister

Office A.A. Quartermaster
North End Folly Island S.C. Oct. 10/63

Dear Parents + Sisters

I rec'd a letter from Laura yesterday. I am glad the visitors have got home again all safe and sound. I sent a box to Mr. Comstock yesterday containing the clothes + other effects of George Clark. In the box is a bundle of letters and some few little trinkets done up together and packed in a cigar box. If you call on Mr. Comstock I think he will open the box and give you cigar box which lies just under the cover of the box. I am very well at present and enjoying myself first rate. We have all the oysters we want to eat for nothing. Every 2 or 3 days I take a boat & crew & go up the river & gather 3 or 4 bushels in half an hour.

Fish also are very plenty but as it takes longer to get them than it does oysters I cannot get time to go very often. I had some boiled cabbage the other day for the first time since I left home. I tell you it tasted nice. Apples are plenty at 5 cents a piece. I am afraid operations are entirely

Interior of Fort Wagner on Morris Island, S. C. (1865)

suspended here for the winter. The weather now is lovely. Do you have to pay any additional postage on my letters when I put on such old stamps as I sometimes do. Inclosed I sent you twenty dollars No I'll send it the next time I write. I send you two darts from the buck of the fish called the Stingaree. Dont prick yourselves with them for their wound is very poisonous. I am gathering some more sea shells. As soon as I have a sufficient quantity I will send them home by express. There is no news at present. A few days ago one of the North Carolina regiments stationed at {unknown word} mutinied and the rebs had to send up 2 squadrons of cavalry and a large force of infantry to quell its troops.

[E Cook]

Letter from Private A. Lyth to his Brother

General Hospital
Hilton Head S.C. Oct 14th /63

Dear Brother

I received your kind and welcome letter of the 4th inst and was very glad to hear that you were all enjoying good health and that Sarah Ann was doing well and getting better I never received the letter that you said Sarah Ann wrote to me about a month ago containing some postage stamps. My own health was never better and I am getting along first rate. I take a tramp down town now every day for the boys that are wounded and cannot get up see you I am some use where I am the weather here now is very warm to what it has been but we have had no weather here yet that we could call frosty weather in fact the thermometer has hardly ever been below 60 degrees. I had a letter yesterday from a friend of mine in the Regt but there is nothing of any importance going on up there at present and very little news of any description and there is nothing new going on here except they have opened a recruiting office for the Veteran Corps and they offer $40 to all soldiers who will enlist in it and I think they are getting quite a number of recruits but I am thinking it will be a long time before they will catch me enlisting again. Any way not until I get out of this term of enlistment. not saying that I am sorry that I ever enlisted or that I am getting tired of the service for I think it is every young man's duty who can come as conveniently as I could to enlist but I think I will see this show out before I step into another one.

The Rebs used to shell the island very considerably but without doing much damage having killed only one man. They have ceased wasting their ammunition in that direction and have not fired on us for about two weeks. The mosquitoes bother me so much and the evening air is so sultry that it makes me feel quite nervous and uneasy and not at all in a writing mood. The Captain thought I confined myself too close to the desk so he advised me take more outdoor exercise and told me to take any horse in the stable and have a ride whenever I felt like it

[A. Lyth]

Ed: The three year terms of the soldiers who enlisted in 1861 were coming to a conclusion. It was difficult for communities to fill their enlistment quota since so many men were already serving in the army. Disgruntled veterans were returning with descriptions of battles, officer errors resulting in losses, living conditions, injuries, and diseases. The federal government was about to lose many of its seasoned soldiers. Conscription was initiated which was supported by the soldiers. It required those citizens in a certain age group who did not enlist to be drafted. Those drafted soldiers could increase the size of the army and thereby shorten the war. However, many soldiers did not support drafting their brothers, fathers, or sons into the army since their families had already made a significant commitment to the war effort. Enlistment incentives of a 35 day furlough and a $400 bounty were offered. In addition, *soldiers reenlisting would receive chevrons to wear on their sleeves. Regiments could stay together if three quarters of the veterans in the regiments reenlisted, thereby pressuring all members of the regiment to reenlist. Their loyalty to the comrades was used to coerce the soldiers to reenlist.*

Chapter 4

Tenting on the Old Campground

Walter Kittridge (1864)

We're tenting tonight on the old camp ground
Give us a song to cheer
Our weary hearts, a song of home
And friends we love so dear.

Chorus
Many are the hearts that are weary tonight,
Wishing for the war to cease;
Many are the hearts looking for the right
To see the dawn of peace.
Tenting tonight, tenting tonight
Tenting on the old camp ground.

We've been tenting tonight on the old camp ground,
Thinking of the days gone by,
Of the loved ones at home that gave us the hand
And the tear that said "Goodbye!"

Chorus

The lone wife kneels and prays with a sigh
That God his watch will keep
O'er the dear one away and the little dears nigh,
In the trundle bed fast asleep.

Chorus

We are tenting tonight in the old camp ground
The fires are flickering low
Still are the sleepers that lie around,
As the sentinels come and go.

Chorus

Alas for those comrades of days gone by
Whose forms are missed tonight.
Alas for the young and true who lie
Where the battle flag braved the fight.

Chorus

No more on march or field of strife
Shall they lie so tired and worn,
No rouse again to hope and life
When the sounds of drums beat at morn.

Chorus

We are tired of war on the old camp ground
Many are dead and gone,
Of the brave and true who've left their homes,
Others have been wounded long.

Chorus

We've been fighting today on the old camp ground,
Many are lying near,
Some are dead, and some are dying
Many are in tears.

Final Chorus

Many are the hearts that are weary tonight
Wishing for the war to cease;
Many are the hearts looking for the right
To see the dawn of peace.
Dying tonight, dying tonight
Dying on the old camp ground.

"The men of Company H will recall with pleasure the period in which we were detached as a permanent picket guard near Pawnee Landing, and would likely need to be reminded of our picturesque little camp under the great magnolia trees, with the large palmetto at the head of the street."[11]

Letter from QM Clerk E. Cook to his Parents and Relatives

Office A.A.Q. M.North End Folly Island S.C. Oct. 21/63

Dear Parents

I have given up drinking tea + coffee since we have been getting in water from the sanitary commission. I bless the sanitary commission and thousands of other soldiers bless them for this great and almost inestimable luxury which they furnish us free gratis. I wish the newspapers would speak of what good the commission is doing and of the opinion that the soldiers entertain towards it for it would encourage the patrons of the commission to greater efforts, and make them happy to know that the soldier received and appreciated the good things that are sent to him and learns that his wants and wishes are not forgotten by those at home

Our batteries have again opened on Sumter and have already succeeded in knocking down the sea wall. There is a heavy smoke hanging over Charleston. But whether it is from shells thrown from our batteries or from fire caused by other means I do not know. We expect every night to hear that our men have stormed Sumter. The firing today is very rapid and heavy and chases away all thoughts of lonliness and fatigue. I had rather hear the firing of cannon and the bursting of shell than the song of the sweetest singer or the chords of the grandest organ. You have no idea of the lonliness that pervades our feelings on the days when there is no firing. It makes us feel sad and almost homesick, but as soon as the cannon begin to roar and the echoes pick up the sound and carry it from wood to cloud & from cloud to wood again, our hearts bound within us and chase away each gloomy thought and drown each homesick sigh. It is our music, and its melody is sweeter to our ears and more touching to our souls than the voice of the lute or the notes of the harp.

[E Cook]

Ed: The United State Sanitation Commission was a governmental agency that coordinated the efforts of women to help with the Union war effort. They raised money, helped in the kitchen in army camps, worked as nurses, and operated lodges for traveling or disabled soldiers.

Letter from QM Clerk E. Cook to his Parents and Relatives

Office A.A.Q. M.
N. End Folly Island Nov. 3rd 1863

Dear Parents

How I should enjoy a short visit or even an evening call. I would to hear the sound of the piano and see my dear old bookcase. I should love to sit in the old armchair and rock myself away as I told you of the scenes I have witnessed and the hardships I had passed. I wonder if the time ever comes when I can again enjoy the pleasures of home. I hope so & you hope so but how many "Hopes so's" have died in disappointment since this war began.

Our regiment has received between 1 & 2 hundred of the conscripts, but only one or two of them are from Buffalo. They are mostly fine looking men but some look thin + poor and adapted to stand the hardships & exposures of the soldiers life. I am almost persuaded to go back to my company and try to win promotion in the proper and legitimate path of duty. I have been offered the position of orderly sergeant if I go back, but I do not think I am entitles to it and therefore I refused to accept it but the Lieutenant in command of the Company has not appointed anyone else still hoping to get me back. All that I want is your consent and blessing for I feel that I should not do right to go, back of own accord without your consent unless I am sent back in the same manner that I was detailed vizaby an order from Head Qrs.

Good Bye from your affection Son, Edward L. Cook
Co. "H." 100th N.Y. Vols.

Ed: Soldiers constantly thought of home and home life, and those thoughts provided an anchor and a hope amongst the rigors of camp life and the terror of battles.

Letter from QM Clerk E. Cook to his Father and Mother

HEAD QUARTERS, Co H, 100th Reg't N.Y.S. Vol. Infantry,

Camp, Morris Island S.C. Dec 21st1863

Dear Father + Mother

I received your kind and welcome letter of Dec 2d and I was very sorry to hear that Sarah Ann is so sick again but I hope she is better by this time. I wish you would ask her if she received my last letter I wrote her when I was at the hospital for if she has not I want to write again to her. This morning Col. Dandy, Lt. Stowits and some more officers of our Regt have started north on recruiting service beside a man from each company in the Regt if ever you come across Lt. Stowits you can introduce yourself to him he is a very nice man and he will tell you a good deal about the 100th Regt. I was on guard duty at fort Shaw this morning when they left or else I should have sent a message by the man that left our company. But when the recruiting office open in Buffalo if John goes there and inquire for Lambert S. Melvin he will find him and I should like him to do so. Melvin is a corporal in our company he is a Michigan man and an honest good hearted fellow by the way don't mention to him that Capt. Dye ever offered me a corporalship for Capt Dye not liked by any of the company. On the 17th all the troops on this island had to turn out to witness the shooting of a deserter. he was a substitute and belonged to Co G 3rd N.H.V. he had got a pile of money as a substitute. All the troops were drawn up in line on the beach in the afternoon he was placed in a ambulance on his coffin at one end of the line and marched the whole length of the line the band playing the 'Death March' all the time he seemed as unconserned as if he was going to a picnic part of the way he lay on his coffin leaning on his elbow and part of the way siting up they came half way back up the line and stoped directly in front of our Regt about 50 paces from our company his coffin was placed close to the water's edge. he then stood on the side next the water the chaplin said a prayer. the he said something which we could not hear then he took off his hat and his shirt Just as if he was going to work then he knelt on his coffin a handkerchief tied over his eyes then the motions were given and they fired and he fell, he hardly had struck the ground when a large bird lit on his body and before he was shot there was not the appearance of a bird in the vacinity and they could hardly drive the bird away he was then picked up and streached out on his coffin and all the troops marched close past the coffin there were six holes through his body There is very little going on here at present I was on duty in fort Wagner one night and the rebels did everlastingly pop over the shell that night but did no harm our men fire an occational shot into the city my love to you all

From Your Affectionate Son, Edward

Letter from QM Clerk E Cook to his Sister

Office A.A.Q. M.   Tuesday
N. End Folly Island S.C. Dec 22/63

My dear sister Laura

A deserter was shot on Morris Island last week. He was caught in the attempt to desert and sentenced to death by Genl. Gillmore. Some of our boys went over to see the execution. They said the man acted very cool and collected. He rode up to the place of execution in an open ambulance seated on his coffin. He leaned back upon his elbows and threw one leg over the other and looked out upon the regiments of soldiers drawing up in line to witness the scene of his moments on earth as composedly as if he were going to a fair and gazing on a crowd of visitors. Having arrived on the ground he bowed in prayer with some chaplain for a few moments, then deliberately laid off his coat & overshirt. His eyes were bandaged and the word was given – Fire! He died instantly and was laid out on his coffin. The line of soldiers was marched around the corpse and the ceremony of the execution was completed.

[E Cook]

Letter from QM Clerk E. Cook to his Parents

Folly Island S.C. Jany 28/64

Dear Parents

I was much pleased to receive a letter from you about a week or {unknown word} ago. It came just about to time that as moved our office to Gen. Vogdes head quarters and I was so busy that I did not have time to reply to it by the return steamer, so I will answer it now and have it in good time for the next steamer. I wish I could receive a letter from you much oftener than I do, but I suppose your time is fully occupied in daily duties and leaves you little leisure to dip the pen and write the lines. I think that the soldier will know how to value the services of a wife or mother when he returns to his home, for his experience down here is a lesson that will not soon be forgotten. He will know how to value her ceasless industry and tireless energy. What better lesson can be taught him than the lesson of experience. The soldier has to cook, wash, mend clothes, darn stockings, and in fact perform for himself all those little things which his wife or mother used to do for him & which we would never have learned to appreciate if he had not turned himself into a bold volunteer. Anxious wives and loving mothers bless the day when your sons + husbands joined the army, for when they return to your pleasant homes and cherished society they will value your love and the blessings of home far more than they ever could if they had never been separated from them. An absence of 3 years from everything we hold most dear is a long time to look forward to, but how precious will be the hour when we are again permitted to join them. I think that the happiest day of my whole life – past + future – will be when I return to my home and find all there whom I have left. But if one should be among the missing whether sister, parent or my dear old grandmother I think the happiness should be destroyed. How many hours I have spent in thinking of my reunion with the loved ones at home? I almost fancy sometimes that I am on the point of meeting them, and my happiness is almost complete but alas the dreams of day do not last and my happiness is soon destroyed. Now Lila you must write more naturally & not spend so much time in your composition. If you can't think of some big word to fill in a sentence don't let you letter stand waiting until you do think of it, but put in some smaller one, and let it go at that. Remember you are writing to your brother and not to anyone who is going to show your letter around among his friends and have a general laugh if a slight mistake is made in the rhetoric, composition, or orthography. A sister's letter is sacred property and is read only by the eyes for whom it is intended.

Write free, write easy, write naturally, write news, write pleasantries, write anything that you think will interest one who has an interest in your interest and I promise you that your letter will be interesting and most heartily welcome to the recipient. I suppose I have misspelled a dozen or less words already in this letter but I am not going to run all around the department to try and borrow a dictionary to prove them. I will leave that for you to do & tell me in your next letter and correct them so I will not make the same mistakes again.

[E Cook]

Letter from Private A. Lyth to his Father and Mother

Morris Island S.C.February 11th,1864

Dear Father + Mother

I take the present oppertunity of writing you these few lines hoping they will find you all enjoying good health as it leaves me at present. We were paid off day before yesterday so that all the Regt are in good spirits I have sent you a picture with this of our camp at Gloucester Point Va if you look to you right hand when you look at the picture and pick out the third tent in the second row you will see the tent that I used to boarde in and I don't know but you may find me out in one of those companys that are drilling I dont know. But I will leave it for you to find me out

Today our Lieutenant got a letter from St. Helenas island from a man named S.M. Barbarow inquiring any particulars of Edward Townsend or if he knew of his where abouts for he said it would be confering on both him and his afflicted family a great favor. Now I had to go to all the boys in our company and find out if any of them knew what became

Morris Island S. C. Camp July 1863 Haas & Peale photographers

Morris Island S. C. Camp July 1863 Haas & Peale photographers

Morris Island, S. C. The "rogue's march" drumming a thief out of camp (1863)
Haas & Peale, photographers

of him that night of the charge and to write the answer to his letter. I found out all I could and it is quite evident that he was killed that night near fort Wagner. He was last seen a few rods from the fort and it is supposed that it is near there where he met his fate but it was so dark at the time that the boys could hardly could recognise one another.

[A. Lyth]

Letter from Private A. Lyth to his Folks at Home

Morris Island S.C.
February 28th 1864

Dear Folks at Home

I received my box day before yesterday and I was glad to see that the names of you all were marked on some little article It has been so long in coming that of course the two pies were completely spoild and the two cakes were a little mouldy on the outside but all right in but the best of all is those usefull articles that Mary and the handkerchief that Mother sent. The cake Mrs. Yates sent was very nice. The salve that Mr. palmer sent I have not had any occation to use any of it yet and I hope I shall not but I suppose it is very usefull in some cases I am very thankfull to the neighbors for thinking of me

There is a good deal of talk of the Regt coming home in the spring. but I should prefer staying in the field if I have to stop my time out. of course we should enjoy coming home and seeing our friends and relatives and getting amongst civilization again but soldering is too lazy a life for me if we were at home and. I should not like it. I must close now with my love to you all

Your Affectionate Son + Brother, Alfred Lyth

Letter from E. Cook to his Father

Office A.A.Q.M. Seymours Div.
Feby. 29th 1864

Dear Father

I long for the time when I can once more be with you all – at home to stay. I want to see you all and see the old city of Buffalo but still I do not want to go home until my time is expired and I can go home to stay.

My time is just half gone. If it has passed as quickly with you as it has with me, then it does not seem very long; and I hope the last half may roll round just as quickly + as pleasantly as the first. I am in hopes that I may not have to remain during my full term of enlistment. It is very probable that the war will find its close during the present year, but if it does not, then I am willing to stay until my time is out and in the interval render to my country any service which it may be in my power to offer in the line of duty, be its nature what it may. I have now been in the Q.M. Dept. upwards of a year. I know that I have been of service to this Gov't. in this department and I like the duty very much better than being in my company (although by my absence from the company I lose all chance of advancement in the line of promotion) yet whenever my commander sees fit to recall me I shall return willingly & cheerfully to any duty which may present itself for my kind regard. I think I can almost see the picture of the "Peep into the Sitting room" which you described in your letter. I can imagine dear old grandma sitting in the arm chair reading her bible {unknown word} sitting quietly looking at the fire and twirling her thumbs thinking of Edward, George, David, Harriet, Eb, Eliza, Grace all in rapid succession and wondering what each and all of them are doing and thinking how she should like to see them all. Alas! some she will never see again and some will never again see her.

Morris Island S. C. Camp Scene July 1863 Haas & Peale photographers

Then next comes yourself sitting at the table & for the first time in a year writing a letter. This is the most difficult part of the picture for my weak imagination to paint. I can see you sitting at the table with your specktacles under your nose and your eyes peeking over them onto the newspaper in your hand intensely engrossed in the perusal of the president's message or the telegraph column; or I can see you lying down on the lounge, or nodding over the sleepy proceedings of the City Common Council but I can't see you writing a letter. Then there is mother, away off in the dark of course, straining her eyes to make out some outlandish and unintelligible word that has puzzled her brain ever since she received the letter. Laura is writing to me. I wonder if she knows how I appreciate her sisterly kindness. She has been very good to me and very faithful in keeping her promise of writing to me often and she will be rewarded some time or other for her kindness and be glad to think that she has contributed so much towards making the life of her brother pleasant & happy, by keeping up a communication between him and his cherished home. Then there is little roguish Gracie and Annie + Lilie just come in + by & by the august parents – Steve & Mary – come poking along and then the room is full and the picture is finished but not complete. I am not there but I hope to be one of these days and then wont there be oh grand old jollification and happy hearts for a little while, I don't care how soon this war is ended and we are dismissed and paid off and allowed to return to our homes.

Tell Lily that she owes me a letter and I want her to write it and send it to me {unknown word}. Have her tell me about her music lessons & her scholars. If she has not time to write a long letter then tell her to write a short one and like Mary's a sweet one. I think she is a little bit vexed with me but I don't care. If she is going to play that kind of a side game then I will get vexed too and I will write to her in spite of herself and bore her with letters until she will be glad to write me for the sake of getting rid of my letters.

Our troops captured a small quantity of salt, turpentine, rosin & cotton at Camp "Finnegan", about 8 miles from this city, & also 7 cannon where we first took the place but on 20th {unknown word} in the fight at "Alustee" we lost 5 cannon so are not much a head in that line.

Give my love to all of the folks and write to me again as soon as you can for your letters are very welcome and cheering when I feel at all sad or despondent.

Good Bye from your aff Son
Edward

Letter from Private E. Cook to his Sister

Office A.A.Q.M. Seymours Division
Morris Island, S. C. March 1/64

My Dear Sister Laura

Morning - It rained last night & is raining still so the fight will most likely be delayed until the rain ceases. All our men are under arms. I hear that Seymour will not wait for the enemy to attack us but will go out to meet them. I do not expect to be in the fight but if our men are driven {unknown word} the entrenchments, which are only 5 minutes walk from my office, it will be necessary I presume for every man to turn out & defend the city. We must hold its place at all hazards and I am willing to give what little aid I can, or my life if it is necessary for our cause. I hope for your sakes that it may not be necessary for me participate in the fight, but if it is I cannot in honor or in duty hold back a single step. I speak thus at length in order that you may not think that I am possessed with a spirit of bravado or false courage, whatever I do, I shall do it under a powerful conviction of my imperative duty and in accordance with my idea of man's most sacred attribute – honor.

[E Cook]

Letter from QM Clerk E. Cook to his Sister

Morris Island, S. C. March 20/64

My dear Sister Eliza

If I do not commence a letter to you this evening I am afraid you will think that I have forgotten you. I shall write you a very short letter for I am tired & sleepy and my neck aches. I was on picket last night with gunshot of Sumter and what with the cold & the myriads of fleas I had a wright time of it. After we came in this morning we had to clean ourselves up & go out on Dress parade. This afternoon I took a short & restless nap and this Sabbath has passed and I have accomplished nothing of any account. There is no news from this district.

[E Cook]

Letter from Private A. Lyth to his Brother

Morris Island So Carolina
March 24 1864

Dear Brother John

There is a great deal of talk now about the old men being discharged in June but I cannot tell how true the report is. but I hope it is so for it is a long time since they have seen any civilization and to be three years in the field is too much for any man. I believe that the Board of Trade men would have been discharge with the old men if Col Dandy had not been against it. but as I have got used to soldiering I dont mind it much. I should like if you hear anything conserning the Regt in old Buff. I wish you would let me know The conscripts in our Regt expect when they have served nine months they will be discharged but in my opinion they will be very much disappointed for I think they will have to serve "three years orduring the war". The conscripts in our Regt as a general thing are pretty good soldiers. But the conscripts in the 52nd and the 104th Pennsylvania Regts are a lot of green horn as soldiers in one Regt they were with the Regt 4 or 5 months. before they would trust them with arms at all and even now they dont trust them on outpost duty. I will give you a little instance which happened a few days ago. One of our corporals got a conscript of the 52d on his post. when he posted him the sentinel he gave him the countersign or watch word. then he went away. but in the course of half an hour returned to see that all was right he goes up to the conscript who was the sentinel on post and asked him if he had the countersign. he answered no did you give it to me. yes answered the corpl. Well I must have lost it answered the sentinel upon which he commenced to feel in his pockets and look around on the ground as if looking for the countersign. The corpl could hardly keep from laughing out right but at that moment he observed an officer coming along the picket line so he told the sentinel to halt him as he came up. when the officer got near enough Mr Sentinel call out 'Who comes there". The officer answered "friend with the countersign". Fetch it here says the sentinel. I Just lost it a short time ago. Then the Corporal steped forward and told the officer to "advance and Give the countersign" which he did. then he asked what kind of a man that was on post the Corpl told him a conspt of the 52d the officer gave orders for him to put another man on the post.

Dear Brother I will close this letter now, as I have Just got some writing to do for the company. Give my love to Sarah Ann + Wm and accept the same yourselves.

Your Affect
Brother
Alfred
Co H 100th N.Y. Vols Morris Island

Letter from Private A. Lyth to his Brother

Morris Island, S.C.April, 1864

Dear Brother John

I received your kind and welcome letter of the 23 of March and I was very glad to hear that you were all well and that you were enjoying the winter season by having a jolly sleigh ride now + then I think if you could find 2 or 3 frenchmen every day that wanted to enlist you would be doing well but I advise you never to show an old soldier a recruiting office or you may get what's not quite agreable I hear that the veterans of the 100th are disgracing the Regt by their goings on in Buffalo. But it is just as a great many of us expected for those mostly that have reenlisted are the roughest caracters in the Regt all that our Co has I am glad to say is one amongst the lot that have come home For the last month past there has been a great many robberies commited in the camp and around Head Quarters since four weeks ago some three or four men were caught rolling off a safe with about $15,000 in it from a building near the Head Quarters. as soon as they were discovered they run and all escaped except a man named John Ross of Co F of our Regt who was to drunk at the time to run he is one of the conscripts he has been in the provost Guard house ever since awaiting his trial by Court Martial There has been quite a number of watches stole and amongst the rest our Chaplins gold watch was stolen someone cut his tent and reached in and took it off the nail it was hanging on week before last a couple of men went into Col Dandys tent and took out a box of money belonging to the sutler to the amount of $1300 but they found the box buried in a tent over at the Provost Guards quarters so the occupants were put under arrest and the money recovered There is very little war news here though for the last week back there has been considerable firing from both sides.

[A. Lyth]

Letter from QM Clerk E Cook to his Sister

Morris Island, S. C.Monday April 4th 1864

Weather quite damp & terribly rainy. The wind blow'd very hard from the rear and as it is just about the time for our high spring tides it played the deuce in our part of the town. The sand bank – a kind of natural sea wall at our end of the Island is only about 3 or 4 feet above high water mark and when you cross over that you find yourself in a kind of hollow basin. This basin is always dry in ordinary times & tides, but if the tide is a little higher than usual & the wind blows rather briskly from the sea it will carry the water right over this bank in one long continued sheet, and fill up the basin to a level with the sea. The basin is somewhat concave and when filled with water is in many places over a man's head. Thus it was this afternoon; the water came pouring in upon us in a perfect cataract. The occupants of about 50 tents were driven out of their quarters. The water entirely surrounded the little hill on which one officer stands and we were left on an Island with the water a foot & a half deep all around us. The water about reached the level of our 3rd step & the waves came splashing their foam right into the doorway. I tell you it was a grand sight to see the long sheet of water come pouring over the seawall, and to watch the waves as they rose & sank and moved onwards until they came right up to our doorstep. Yes it was fun for us who knew that the tide would not rise high enough to drown us out, but it was not quite so pleasant for those poor fellows who were forced to leave their quarters and stand out in the rain until the tide went down. The only inconvenience I experienced was being obliged to pull off my stockings & take off my shoes and wade through the water to the supper table. Our stables were completely inundated and the poor horses & mules about 200 in number were compelled to stand up to their haunches in the cold water for about two hours. Some of the tents that were drowned out were built on frames & had board floors laid in them. These were lifted from their foundations by the force of the waves, and sent floating off in all directions at the mercy of the water & the winds. It was laughable to see them floating around here & there with 2 or 3 fellows holding on to them for dear life almost, to keep them from being washed out to sea. A party of drunken sailors who were ashore this afternoon on a kind of spree were surprised by the tide which cut them off from their boat and there was no way for them reach it except by wading up to their middles which they did after much hesitation. How we laughed to see the drunken fellow go pitching & rolling through the water. Now I have given you the pleasing side of the picture, but there are some sad and grave features connected with it. Do not think that the inundation was allowed to subside without producing some very disastrous results. It becomes my painful duty to chronicle the death of more than one poor creature. Alas what will be the feelings of their fond friends & relatives in Buffalo when they hear of it. It was high tide about 7 oclock P.M. When the water began its backward march, the waves sighing the requiem over the departed, the night was {unknown word} dark and at 7 o'clock the next morning the tide was high again so that it was not until about noon the next day that the bodies were discovered. Passersby looked on with horror yet no one touched them and, with shame be it spoken to those whose duty it is to attend to such matters they were allowed to remain untouched during the afternoon when a little boy with his dog came along and cried out r-r-r-r-ats! r-r-r-r-a-t-s! r-r-r-r-a-ts!!! Rats!

[E Cook]

Chapter 5

~

We are Marching on to Richmond

E. W. Locke (1862)

Our knapsacks sling
And blithely sing
We're marching on to Richmond
With weapons bright
And hearts so light
We're marching on to Richmond
Each weary mile
With song beguile
We're marching onto Richmond
The roads are rough
But smooth enough
To take us safe to Richmond!

Chorus:
Then ....tramp away
While the bugles play
We're marching on to Richmond
Our flag shall gleam in the morning beam
From many a spire in Richmond

2. Our foes are near
Their drums we hear
They're camped about in Richmond
With pickets out
To tell the route
Our army takes to Richmond
We've crafty foes
To meet our blows
No doubt they'll fight for Richmond
The brave may die
But never fly
We'll cut our way to Richmond

Chorus

3. But yesterday
In murd'rous fray
While marching on to Richmond
We parted here
From comrades dear
While marching on to Richmond
With many sighs
And tearful eyes
While marching on to Richmond
We laid the braves
In peaceful graves
And started on for Richmond

Chorus
4. Our friends away
Are sad today
Because we march to Richmond
With loving fears
They shrink to hear
About our march to Richmond
The pen shall tell
That they who fell
While marching on to Richmond
Had hearts aglow
And face to foe
While marching on to Richmond

Chorus
5. Our thoughts shall roam
To scenes of home
While marching on to Richmond
The vacant chair
That's waiting there
While we march on to Richmond
T'will not be long
Till shout and song
We'll raise aloud in Richmond
And war's rude blast
Will soon be past
And we'll go home from Richmond

Chorus

Letter from Private A. Lyth to his Father and Mother

In the Field Va. near the Petersburg and
Richmond Rail Road May 8, 1864

Dear Father and Mother

I should have a good deal to write to you if I had the time at presant but as I have not I will give you hasty discription of our proceeding since we left Glou Point. On the 3rd the 100th drew four days rations and orders to move at a moments notice. On the morning of the 4th we were got out of our beds at 1 o'clock in the morning but we did not leave camp untill afternoon. We marched down to the landing at the York River where there was a very large fleet of transports awaiting the troops going aboard some Regts were already aboard and all the troops got aboard of the transports at dusk. They having been embarking on both the Yorktown + Gloucester sides of the river. The fleet got under way at 2 o'clock on the 5th and arrived at Fortress Monroe at day break Gen'l Butler and Gen'l Gillmore were runing around the harbor in their little steamers giving orders and they got the whole fleet under way for the James river in a short time. Our Regt gave Gen'l Butler three hearty cheers when he ordered our transport forward. When we got up the James river as far as New Port News we found that a fleet had left there loaded with troops up the river. It was a beautiful day and a most splendid sight to see the whole fleet making their way up the river with their flags flying and the gun boats for escorts we past Harrisons Landing at dusk in the evening and arrived off Bermuda Heights at eight o'clock and anchored in the river. the troops commenced disembarking but our Regt did not get ashore untill morning the 6th. The only houses near were a group of half a dozen one being a church. I went over to them but found no inhabitants except in one and he was an old infirm Negro. he said the people of the houses run away at the first appearance of our fleet. they belonged to the rebel signal corps. The army got on the move before nine o'clock and such a sight I never saw in my life and never want to see again. Most all the troops had a good knapsack and the best new clothing but the day was so intencely hot that when we got on the move we could not carry half our load for three miles the roads were lined with blankets overcoats rubber blankets shirts drawers stockings pants caps portfolias whole knapsacks with all their clothes in them even pocket books were thrown away razors and trinkets of every discription. It is a fact that over ¾ of the army threw away their woolen blankets. Thousands of them bran new Just before we started there was a Gen'l order that each man should have two pair of army shoes and the men drew them but hardly any of them carried their extra shoes a mile. They threw them away shoes that they had never even tried on. Some few pulled of the shoes they had worn a little and put on their new ones but they had to suffer for it for the new ones were not broke into their feet. I threw away my rubber blanket 2 pair of drawers one pair of socks and other things of no value. we marched some 6 or 7 miles and piched our camp for the night but were not allowed to pitch tents. Just at dusk Gen'l Butler came along the lines of the army and they all cheered him heartily. he is a noble looking man to tell the truth he is the only Genl that I have seen that I think capable of commanding an army leaving out Genl Gillmore. As soon as we had got some supper they dug entrenchments in front of the whole line of troops and cut down about 100 acres of woods in front of us to keep the rebels from coming upon us in a surprise party. On the morning of the 7th we were got up at 3 oclock having slept on our arms all night and were got ready to move. we made 2 or 3 attempts to move but did not get started they got some coffee cooked we then sat down + had some breakfast but had hardly got commenced to eat the orders came to "fall in" but the boys were bound to finish their breakfast and did by swallowing scolding hot coffee. We got under arms and ready for the march when we were ordered to take off our knapsacks and pile them in a heap and leave guards over them. then we began to suspect there was going to be some work and not far distant we were well supplied with ammunition and got started but had only got a few rods when the Co Clerks were ordered back to straighten up the Co papers + accounts. I tried to get someone to do my work for me so that I might go with the Co but it was no go so I had to go back.

There were two Brigades started out. They had not been gone over an hour and a half before we heard firing and then it increased I got through writing about noon and the papers sent off to Washington when the firing got to be awful. I was half crazy then as I wanted to be with my chums so I buckled on accutrements took my gun and started for the front to try and find the Regt and I run on to a line of pickets who would not let me outside so I cut into the woods and came to an old barn where they were cutting off legs + arms pretty fast and dressing wounds. I then struck off into the woods again to try and get round the pickets and got to where the bullets were flying pretty thick in the woods when I run across one of the 100th boys coming in with a finger shot off. I stoped and dressed his finger and we both then started to find the Regt he to look after his cousin an me to find my Co but we run on to the pickets again and they would not let us past but gave us only ten minutes to get to the rear out of sight. We turned back and got into camp about four oclock and found some of our boys in camp wounded. Shortly after that the firing ceased and the Regt came in about ½ past five o'clock. we had coffee cooked ready for them so they sat down and drank a cup of coffee and eat a couple or so of hard tack with no meat and made a supper then we fell in and moved about a quarter of a mile to the rear where we stacked arms in a field an slept under the heavens for a roof all night. What battle they call that which we fought yesterday I do not know but all we had was in was 8 or 9 Regts of Infty and a few peices of artillery there was more rebs than there was of our men. the object of our men was to tear up the Petersburg + Richmond R Road which is about two miles from our presant camp the rebels were in a gully on the opposite side of the rail road and had a good many peices of artillery planted.

P.S. the rebs kept our men in check a long time and made two or three flank movements on us but could not drive us at last our Regt + the 49th M.S.N. + 48th N.Y.V. and another Regt made a charge on the track and drove the rebs tore up about ½ a mile of the track and telegraph line set fire to the rail road stays having piled them in a pile and then fell back Just as reinforcements were coming to the rebs This morning we fell back ½ a mile further to the rear and other troops took the line in front we drew rations a some were nearly famishing I made a good hearty breakfast out of 4 hard tack + about ½ a pound of raw salt pork and a cup of coffee. In the engagement I could not tell you how many either side lost but our Regt lost only between 50 + 60 killed wounded and missing Our Co only had two wounded in the hands and I have been very busy this morning making out their descriptive lists and papers to send them to the hospital we had 4 officers wounded but none killed there was one of our Colonels killed in the fight but I don't know what Regt he belonged to. The Regt is all out at work now building a fortification in front of our camp about ten rods from where I am writing. there is an artist taking a sketch of the work and I have got to go and look after drawing some rations for the Co so I will close with my love to you all. I forgot to say a small mail arrived this morning and I got two Harpers Address Gloucester Point Va. but there is some of our mail laying back somewhere which we shall get soon. Enclosed you will find the photograph of our 1st Lieut and Co Commander he would have been our Capt when Capt Walbridge left us but he wont be promoted for he wants to go home when his time is out which will be in the fall but if he accepts a captains commission he will have to swear in for three years more and he dont want to. He has been in every battle that the 100th Regt has been in and was never wounded but has had balls give him close calls often Yesterday a ball passed through his coat. I will write soon if I have a chance and write to me often. Give my love to Sarah Ann + Wm

from your Loving Son
Alfred Lyth

Letter from 2nd Lt. E. Cook to Parents

Office Asst. Quartermaster Bermuda Hundred , June 7th 1864

Dear Parents

I sent a letter to Laura this morning. And now I have the pleasure of informing you and all the rest of my friends that unexpectedly and unasked I have received a commission as 2nd Lieut. in the 100th N.Y. Vols. I shall return to my regiment tomorrow and try to perform my duty to my country and to my friends. I trust that neither may ever have cause to blush for my conduct on the field. Pray for me that I may always be blessed with courage to stand up to my duty to God, to my country and to my fellow man. Until you hear from me again you may continue to direct to Co "H" 100th N.Y. Vols. Do not attach any rank or title to my name but direct simply to Edward L. Cook. I do not fear to face the enemy, but on account of my comparative ignorance of military matters I should have preferred to be with my company as sergeant.

[E Cook]

Letter from 2nd Lt. E Cook to his Parents

In front of Petersburg Va. Friday June 10th 1864

Dear Parents

The force sent out Wednesday night advanced to within two miles of Petersburg but finding the enemy too strong for them and fearful that if they delayed another night then retreat would have been cut off, they immediately returned & arrived in camp last evening. They did not succeed in destroying the bridge, but without any proportionate loss on our side the cavalry took between 40 & 50 Prisoners, who had every appearance of belonging to the rebel militia force. Many of them had on clothes of a far finer quality than are worn by the rebs and some had on Hats looking as if they had left their daily avocations at a moment's notice and rushed to arms for the purpose of defending their city from the assault of our troops.

[E Cook]

Letter from 2nd Lt. E. Cook to his Parents

Bermuda Hundred, Va Asst. Quartermaster's Office,
June 22nd 1864 Wednesday

My dear parents

Nothing of any importance has transpired since I wrote you last. Petersburg is virtually in the possession of Grant for he can take it any time he chooses but the opinion seems to prevail here that he does not wish to occupy it at present, but chooses rather the course of investing, instead of invading, thereby detaining in a position favorable to his plans a large portion of the enemy's force while he operates in with much greater effect upon some distant point when his blow is least expected.

Thursday June 23rd 1864

Uncle Abe has paid us the honor of a visit at this front but we unfortunately did not know of it until he had gone. There is almost continual fighting along in line either at one front or another but very few casualties occur. The regiment has crossed the James River, in company with several regiments, at a point 10 mils this side of Richmond and have commenced fortifying. This is a new and {unknown word} move on the part of Gen. Grant. No one can conjecture its meaning or significance. At the same time that my regt. and the others, all under command of Brig. Gen. Foster, crossed the James, another, and a much larger body of troops crossed the Appomattox in an exactly opposite direction.

What do these moves mean?

[E. Cook]

Letter from 2nd Lt. E. Cook to his Sister

Bermuda Hundred Va. July 18/64

My dear Sister

Last Friday & Saturday were, I think, the "bluest" days I have experienced since I entered the service of "Unkle Psalm". I felt sad, very sad, during both the days, and it seemed to me as though some of my friends at home were sick or about to be visited by some calamity. Your letter partly verifies this experience, but I am happy to learn that matters are no worse. I am glad that mother is recovering from her attack of Cholera Morbis, but fearful that your next letter may not convey the wished for intelligence that she is fully well again. I hope to hear from you again very soon and learn that you are all well once more. Poor Father is down again. I wish with all my heart that the time had come when I could be with you all once again and in a position where I could earn enough to relieve father and mother from any more hard work. I hope that none of you are denying yourselves any of the comforts of life on account of prices of produce.

Our orderly (messenger) went out to Petersburg last week with some messages, and he represents the state of the troops as very critical. They are complaining bitterly of their condition and are almost cursing the officers who are high in authority, and vowing that they will never charge on the rebel works at Petersburg. They (our troops) are dirty, poor & ragged, tired, desponding, and care less both of their own fate & the fate of the country. They have to watch incessently day and night, and if they get any sleep at all they have to catch it during the day when the sun is so scorchingly hot that the rebel gunners are glad to cease firing & leave their guns to seek for themselves some shelter from the scorching sun rays. Our poor men are in danger not only on the battle field and in the zigzag trenches but even their camps and of little shelter tents the fatal bullet finds its way and picks of many noble sons and fathers. They are safe nowhere and at no time. They cannot feel thankful, when after lying 48 hours in the dirty, dusty trenches, they are relieved and sent back to their camp for the same length of time, because they know that even there they are not safe from the enemy's death dealing missiles. While our orderly was passing down the camp of his regiment a bullet came whistling towards him and fell at his feet. If he had been advanced a few steps farther it would have entered his body. The men say that they have been hurled into battles and urged on to charges and have lost 80,000 of their comrades and they ask "What have we accomplished by it?" "Nothing!" "We are no nearer to Richmond than we were when we started, and we will not fight any more, all the officers in the army shall not compel us to charge again" Thus they talk, and those who do not know the hearts of soldiers, or are not soldiers themselves, are alarmed and fearful that something dreadful is going to happen if another battle occurs.

Have you any fears for the result of the war? I have not. With such men as our army contains to fight for us and with such a cause as ours to fight for, we must succeed – there is no such word as fail. I still have every confidence in Grant and trust that my confidence may never appear to have been misplaced.

The raid up North has excited no particular interest in the army, and if it had been for the great scare which it has produced at home, and the great sensation which it has caused among the "newspaper dailies" I should not even have deigned to mention it. It is all over now and the rebs have got back with whole skins and unbroken organisation just as I bet they would when I first heard of the raid. Nobody wanted to <u>check</u> their depredations or catch <u>them</u> when they offered our people a good opportunity to cut them off and use them up. One of the screws in the machinery of our government has been loose a long time and I am forced to believe the thread is worn off and it can never be tightened up again.

I think Grant is going to give up the hope of whipping the rebs at Petersburg for the present. I cannot imagine what will be his next move but I believe he will leave only troops enough to hold the works and withdraw the main portion of his army to some other point. He has failed in this attempt but it was not from any fault in the plan (which seems to have been a good one and promised complete and prefect success to our army, and a most terrible & telling and decisive blow to the cause of seceshion. Man proposes & God disproves. A short delay of an hour, of a single hour, or the unaccountable panic that seized the niggers, lost us a battle, which if it had been gained, by us, would have proved to be the most important and decisive one of the campaign either in this department or any other. But we have failed and must submit for it is the will of God, and He doth all things well. It will only prolong the war for an additional length of time, but perhaps each delay will only serve to make our peace more lasting & complete when it does come.

I am getting tired of the service and if the war continues another year & I do not get out of it honorably at the expiration of that time I think I shall be in favor of Peace on any terms.

[E Cook]

Ed: Edward complains about the trench warfare in the Petersburg campaign but remains optimistic as to the outcome of the war. The "raids up North" refer to the Battle of the Wilderness in which Grant suffered a total of 55,000 casualties during the campaign. Also, in May, 1864, the Battle of Cold Harbor was fought and an additional 12,000 men were lost. Northern newspapers began to refer to Grant as the "butcher."

Letter from 2nd Lt. E. Cook to his Sister

Bermuda 100 Va. Aug. 14th 1864

My dear Sister

You speak of Capt. W. as being so universally liked. He is indeed a fine young man and of very promising aspects. I like him very much but, although I have allways stuck up for him in every other respect yet I have always said & still say that he is like the large majority of others offices, viz, he has <u>no honor or respect for us enlisted men</u> farther than it will advance his own interest in some cases (like my own) to treat a private with a little more than the usual portion of "Regulation" courtesy meted out by officers to the men under their command. I suppose he said that he thought very highly of me. Of course he would tell you so because he could not or dared not clothe his thoughts in any other words. If he has truly said what he meant he would have said "I value his ability, his knowledge of my business, his services" but any other enlisted man that could fill my place would do him just as well. It is a prize to a man to have a clerk who can take charge of his business for thirty day and keep things straight while he is home enjoying comforts & luxuries; and anywhere else, except in the army, such a clerk might have a claim on the affections and indulgence of his employer, but here it is not so. An enlisted man is no better than a dog – he can come when he is called and go when he is sent, without a murmer or a question. If a "<u>valuable clerk</u>" is enlisted he must ask for none of the priviledges & conveniences that are furnished to the civilian clerks. If an enlisted "valuable clerk" is sick, no matter how dangerously, and it comes under the notice of his employer, he is told to go to the doctor and get a dose of quinine. Perhaps the man is unable to walk there but that makes no difference, he must go & and return as soon as possible to resume his work. The case is different with the civilian clerk. If he is ailing slightly he must go to his quarters and have the doctor sent to him and the enlisted clerk must do his work while he is away. The <u>ability</u> of the one is no greater than that of the other, his <u>services</u> are really not so valuable. What then constitutes the difference? Simply this, one works in a uniform and draws $13 a month and is a slave, subject to orders; the other is a Civilian, wearing his own clothes, draws his $100 a month and is either his own master or else is master of his employer. I dont often grumble do I? I generally look on the bright side, but I must still declare that are enlisted mans experience is that of a dog or a slave.

In one of your letters you spelled asylum with 2 S^es. It only has 1 S.

Don't run down Genl Grant yet. He was not the one to blame for the Petersburg failure. Abraham Lincoln is the man for next president.

Good Bye write again soon + direct as heretofore.
Your Loving brother, Edward L. Cook

Letter from 2nd Lt. E. Cook to his Sister

Camp of 100th N.Y. Vols.
Near Petersburg Va. Friday Sept. 23/64

My dear Sister Laura

There is a rumor that Sherman has Atlanta and, if it is true, I think very likely the rebs will allow no communication between the pickets for a day or two. There were no particulars rec'd of affair but the general impression seems to be that Hood has evacuated and is coming up to assist Lee in retaking the Weldon road. I fear for Grant but trust he is prepared. We have received a few reinforcements within a day or two and they have all marched to the left towards the Weldon road. I have never yet lost confidence in Grant and I am not going to despair now. If he had only had 50,000 fresh troops at the time of the Deep River affair and when he took the Weldon road this war would today be 6 month nearer the end than it is now, and if we can only get a few more troops to enable us to hold our ground against the combined forces of Lee & Hood we can perhaps do as much good we could by a fierce battle. We have now fortified ourselves so strongly at this point and have so many guns mounted that our artillery can hold our position here with a very small force of infantry for picket duty and I think it is very likely that if Hood does attempt to reinforce Lee, our corps will be ordered to the Weldon road to assist in defending our position there. I think Lee will have a hard task to drive Grant back from his present line of works. Things are coming around all right by & by and I hope it will be very soon.

The weather is damp and disagreeable. I have to go on picket again tonight and be gone 3 days & nights. The last time I was on picket I was placed in charge of Co "J" on the left of the skirmish line. There is no continuous trench on the left skirmish line and, therefore, as the rebel lines and ours are in close proximity, they being on the top of a small rolling hill and we at the base, it is extremely hazardous in relieving the men which can be done only at night when they cannot see us, and very silently that they may not hear us. The rebs have the advantage of us at that point for they have a trench all along the front and can relieve without danger to themselves. I was never on this line but once before and that was the first time we ever went on picket here. Then the rebs and us were on the very best terms and we used to expose ourselves in open day, and even went so far as to meet half way between the lines and exchange little trinkets. At that time it was the best part of the line for there was no picket firing either day or night but now it is the very worst part of the line and the only part that is fully exposed to the fire of the enemy and that has no protection or approaches. Well when I took my relief out I was given a small number of shovels to complete the pits & form a continuous trench. I was told that the work had been commenced and was nearly finished and that I could finish it with my men in one night. I moved my men forward down a ravine until I approached the right part of the left line. Here I found the officer (belonging to the 10th Conn. Vols) who had charge of the line the night previous. I tried to get some information from him about the number of posts +c but he was crouched up against the side of his pit and all the information I could get from him I could put in my eye. He said he had not been along the line and kept begging me to come in the pit out of danger and send my men along the line alone. My orders were to halt my men at some safe point and send them out in squads of threes to relieve the old pickets. I might have done this if I could have obtained any information from the 10th Conn officer, but as I could not, I had to go along the whole line and find out where the posts were and how many they were and how many men it required before I could post my men on a post. This I did within stones throw of the rebel line. I relieved the old picket and posted my men all right and to my own complete satisfaction and never lost a man or had a man struck. I think I hear you say "brave boy" "courageous act" "wonderful preservation" +c. All this would have been true under certain circumstances, but it happened on this particular occasion that the Jonnies did not fire a single shot which probably accounts for the fact that nobody was hurt. Well when I had my men posted I tried to start them at digging but the ground was so hard that the shovels would make no impression on it. I then went away back to the rear and tried to get picks but I could not get them and returned to tell the men to use their bayonets as far as possible but, during the interval that I was gone the moon arose and the firing commenced. I started to go along the line again but the bullets came ahead of me & over and behind me and when I got about half way I dived into a pit until the moon got behind a little cloud and then I started back for the pit where I staid for I knew if I got to the end of the line I should not be able to get back until the next night unless the sky clouded up so the rebs could not see me. I told the men in the pits as far as I went what to do & then left them to themselves. The next night when I went round with new relief I told the officer in charge just what was wanted and gave him instructions so that he could make twice the headway that I did the night previous. I came in all right and brought all of my men in safely but you can judge whether it was a hot place or not when I tell you that the men fired from 100 to 250 rounds of cartridges each and the rebs fired full as much as we did if not more. But I must close for I have 2 or 3 more letters to write to day. I was down to Bermuda Hundred day before yesterday and saw Capt. Walbridge and the boys. The Captain did not even invite me to stay to dinner but perhaps it was because he had no conveniences. I had dinner with the clerks and was well satisfied. The Captain looks well and received me very kindly. Give my love to Grandma and tell mother that I have received her letter and will answer it soon. I will also write to Aunt Harriet the first opportunity. Good bye.

Write as soon as possible. Some poor soldier has gone to his last home – I hear the band playing the doleful "Dead March"

Your affectionate brother, Edward L. Cook

Ed: The Siege of Petersburg was the most prolonged of the war. It lasted from July, 1864, to April, 1965. It was a series of battles designed to wear down Lee's army. There was a change in fighting tactics in the last two years of the war. Open, exposed conflict gave way to trench warfare. The conflict was less bloody, but there was an ever present danger of mortar shells and sharpshooters. The dullness of trench life affected the morale of the troops.

Letter from 2nd Lt. E. Cook to his Sister

Camp 100th Regt. N.Y. Vols.Near Petersburgh Va. Friday Sept. 27/64

My dear sister

I received three papers from home to night. The last time I wrote to you we were on the point of marching. We broke up camp that same night and marched to the rear a distance of 2 miles or so. We were relieved by the 2^{d} Corps. We are encamped in a field between two woods. We are out of range of bullets and out of line of shells. The rest of our Corps is encamped in the same field. We are altogether again the camp of one regiment joining right on to that of another for the distance of nearly a mile. Oh! it seems so good to be once more out of range where we can sleep above ground and not have to live in holes and have {unknown word} and proofs and earthworks built above and around us. I never experienced such a perfect feeling of relief as the first day we pitched our camp in this position. In our old camp we could not step out of our tents without hearing a bullet go ping or pish or burr, over our heads & then chug as it struck the ground. Our men are feeling as merry as crickets & happy as birds. The reversion of feeling experienced for us all on account of the sudden and unexpected change from a position of constant danger to one of perfect safety is almost miraculous. I cannot describe it but I can realize it and one must needs be placed in the same

141

situations to rightly understand it. It was not fear, that in our other camp, kept down our spirits and destroyed our natural flow animation. It could not be fear for we never for a moment hesitate to go from tent to tent or lounge about in the company tents and talk and transact business even when the bullets were flying the thickest. What was it then? It certainly was something – a constant knowledge of our danger and a knowledge that at any moment we might be called to face our Maker, and give an account of our stewardship. There certainly is such a change in the feelings of the men that they seem like a different set of individuals. I only hope that we may continue in our present camp for some length of time but I fear not.

If I had my choice now between commission in the line and his situation with a chance of retaining it until my time expired I would throw up the commission and accept his place. He is not only comparatively free from danger but he is his own master. He does not have to be up and under arms every morning before daylight. He can go to bed when he get ready & get up when he sees fit. He is always sure of having a place to lay at night. he has no guard or picket duty to perform, he can go when he wishes and come when he will. His work is all done during the day and when it comes night he can lay down to quiet slumber, undisturbed to rest and dream of home and friends till morn nor think of danger nor start up at night to hear the loud drums roll or bugle call to arms. He now is safe, secure from every danger incident to war with prospects fair of seeing home and friends once more. There let him stay nor shall an act of mine do aught to call him back again to duty in the ranks.

[E Cook]

Letter from 2nd Lt. E. Cook to his Sister

Camp 100th N.Y. Vols.

In the field before Richmond Va.

Oct. 25th 1864

My dear Sister

This will be one of the strongest positions in the whole cordon that Grant is throwing around Richmond and Petersburg. When it is finished a few men can hold it against a vastly superior force and thus enable Grant to remove the bulk of his army to some other point either to assail the enemy's position and force an entrance into the City or to take and hold another position towards the completion of his vast encircling chain of forts and breastworks. The works goes forward almost imperceptibly, but like a vast moving body its momentum cannot be resisted. It carries everything before it. Grant does not make a move until he is ready to make it. His army lies apparently inactive for a time, everything seems to indicate that the campaign is closed, and men and officers begin to build their winter operations, but all the time Grant is not asleep - he is cautiously and silently working in some unexpected quarter – adding weight to the vast mass that he intends to move, concentrating everything towards the complete success of his plan and when everything is ready, when a move is least expected and where it is least anticipated, he puts the mass in motion and it rolls on and on and over every obstacle until the design is accomplished and the plan carried out completely & effectually in all its points. This is Grant. He is now apparently inactive, engaged merely in {unknown word} up defensive work, but in reality working out beneath this calm exterior a plan of stupendeous proportions – a mighty storm is brewing + soon it will reach its proper temperature and then it burst over our enemy and overwhelm them in its onward flood working ruin in their army and destruction to their hopes. This is my conviction and my prayer is that I may not be swallowed up in the flood but live through it all to raise my voice in thanks to Him who giveth victory to the righteous and causeth desolation to swallow up the wicked. Give my love to Grandma and all the rest. Write soon

Your Affectionate brother
Edward L. Cook

Letter from 2nd Lt. E. Cook to his Sister

Camp 100th N.Y. Vols.
Before Richmond Va. Jany 2/65

My dear Sister

I wish you a happy new year. The weather? it is very cold. My health it is good and everything goes along well. I wish Lili you would not write just such gloomy letters Every day around a soldier is gloomy enough without their gloomy letters from those who should try to enliven & cheer him up. When a person cannot take a short walk in any direction without coming across the grave of some fellow soldier and {unknown words} are right in the midst of camps & companies I should think his life might be dismal enough to merit a little syrup {unknown word} & cheer from this friend at home who are surrounded with blessings that they do not know how to appreciate. You are growing up to fast and second (I won't mention name) wishing you were dead. Anybody that did not know you would think you were an old maid dying for love & a husband. When you have been disappointed in Love as many time as I have you will learn to look upon such matters Lili Soffi Callie and not mourn yourself to death over a slight change in the would be programme. Just think, of the many losses I have sustained Abby Stone, Alice Smith, Mary Clemmens, Mary Adams,

Earthworks in Front of Petersburg Va. (1865)

Petersburg, Va. The First Federal Wagon Train entering the Town April, 1865
John Reekie photographer

Nelli, Fannie Porter, Nellie Sherman, Ella Halsey, Mattie Butter, Susie, Nellie Hines, Lottie McLane, Sadie Lyons, Em Anthony and a million & two others too numerous to be mentioned. I suppose you think because I write in this lively strain that I am not in earnest but I am. I have taken each one of these disappointments deeply to heart have grown so that now I dont weigh anywhere near 280 pounds. Alas!

Your Loving Brother, E. L. Cook

P.S. If I knew that you all desired to see me home before my time of service expires which is now but little more than 7 months I would try and obtain a leave but if I consult my own wishes and inclinations I shall not return until I return to stay. Wont that be a happy day when we meet again and not to part until some power stronger and more terrible than rebellion summons us to our last long home beneath the clay upon which we now tread in the full vigor of life & manhood.

Ed: Edward, like all soldiers, needed to hear good news from home. His sister, Lili, didn't understand that basic tenant.

Letter from 2nd Lt. E. Cook to his Sister

Camp 100th N.Y. Before Richmond Va. Jany 14/65

My dear Sister

I have just returned from a trip down the {unknown word} River to start off our regiment. They left fort Monroe and I suppose they are now in old Buffalo. I saw the old settlement of Jamestown the home of

Capt. John Smith + Pocahontas. I send you enclosed a sprig of willow which I wish you to plant. I send home some relics which I wish have preserved.

You would walk down to his house on Niagara Street and get them of him. There are three plants the smallest one was cut from the old Churchyard + all the rest + write soon

Your Loving brother, Ed

Letter from 2nd Lt. E. Cook to his Sister

Camp 100th N.Y. Vols
Before Richmond Va. Jany 27/65

My dear Sister

I have a little time to spare today and as I am at present in command of the regiment I am my own master and therefore no one can blame me for employing my time as I see fit. It commenced about five oclock this morning to rain and freeze and has continued steadily all day but the cold has somewhat decreased in intensity and now it is raining without the freeze. I think you are about right in regard to the class of young men left at home. I dont think it would be possible for me to remain at home in active while my country was pouring out her life blood in a terrible struggle for freedom and existance. It is the duty of every man to come forward at his country call and offer his arms and his life if need be for her salvation and support.   I have never regretted that I joined my country's cause and if I live to get through this how I shall bless God that I was permitted to lend my fickle aid to the cause of liberty and union.

[E. Cook]

Letter from Capt. E. Cook to his Sister

Camp 100th N.Y. Vols
Before Richmond Va. Feby 23rd 1865

My dear Sister

Your letter is at hand. Tom was home on a furlough at the time he married but has returned to his duties again I think I should prefer to wait until I went home for good before I tied to a piece of calico. The honeymoon of such weddings is most to short to pay for the anxiety and fear of the following seperation.

I received the shirt you sent me and am highly pleased with it. How are Mr. Sees children getting on ? Did Horace Riley say anything about them. I wonder if Cornelia See has got over her mad at me. I received Emma Anthonys letter and answered it but no reply has yet been returned. I have got my Captains straps. I think that bar is worked in splendidly. The bullion of which the straps are made is not gold but is simply galvanized on a silver base but then they are good enough for this climate and where it rains all day + freezes all night.

I think I have got now as high as I wish to go for if I am mustered again I shall have to serve another three years and I do not wish to do that for I want to get out of the army when my time is out. I am beginning to count the months. By time you receive this I shall have been in the service nearly 2 years + a half and six months more will see me on my way home if God spares my life and preserves my body from injury + illness. I received the silk thread you sent me and now I should like a few threads of red silk to sew up my sash which is commencing to unravel in several places. I will also intimate that I always have to borrow when I want to sew on a button with <u>white</u> thread. I received those last envelopes with my initials today. They are very neat indeed but the back

148

of them does not run up high enough to prevent the mucilage on the flap from adhering to the letter. The note paper is most excellent but you fold it the wrong way when you wrap it in the newspapers. If you would double it lengthwise instead of crosswise it would be much better. I am not acquainted with Edgar Benson. I will call on Horace Riley if I ever pass through New York. I am glad that Uncle Eb has got such a good situation & hope that he may be able to remain in it until his time is out. I suppose you have heard the news about Charleston and Columbia. We gave three cheers on the color line day before for the victory I hope the news may not prove a chimera like some other reports that have been circulated. There was a wide spread rumor through the camps yesterday that Petersburg had been taken by our troop after several hours hard fighting but as there is no confirmation of it this afternoon I take it to be unfounded. The mail is ready to close so I must stop. Goodbye.

Ed

Letter from Capt. E. Cook to his Sister

Camp 100th N.Y. Vols
Before Richmond Va. March 11/65

My dear Sister

Whenever we have battalion drill or inspection I have to go out and we generally have one or the other about every other day which occupies about 3 hours each time it steal away very many valuable moments that I would like to devote to corresponding with my friends. I expect to go on battalion drill this afternoon and if I do I must cut this letter short. We were reviewed by Genl Grant this last Sunday. He was accompanied by a large staff & numerous ladies. Our division at a review last week was reported to be the best in the army of the James and that probably is the reason why Gen. Grant came over to see us as he did not review any troops on this side but our division (the 1st Div. 24th A.C.) We did look splendid & no mistake and marched like clockwork I tried hard to steal a look at the ladies who were seated in ambulances but the dust was blowing toward them and they were compelled to keep their veils down I was extremely sorry of course at this heavy disappointment but I bore it like a hero. Genl Grant is of a very ordinary appearance so much as that the presence of ladies attracted all attention from him. Of course up north where you have lots of ladies & few Lieutenant Generals the case would be just the reverse.

I think this review is precursory to a move indeed an order was circulated yesterday saying that as this army was liable to move at any moment no more Leaves of absence or furloughs would be granted except in very urgent cases. I received my straps, bars, stockings, slippers, valise & stockings all right. What did you pay for the valise? It is a splendid one and will last a person his lifetime. The weather is lovely. Tell Mary + Laura I will try and write to them to night if I don't get too sleepy by the time I get through with the examinations. I received the red silk thread you sent me. There goes the call for drill so I must stop writing. Give my love to all the folks. We are going to get paid off this week if we don't move and then I will send you some money. Write soon and tell me all the news about everybody.

Your loving brother
Edward L. Cook

Letter from Capt E. Cook to his Parents

Camp 100 NY Vols In the Field near Appomattox Station Va
I think it is April 12th 1865

My dear Parents

I have lost all track of days + dates. Genl Lee surrendered his command last Sunday just one week after we charged fort Gregg. I have received no letters since I left before Richmond except one from Laura in which she acknowledged the receipt of $50 #. Since I sent the 50 dollars I have sent 100 more but have not heard that you received it. We have had some hard marching + were well paid for our work. Our brigade fought the last battle but our regiment was not in it as we were selected as rear guard two days before the fight.

Our regiment is in the 3rd Brig 1st Division 24th Army Corps,

Col. Dandy commands the brigade

Gen. R.S. Foster "   " Division

Gen. Gibbon "   " Corps

" Ord "   " Army of the James to which our corps belongs.

Our corps has done good service in this campaign. It is said that Genl. Lee made the remark that he surrendered to the 24th A.C. for the Army of the Potomac could never have whipped him but when he made a dash expecting to fight only Sheridan's Cavalry he always found the infantry of that Gd d-d. 24th Army Corps. When we took fort Gregg the rebs inside asked us what we belonged to when we told them the 24th A.C. they said they thought + knew we were not the Potomac Army for they never stuck to a thing as we did.

We are again under marching orders but we do not know where we are bound for. The war is not yet ended but I think it soon will be. One more good hard battle will finish up everything. Johnson will soon have to surrender or be cut to pieces. I enclose herewith an article clipped from the herald it will give you a better idea of our movements up to the 2ᵈ April than I can write you.

[Ed Cook]

Letter from Private A. Lyth to his Brother

Richmond Va. April 15ᵗʰ/65

Dear Brother

Before this reaches you I shall be with my Regt We left City Point yesterday afternoon and came up the James river on a steam boat Just below this city the river has been blockaded in 8 or 9 different places. In coming through one place where our men had just opened it large enough for a boat to pass through our steamer struck and nearly capsized and in the excitement 15 men jumped over board and got a shore when the boat righted again and got through they were left behind and had to walk to the city. we landed after sunset and marched through the city to Head Quarters and we went through the part that was burnt down which is about 30 of the finest squares in the city in marching through the streets **the boys sung a lot of patriotic songs such as 'Rally Round the Flag Boys', 'Red White + Blue', John Browns Body +c** Our Regt is somewhere outside this city part of our Brigade is doing provost duty in the city and they tell us just before Lee surrendered our Regt was in a fight and lost heavily. My headquarters are now in a tobacco wharehouse on Franklin Street. I will close now with my love to you all

Alfred

Petersburg, Va. Pontoon Bridges across the Appomattox River May 1865
Timothy O'Sullivan, Photographer

Rally Around the Flag

George F. Root (1862)

Yes, we'll rally round the flag boys, we'll rally once again,
Shouting the battle cry of freedom,
We will rally from the hillside, we'll gather from the plain.
Shouting the battle cry of freedom!

Chorus

The Union forever! Hurrah, boys, hurrah!
Down with the traitor, up with the star;
While we will rally round the flag, boys, rally once again,
Shouting the battle cry of freedom!
We are springing to the call with a million freemen more,
Shouting the battle cry of freedom!
And we'll fill our vacant ranks of our brothers gone before
Shouting the battle cry of freedom!

Chorus

We will welcome to our numbers the loyal, true and brave,
Shouting the battle cry of freedom!
And, although he may be poor, not a man shall be a slave,
Shouting the battle cry of freedom!

Chorus

So we're springing to the call from the East and from the West,
Shouting the battle cry of freedom!
And we'll hurl the rebel crew from the land we love best,
Shouting the battle cry of freedom!

Chorus

Hurrah for the Banner of Red, White and Blue

Song of the Irish Regiment by Thomas M. Brown (1864)

1. Hurrah for the banner of Red, White and Blue,
To be the proud flag of stars, we will ever be true;
To black hearted traitors, the dark day shall rue,
When they spurred our brave banner, the Red, White and Blue.
When forced to leave our own Green Isle
To seek a home, on the stranger's soil.
Its gleaming stars and rainbow bars
In welcome floated o'ver us.

Chorus

The hurrah for the banner of Red, White and Blue,
Three cheers for the banner of Red, White and Blue,
And a cheer for old Ireland and Liberty too,
God bless our proud banner of Red, White and Blue.

2. By Clontarf's princely glories, that never will die;
By the heroic mem'ries of famed Fontency,
By each battle field where wild Irish cry;
Rang out the proud watchword we'll conquer or die.
By Montgomery's patriot name,
By Warren's blood McDonough's fame,
We raised the cry, to live and die
For Liberty and Union.

Chorus

3. 'Twas said we were false when we swore to be true,
That we wouldn't "cotton" to the Red, White and Blue;
That we couldn't love Ireland and American too
That we would "recede" from the Red, White and Blue.
Ring out our old wild Irish cry;
Fling out the starry flag on high;
Beneath its folds we'll do or die,
For liberty and Union.

John Brown's Song

William Steffe (1858)

John Brown's body lies a mouldering in the grave
John Brown's body lies a mouldering in the grave
John Brown's body lies a mouldering in the grave
His soul's marching on!

Chorus:
Glory Hally Hallelujah!
Glory Hally, Hallelujah!
Glory Hally, Hallelujah!
His soul's marching on!

He's gone to be a soldier in the army of our Lord
He's gone to be a soldier in the army of the Lord
He's gone to be a soldier in the army of our Lord
His soul is marching on!

Chorus

John Brown's knapsack is strapped upon his back
John Brown's knapsack is strapped upon his back,
John Brown's knapsack is strapped upon his back,
His soul's marching on!

Chorus

His pet lamps will meet him on the way,
His pet lamps will meet him on his way
His pet lamps will meet him on the way
They go marching on!

Chorus

They will hang Jeff Davis to a tree,
They will hang Jeff Davis to a tree,
They will hang Jeff Davis to a tree
As they march along!

Chorus

Now, three rousing cheers for the Union!
Now, three rousing cheers for the Union!
Now, Three rousing cheers for the Union!

Letter from Capt. E Cook to his Parents

Camp, 100th NY Vol outside of Richmond, VA
May 3rd, 1865

Dear Parents

Give my thanks to Mr. [ ] for his portion of the contents of my box. I have not got much time to devote to letter writing as I have lots of company writing + business. I am just getting over an attack of the dysentery and ague. I kept up first rate on the march but as soon as we had halted where we were going to stop I was taken sick. I should have written to you before if it had not been for this. I am almost well now and feel better to day than I have before for about a week. We came through Richmond and marched about 3 miles + encamped where we now are within about 2 miles of the city by the shortest route. Our camp is in a very pretty spot near a farm house and in a very pretty little grove of oaks + hickorys. I have lost the key to my watch. I wonder if [ ] has got one that will fit it. There are all kinds of rumors about our going home. Now that the war is over I am awful lonesome and homesick and I want to get out of the service. I hear that Charlie Wallbridge is Colonel to Chief Qr. Mr. of the 10th A.C. at Raleigh. Write to me as soon as you get time and tell me all the news. I have not seen Geo. Stoddard since I left the north side of the James.

Good Bye
Your Aff Son
Edward L. Cook
Co "H" 100th N.Y. Vols
3[d] Brig. 1st Div.
24th Army Corps
Richmond Va.

Richmond, Va. General View of the Burned District April, 1865
Alexander Gardner photographer

Letter from Capt. E. Cook to his Parents

On Picket near Richmond Va.
May 9th 1865

My dear Parents

I suppose you all think that now the war is ended there is no use in writing any more to your letter boy. What does he care about hearing from home now that there is no more fighting? I have received just one letter from home since we came here. I received a weekly express yesterday I sent home 2 or 3 papers a few days.

Two corps of Genl. Meade's army of the Potomac passed through here two or three days ago on their way to Washington. We expect two corps of Genl. Sherman's army through here in a few days. The rebs say that they do not wonder any longer that Genl. Lee surrendered to Grant. They think we have got all the men we wanted to whip them out. It took upwards of 7 hours for the soldiers of the 2^d + 5th Corps to pass a fixed point let alone to supply baggage + ammunition trains. We supposed we were going right on to Washington but things look now as if we were going to stay in Virginia until our time is out. What do you think about my coming home for a couple of weeks? They are granting furloughs + leaves of absences to go out of the Dept. for 20 days. I suppose it would cost between 50 + 100 Dollars to go home whereas if I wait 4 months longer I can go home for good, but if you all really wished me to come home on a short visit I think I would try and accommodate you. I wish they would muster us out of the service tomorrow. I am 10 times more anxious to get home now that the war is over than I was while we were fighting all the time.

[E Cook]

Richmond Va. General View, with ruins, from Gambles Hill April, 1865
Alexander Gardner photographer

Chapter 6

When Johnny Comes Marching Home

Patrick Gilmore (1863)

When Johnny comes marching home again,
Hurray, Hurray,
We'll give him a hearty welcome then'
Hurrah, Hurrah;
The men will cheer, the boys will shout,
The men will cheer, the boys will shout
The ladies, they will turn out

Chorus
And we we'll all feel gay,
When Johnny comes marching home.

2.
The old church bell will peal with joy,
Hurrah, Hurrah.
To welcome home are daring boy, Hurrah, Hurrah;
The village lads and lassies say,
With roses they will strew away.

Chorus

3.
Get ready for the Jubilee,
Hurrah, hurrah,
We'll give the hero three times three,
Hurrah, Hurrah
The laurel wreath is ready now,
To place upon his royal brow.

Chorus

4.
Let love and friendship on that day,
Hurrah, hurrah,
Their choicest treasures then display,
Hurrah, hurrah,
And let each one perform some part,
To fill with job the warriors' heart

Letter from Private A. Lyth to his Brother

Camp 100th N.Y. Vols near Richmond Va May 19/65

Dear Brother

Having a little spare time on my hands at present I thought I would write you these few lines to let you know that I am well and in good health. We are having very pleasant times here at presant and by all appearances we are likely to stay here for some time yet. Last Saturday all of our corps had to turn out in light marching order and go to the city to receive the 2nd and 5th army corps as they passed through here on their way to Washington. They commenced to pass at a little after 8 o'clock in the morning and were passing all day until dusk in the evening before the last passed through and I tell you it quite astonished the rebels to see so many troops but when they were told that all they had seen that day was only two army corps some of them would hardly believe it for they thought it was the whole of Genl Grants army. I went to town to see them and I came across a good many of the boys I was acquainted with and I had a good time of it as I did not have a gun to bother me and I could go where I pleased. Yesterday part of Sherman's army commenced to pass through here on their way to Washington Sheridan's Cavelry were passing all day and the infantry and Artillery commenced early this morning to pass through the town and I guess if they march all day to day they will not get through then It is thought that our corps will be kept here until they get the 25th corps which is all negros well drilled then it is said they will releive us Some think after Sherman's army has all passed on to Washington that we will follow them up to be on the big review there. if we do I shall be home in the course of a couple of months with my discharge in my pocket if we do not I am good to remain here until my time is out which is only a little over three months now

I with three or four more boys of my Co went to the theatre night before last in Richmond but when we got there we found it was a negro minstrels had the theatre and was going to perform we were very glad of that so we bought our tickets and went in to see the fun. We are having very fine weather here and the farmer's crops are looking nice wheat is heading out fine potatoes are 6 and 8 inches out of the ground peaches are hanging thick on the trees about the size of plumbs. Early cabbage is begining to head up and we have had lettuce + onions three weeks ago

I forgot to tell you that just across the river here there is a large brick + tile yard in the city of Manchester. We went past it when leaving this city for Petersburg a few weeks ago. Next week I am going to apply for a pass to go to Manchester to see the place and their machinery. Dear Brother I must close now hoping these few lines will find you all well and in good health. Give my best respects to Lewie and Miss Kepplar and the rest of the folks

Your Affectionate
Brother Alfred Lyth

P.S. write soon

Washington, D.C. Units of the 20th Army Corps passing on Pennsylvania Avenue near Treasury May 1865 Matthew B Brady photographer

PART II

✧

VALUES, BELIEFS AND OBSERVATIONS

Ed: Soldiers brought with them to the war their views of their northern culture as well as the southern culture, death, politics, and religion. Since many in the regiment were from the same area, their initial opinions about these topics were probably reinforced by the others. However, it is important to consider how these opinions may have changed or been hardened by their experiences during three years of service. By selecting passages relative to these areas from their letters, it is interesting to observe their various comments and opinions.

EDWARD COOK AND ALFRED LYTH: THOUGHTS ON NORTHERN PERCEPTIONS

Ed: The Union soldiers strongly believed in the justness of their cause and the superiority of the northern way of life. As Company H moved through the South, the soldiers recorded in their letters observations that included camp life, climate, agriculture, sea life, towns, plantations, and blacks. Insects, sand, poor roads, and unusual fish and shells also did not escape their scrutiny. While the towns and cities of the North were central to politics, education, and business, the agrarian culture in the South revolved more around the farms and plantations. Such decentralization represented a primitive and undemocratic government to the northern soldier.

The letters to home also reflected their judgmental views. The decaying houses and towns, poverty, and dirty, ignorant and lazy blacks in squalid Negro cabins provided topics to convey to their families. Of course, basically they came into contact with Negroes mostly on the small, minimally populated coastal areas and islands.

Their letters reflected a lot of antipathy towards Negroes. While initial prejudices were softened by contact, they attributed stereotypes to them and commented on their dress and demeanor. Also, the cheapness of their labor was a factor of concern as well as the association of Negroes with the war itself. As the war dragged on and hardships mounted, the Negroes became the scapegoats for the war itself. The anti-Negro sentiment took the form of disparagement of physical characteristics as well as their gullibility and ignorance. However, many Union soldiers talked about the Negroes amiability, religion, intelligence, and eagerness to learn. They also commented on the support given to the soldiers by the Negroes who gave valuable information as to southern troop locations and stored southern valuables. Those Union soldiers who visited the Negroes cabins were welcomed, fed, and housed. Some Union soldiers taught the Negroes to read and write, and some attended the Negro church services.

In the summer of 1862, the Congress approved the enlistment of Negros into the Union Army which was opposed by the majority of Union soldiers. They were initially used for noncombat duties in the camp. However, the report of the performance of the 54th Massachusetts black unit at Fort Wagner won over many soldiers as to their bravery and ability to fight.

Gloucester Point Va. Sept. 28th 1862

Dear Parents this is the Sabbath and although we have no service, it seems different from a week day. We slept in a tent last night and it is the first time we have slept under a covering since last Tuesday. I mailed a letter to you from Fortress Monroe on Friday day before yesterday. I had not been returned to the boat many minutes, after going to the post office, before we received orders to proceed to Suffolk opposite Norfolk in Va and before we had time to cast of the ropes + let the boat loose another order came out as the first order and again in a few minutes came a 3d order telling us to proceed to Yorktown. This is the way that business is done in the Army; there seems to be no certainty or decision in anything relating to Army Matters. We sailed from the Fortress about 1 oclock P.M. of Friday + arrived at Yorktown about 8 o'clock P.M. of the same day. Our ride up the York River was very pleasant, the water is salt and I sat for an hour or two watching the different kinds of sea fish that we passed on our way up. There is a kind of thing here that they call the sea nettle, when it touches you it stings like a nettle and it is nothing more than a kind of thick transparent colorless jelly and yet it has life + breathes in the water. In the evening whenever the water is disturbed it is all alive with spots of light or phosphoresant fire. It looks splendid in the evening, I can tell you. We marched from the boat up the hill about ½ a mile + found ourselves within the lines of our regiment. You cannot guess how pleased we are to be with our regiment after being on the road so many days. We had to tent with some of the other boys last night but I suppose our tents will be here today so we can put it up by night.

We all went outside the first line yesterday after dinner and got some oysters to eat about 3 dozen raw and if we had time I might have eat dozen more. They are very cheap here at present I am going out on the river a little ways tomorrow and get some more. They are very plenty up the river about ½ a mile above our camp and all we have to do is to pull off our clothes + wade in after them. We have not had 1 unpleasant day since we left Buffalo. Some of the days are very hot + sultry but the majority are quite pleasant. The days pass by very quickly but it seems an age almost since we left Buffalo. I have not been homesick since we left Buffalo. I would not return now if I could. Yesterday I took a salt water bath for the first time in my life. I enjoyed it first rate. There are lots of salt water fish here if I only had hooks + lines to catch them with. I have sent you a letter asking for some things and I wish father would put a fishline in + 1 or 2 hooks. You might send them in a letter for that matter if you like. That cotton cloth you gave me will come in first rate for cleaning my musket, but woolen cloth is better + I don't care if you send me a few scraps of old woolen cloth with the other things. Tell father to ask if they ever got that roll of sheet lead if not they can get it of Ensign by paying $1^{00} charges!

Let Father tell the directions so they can write to me. In Barnum's Museum where the have the sea fish, the have to keep them in sea water and as they would soon die if the water was not changed very often and as there is no easy mode of getting sea water how do you think Barnum manages? He has an arrangement fixed up by which a continual stream of fresh air is forced into each one of more than 100 Glass vases thus keeping the water constantly pure + wholesome.

Coming through Washington some little Negro girl was telling about a man shooting a dog + she felt very bad about it. She said "De dog diddent say nuffin to de man + de man up + shot him."

The negroes here seem to be more intelligent than the white folks and talk with less brogue than the white folks. If you had your eyes shut you could not tell the difference by hearing them talk. Write as soon and as often as you can + send along a paper once in a while.

[Private E. Cook]

Camp at Gloucester Point Oct. 2^d 1862

The sun is very hot but the air is not sultry as it is in Buffalo. The nights are not near as cold as they were at Alexandria. I was sick Sunday night but was all right again in the morning. We are right on the bank of the York River where we have saltwater to bathe in if we desire it. There are beautiful springs of pure cool spring water all along the bank of river oozing out of the sand so we do not have to use our filters. We feel that this is a great blessing after using the nasty muddy water at Alexandria. We could get pretty good water at Alexandria but we had to go about a mile or a mile + a half to get it. All the water near the camp was very impure.

I cannot help speaking of the sunsets and sunrises in this country. They are perfectly lovely. The sun rises now directly out of the Chesapeake bay and as I go down to the river each morning to perform my ablutions I am compelled to stop and witness the first appearance of old Sol as he rises his face up out of the water. The sun rises grandly but it does not compare with the evening sunset. We are where we can watch it until the last moment. The sky is almost always cloudless until after sunset and then as he sinks below the horizon the clouds begin to show themselves and gradually grow more + more distinct as the sun sinks lower and lower; then the rays shoot up and change colors almost like the northern lights the edges of light vapory clouds in all shades.

[Private E. Cook]

Camp at Gloucester Point Va. Oct. 3[d] 1862

G. Stoddard and I went out in front to the picket-line this morning and bought a peck of sweet potatoes. I dug them myself while Jeff the Negro slave stood by and looked on said "dat he wave glad dat I wave diggin dum kase his head ached right smart." I dug just for the romance of it. The slaves and free Negroes here have no idea at all of miles or distance. If you ask them how far it is to a certain place the invariable answer is a "right smart distance". "Well but how many miles is it?" "Dunno sir but it are a right smart distance I know dat." In the rear and on the right of our camp near the bank of the river stand the ruins of an old house. It has been pulled down I suppose because it obstructed the range of the gunboats on the river. All that remains of it is a tent. He is an old bachelor and is living now in an old shanty with the tent over his roof to keep it from leaking. He is very wealthy and owns the land where our camp now is. One of our boys saw a pair of children very light colored playing before a Negroes house and he asked an old negro at the door whose children they were. "Dey is my daughter's children" "Where is her husband?" "She dun got no husband" "Well then they ain't her children are they?" "Dey is her children" "Well but how can that be?" "Oh I know how dat can be well enough deys Massa's children too dey is. Yah! Yah! Yah!" The soldier then went to the mother and said "Are those your children?" "Yas dose is my children" "Are you married?" "No I isent married." "How then can they be your children?" "Oh Massa know dat, he know how dey be my children. Deys Massa children." This is slavery and southern chivalry.

I cannot help speaking o the sunsets and sunrises in this country. They are perfectly lovely. The sun rises now directly out of the Chesapeake Bay and as I go down to the river each morning to perform my ablutions I am compelled to stop and witness the first appearance of old Sol as he rises his face up out of the water. The sun rises grandly but it does not compare with the evening sunset. We are where we can watch it until the last moment. The sky is almost always cloudless until after sunset and then as he sinks below the horizon the clouds begin to show themselves and gradually grow more + more distinct as the sun sinks lower and lower; then the rays shoot up and change colors almost like the northern lights the edges of light vapory clouds in all shades. I have managed to tip over my inkstand but I enclose a little slip containing the words that are blotted out so you will not be at any bother to make it out. Do I write plain enough?

In the evening we generally go down to the river and take a bath to keep ourselves clean. There is great danger in a camp of getting lousey and we are afraid of it.

Last night we got a lot more men for our regiment they being alot of exchanged prisoners which were taken at the Battle of Fair Oaks + we expect a lot of new Recruits to night I had a good Bit of fun with a little nigger boy out on the picket lines the other day. he was about the size of Bill and had lips as thick as my fist he is a slave but is quite a sharp little fellow and said he was a regular secesh and he said he wanted the south to whip the north because he said if the north whips they will take the niggers up north and freeze them all to death and kill them he sung us some nigger songs and some secesh songs that the secesh soldiers had learnt him when they were camped here

When Eliza's Laura's letter was handed to me out on the line it was so dark I could not read it so I went into a house that stood nearby the post, occupied by a Mr. Shakleford, and obtained permission to read my letter by his light. The candle was nearly burned down he ordered his slave, a thick lipped negress, bring another candle. She did so and stood holding the light for me while I read. Wasent that an incident and quite romantic. Picture a sallow thin faced man with broad hat + straight coat in the background, in the foreground a young soldier reading a letter beside a table, while a shining faced + sparkling eyed negress stands grinning behind him as she bears up the flickering candle for him to see to read; on the right and in a doorway sits the mother sits a crib to sleep her young infant, while on the left and leaning on the table are 2 or 3 young children who eye with strange curiosity the group before them. It half reminds me of some of those dear old scenes we read of in the times of "76". Another thing I saw this morning reminded me very much of the old revolutionary times. About eight oclock this morning some person from outside the lines drove up to the second post to the left of us with a 2 wheeled cart load of provisions of some kind. The animal that drew the cart was a steer + was driven with a bit + lines the same as a horse. (The bit was made of a piece of wire + the lines of roap.) The man drove up to the line + was halted, the Lieut. came up and passed the cart load of provisions but the man had to remain outside. As the animals, the owner handed the lines to someone inside and that one took charge of the cart + unloaded it and then returned it. thus we pass stuff into the lines but allow nothing to be passed out. We consider that everything that comes inside the lines is just so much taken from the rebels, whether it is intended for our troops, or those families that live inside.

The next day we turned a secessionist out of his house and are going to occupy it as a hospital and we set him adrift on the other side of the picket lines The reason of turning him out of his house is that he + his wife in particular were continually throwing out hints threats talking secesh and abusive language to the guard that was put over their property to keep the soldiers from molesting anything cursing the Yankees to the officers which would often call and see them so being in need of a hospital on this side of the river and this house being the very thing Uncle Sam politely helped secesh to move as Uncle Frank once politely helped us to move as was quite natural old secesh was a little vexed particularly the old woman as she said she was sorry she had not poisend a few of the yankees before this The old feller threatened to destroy the house but he was too closely watched for to get an opportunity and imagine his chagrin when the boys were helping him move of their retaining a keg of powder which they found snugly stowed away in a corner of his celler. However he is now with his friends on the other side of the picket lines today.

[Private E. Cook]

Camp at Gloucester Point, Va. Wednesday Oct. 8th 1862

The boys returned from their fishing last evening with 4 large sea crabs and this morning we boiled them and had quite a relish. They are much finer flavored than oysters and taste very much like lobsters. You will recollect that in one of my letters I spoke of the thing they called a sea nettle – a kind of sea fish that looks like a piece of transparent jelly about the size + shape of a silver dollar with 3 or 4 long root-like appendages. I had one of them in my hand the other day; it did not affect the palm of my hand but as soon as the back of my hand touched it, the hand commenced to smart as if it was stung or burnt. Last night the boys had one of them on the dock and as soon as it came it commenced to glow like a coal of fire, so we think we can now answer the question "what is it that makes the sea look as if it was on fire?" I think it is these sea nettles that make it appear so as they come to the surface. The boys have gone fishing again this evening and perhaps may return with new developments.

[Private E. Cook]

Camp at Gloucester Point, Va Monday Morning Oct. 20th 1862

I left off my story last night at Yorktown, which place I visited Tuesday Oct. 19/62. There was one or 2 things that I saw there that I wished to speak to you about. One of them was the chimneys. Every Southerner seems to have a particular hatred of chimneys, and so strong is that hatred that they turn their chimneys out of doors. It looks so odd to go along and see sticking out and up at the back end of the house a long chimney. It looks as if the chimney was built first and then the house added on.

Did I ever tell you what constitutes a village in this country? It is 1 courthouse 1 shop + 2 dwelling houses with a black smith shop in front of one of them. Only the C.H. + shop are absolutely indispensable; the dwelling houses are not necessary.

[Private E. Cook]

Camp at Gloucester Point, Va. October 24th 1862

The city contains less than 300 inhabitants and not more than 20 or 30 houses it is built on the sand of the sea shore and has a decided bleak appearance like an outcast and out of the way village. There is a large military R.R. Depot at the boat landing and this I presume is what has laid the foundation for a city at such a strange point as the sea shore sand.

[Private E. Cook]

Camp at Gloucester Point, Va. Friday Dec. 12th 1862

The day was very lovely but not very warm. It was my turn to go on Cap. of the Guard so I was put on Picket Guard and had charge of the 3 posts on the left of the centre line and guarded one fork of a road.

There was a large house set back from the road a little ways called "Elmwood" and in the rear of the house was another large two story building used for a slave house or nigger residence. They had Geese, ducks, turkeys + chickens in the yard. I had a good dinner of chicken soup made of chicken boiled with unsifted corn meal. I tell you it was "bully! The nigger made me some hoe cakes + gave me a lot of nice turnips. I thought I fared pretty well for that day. The nigger houses are very poor affairs generally having no floor and only one room. The windows are made of old clothes. The slaves are very poorly clothed and their clothes are ragged + torn. They tell me that they have not received any clothes this year. The night was cold and I could not sleep a wink all night. They told me to put out my fires at night but I did not do it. I kept a few embers burning all night which made things a little more comfortable, and I managed to get through the night although it seemed terribly long before daylight appeared and I was right glad when the first red streakings of the morning light came shooting up the Eastern sky. The old nigger that lived in the slave house was "Uncle Pete" and a queer old "Pete" was he. He put me in mind of "Uncle Tom". A colored gal came up to the line this afternoon and gave me two big sweet potatoes. I had quite a talk with her.

[Private E Cook]

Camp at Gloucester Point Va. Dec 23ᵈ 1862

In the Harpers Weekly you sent in the box there is some very splendid illustrations of the army. There is one of where the cavelry are deployed a scrimeshers it reminds me of our tramp that we had out to Gloucester Court House The most amusing feature of that march was to see the niggers They would flock to the roadside by hundreds some bowing and saying how is you masser. Youre grining Some shaking with fear and some of the knowing ones kicking up all sorts of cappers It is quite a show to see such a lot of the colored race together some great big thick lip and as black as midnight some little bit of monkeys that can hardly crawl. We met a nigger on the road out there who had a pair of what he called new shoes. I never saw such shoes I think the {unknown word} was about ½ {unknown word} it was green in places and quite rotten one shoe was about half an inch longer than the other one was {unknown word} the ties and the other peaked and such workmanship never was seen it looked as if they had been cut out of a dead pig with a skull hatchet it is no used me trying to describe them shoes I was astounded he said he had to pay 5 dollars for them and they could not be bought for less and a pair of {unknown word} such as we should get in Buffalo for 5 ½ or 6 dollars he said cost from 35 to 40 dollars.

[Private E Cook]

Carolina City, N.C. January 2nd 1863

We are considerable farther south than we were in Virginia but we are right on the sea shore and it is much colder I think than it is in Virginia where we left. All the male inhabitants from little boys 10 years old + upwards chew tobacco and all the females from little girls to old women smoke pipes + chew snuff on the end of a stick. It makes me sick as I write about it. It is the most disgusting habit I ever knew. The corners of the girls mouths are constantly dirtied up with the nasty snuff. Instead of having carpets they sprinkle their floors with fine sand and use the whole room for a large spit box. The girls squirt the snuff juice out of their mouths and between their teeth as far and as forcibly as any man who has chewed tobacco for years. The soil of this point is sandy dry + unproductive. Scrub or live oak flourishes abundantly and of swamps there are no end. The pine tree also grows extensively and they make tar here in great abundance. There are not near as many slaves here as in Virginia and the rank South feeling is not found here. All that the people here want is to be let alone. I am writing now in a secesh house just behind our company

I am enjoying very good health and I hope you are doing the same. It is very good weather here yesterday it was a little cold as the wind blew from the all day but today it is very warm not only warm but the sun shines down very hot upon us The people in this vicinity are not such rank secesh as those in Virgina some profess to be union and others dont seem to care how the thing goes only the war was settled.

It is a curious fact that in this part of the country that both men + women and even children to as small as sister Fanny either smoke or chew tobacco in the house I am writing there is an old woman + 3 daughters one about 19 the other 16 or 17 and they both smoke and the old woman smokes the other is about as old as fanny and she smokes when she gets a hold of a pipe then she has 2 sons one about the size of Billy the other smaller and they both chew and smoke tobacco. You must keep on writing a usual as we shall get the mail here twice a week if not oftener and I shall always continue to write as usual myself Give my best Respects to all the neighbors I send my love to you all so no more at present from

[Private A. Lyth]

Carolina City, N. C. January 16th 1863

After Breakfast, I walked to Newbern again and got there just in time to take the nine o'clock train for Carolina City. It is cold + rainy today and coming down on the cars I grew quite chilly from having perspired freely on my walk from the 67th camp to the city. The line of road from Carolina City to Newbern is very dreary. I do not think there are six houses along the entire 30 miles. The wood is all pitch pine and nearly every tree has been barked + scraped for the pitch that flows from the tree. You have seen the Virginia pine, but the pine that grows here is as much worse than the Virginia pine as that is worse than our own

Northern pine. North Carolina is a great state for tar making. The tar is made from the pitch or gum that flows from the pine.

[Private E Cook]

Beaufort, S.C. Monday Feby 2ᵈ 1863

Another pleasant day. Our Boat made another short trip this afternoon and now we are lying at the landing of Beaufort S.C. Thursday afternoon we left the harbor of Beaufort N.C. and Friday Feby 13/63 The weather is still warm and at times even sultry. The nights are cool and are always accompanied by heavy dews which has given many of us a severe cold in the head. I had a sore throte the other morning but it worked off during the day. The first night the troop landed on this Island they burned up a negro settlement. It seems one of the negroes shot a soldier of the 9ᵗʰ New Jerseys which so exasperated some of the members of the regiment that they burned up every negro house they could find, furniture and all. The negroes put on a good many airs since they have raised a regiment in the part of the country and they had made their brags that they had cooled down and scared our regiment of white soldiers who landed on this Island and they thought they could do the same to these troops, but how vain are all the calculations + expectations of ambitious man as the smoking ruins of their once loved homes will now bear witness

Beaufort is up the river about eight miles above Hilton Head. The river is very narrow but so deep that the largest ships can run up to Beaufort. But just above here the river divides into two forks and is not wide enough to allow of the passage of vessels. The harbor at Hilton Head, which is nothing more than the mouth of, Beaufort is called the finest harbor south of New York. Hundreds of vessels of the largest build could anchor in it with perfect security to themselves and to each other. At Hilton Hd, there are 2 rebels forts – "Forts Walker" + "Beauregard" – on either side of the harbor which were captured by our forces last spring I think it was. I believe it was here that Capt. Budd U.S.N. of Buffalo lost his life while rowing up the river to make a reconnaisance. This whole vacinity is called "Port Royal". If we land here at Beaufort as they say we are going to do tomorrow morning I shall be able to give you some kind of a description of the place. As I see it from the vessel it appears very neat + clean with many very pretty Southern style residencies. The regiment that guards the place is a negro one. Their uniform is a dark blue jacket + red pants. They appear similar to show monkeys at a little distance but they feel as proud as a pet Peacock. I have rec'd. no letter yet.

[Private E. Cook]

Beaufort , S.C. Tuesday Feby 3ᵈ 1863

The two regiments on board this vessel disembarked this morning for a day or two while the boat hands clean the ship. It was a great joy to the boys to see their feet on land once more. It will give them an opportunity to clean themselves and wash their clothes if nothing more. Close by the landing is a cotton mill that runs 9 gins. All the hands employed are negroes – men + women – except the overseer who is white.

When reading of Whitney, the inventor of the cotton gin, I have many times desired to see the operation of one of these wonderful inventions and here unexpectedly the wish is gratified. The machines used in the factory here are of very simple construction. They are run by steam power and the work is performed by a roller around which is glued a leather strap running diagonally like a screw. As this revolves it pulls the cotton from the seed with great perfection. After witnessing the operations of the machines I went out on the beach and had a hunt. I found one big one about 20 little young ones and 50 nits. I gave my clothes to the wash woman and told her if there was one on them when she returned them

I wouldent pay her a red. These are the first I have found on my clothes since I enlisted, but this is the result of living on board of transports. In the afternoon I took a stroll around town. Those who have been here for some length of time say that when they first came here it was one of the loveliest places they ever saw; Every yard was filled with flowers and every street shaded with beautiful trees. Orange trees are common and Lemon trees abundant. The walks were all nicely kept and everything was loveliness, but now the fences are broken or destroyed entirely, the houses are torn and dilapidated, the flowers plants + fine shrubery are trodden down and they say it does not look like the same place. Still there are some beautiful residences here yet but there are no occupants for them except officers + niggers. You have seen orange + Lemon trees but they bear no comparison to those down here. I saw an orange tree today that was as high as a 2 ½ or 3 story house and a large and beautiful tree it was I tell you. They are about as common here as peach trees in Cleveland. Some flowers are in blossom here now. This afternoon I picked a full blown Dandelion. It was a beauty in my eyes for it made me think of home. This is the place which when taken contained only 1 white man. Dont you recollect the papers spoke of him. Well I saw him this afternoon and bought some peanuts in his store. His name is Allen. He is an elderly looking man of medium height, Greyish hair and wears spectacles. I have had quite a spree of it today. It was quite a novelty for us to be in a town of any size. Beaufort formerly contained about 2000 inhabitants. Very many of the houses that were formerly occupied by the residents as dwellings are now turned into stores + shops.

[QM Clerk E. Cook]

Beaufort, S.C. Tuesday Feby 10th 1863

Went to Hilton Head again today and had the rations that I dun yesterday brought up on a schooner. The weather for the past two days has been warm and pleasant. The birds sing so sweetly in the warm mornings that it almost makes me love the sunny South to hear the joyful songs they warble from their little swelling throats.

Hilton Head is quite a business place. It was formerly a kind of a watering place with 2 or 3 large hotels and a few small dwellings. It is now all military. Some of the government store houses for Commissary stores are 500 or 600 feet long. There are any quantity of cannon there ready for shipment where ever they are needed. They have got a horse railroad running on the dock and into all the store houses by means of which they discharge the cargos of the different vessels that arrive at the dock, loaded with government stores. I noticed many of the stores or Sutter shops are built in such a manner that they can be taken apart + moved or transported to any other part of the country. They are patented and are called "Patent adjustable houses". They are made in Baltimore I think and brought down here + sold. They can be taken all to pieces like a play thing in 15 or 20 minutes and set up again in a very short time. They have doors, glass windows, steps, rafters, floor + everything.

[QM Clerk E. Cook]

St Helena Island S.C. Feb 12 1863

We landed day before yesterday at this place which is about three or four miles from Hilton Head. It is bounded on two sides by the harbor and on the other two by the river. It is a very pleasent place there are some large plantations on it. When we landed here it was so hot that the sweat poured down off from us in fact it is the month of July here. When we reached our camping ground we all had to strip and go in our shirt sleeves to pitch our tents and then we had enough to do. but towards night it was very pleasent. We are encamped on a small plantation I should say it is about as large as the lot where the race course is. Upon at the north end of the plantation is the negro huts or houses worked the plantation before the *war broke out.* Just as we had got our tent pitched some boys from another Regt. told us that one of their boys had been shot at by the niggers and that they were very sasy to the soldiers the story got in circulation amongst all the soldiers in this vicinity and it was not very long before there was a lot assembled around the negro shantys then they commenced and went in and took everything that took their fancy. They took all the chickens + pigs they could lay hold on and opened the sweet potatoes pies which were very numerous and took all the sweet potatoes they wanted. I got a good mess of them. Then the negro fled as the soldier commenced to tear down the out houses for lumber for to lay floors to our tents Some of the negros were well suplied with both household furniture as well as clothing in some of their houses I saw some of as fine linen as ever I saw. In one of the out houses there was a sail boat and two or three pots of paint. one of the boys took the pot of white paint and painted the boat all over with it another took and painted the name 'Gen Hunter' on the stern with red. Then they painted it 2 or three colors then a croud got hold of the boat and took it down to the water and lanched her. At night not being satisfied with what was already done the shantys was set fire to which illuminated the whole plantation. Just as some of the men were about setting fire to one of the buildings I steped in to it and saw a loft were the boys had not noticed before I jumped into it and they handed me a candle there was a good many articles stowed away. different things that must have blonged to the Rebels when they had possesion of this place. Then there was a bag in which there was 3 nice shoulders an 3 nice hams I pitched down the shoulders to the boys and 2 of the hams retaining a good ham for myself we have had some of it cooked and it is as splendid ham as ever I tasted. I got a good wash tub which I found very usefull the next day for washing in Yesterday morning we took our wash tub our clean clothes a couple of camp kettles and material for making a fire and went to a spring which is near our camp. I fill our wash tub with cold water and stripped naked and had a good wash so did Tom. Then we changed our clothes and washed the ones we took off and had a regular washing day of it. Our Regt. is very healthey as for myself I never enjoyed better health in my life and I hope you are all doing the same at home.

[Private A. Lyth]

St Helena Island, S.C. March 3rd 1863

On our ramble through the woods we came across a great many wild flowers in full bloom and there are any amount of wild orange + plumb trees the plumb trees are covered with blooms and the peach trees on a plantation that we were on were in full blom There are any quantity of birds of every description and plenty of bull frogs + snakes oft when we are out drilling we get come across snakes on our drill ground.

[Private A. Lyth]

St Helena Island, S.C. Friday March 13th 1863

Windy and dusty. I thought by the appearance of the foliage and everything that surrounds us that they never had any snow down this way but I am mistaken for today we had a tremendeous snow storm of sand. When the wind blows as it does today it reminds me of a good old fashioned winter storm home when the wind whistles through the crevices and the snow come drifting in from every direction. The soil here is light and sandy and the March winds take it up in boat loads and drift over the country and out to Sea. The plantations after one of these strong winds present the facsimile of a snow field at the North. The ridges are leveled down + the furrows filled up until the whole surface is smooth and level as a frozen lake. When the roads are much traveled in dry weather, the ground instead of becoming hard and packed is cut up light + loose and when walking over it, the sensation is like walking in dry snow or flour. I never walk down the road to the boat landing without thinking of tromping through the snow at home.

[QM Clerk E. Cook]

St Helena Island, S.C. Sunday March 15th 1863

Very warm. I presume that it is nearly as hot here today as you will have it in the month of June or July. This afternoon immediately after dinner one of my fellow clerks and myself took a horseback ride out into the country about 6 miles.

Now for a description of my ride. The day was very warm in fact most uncomfortably so and so we could not ride very fast for fear of injuring the horses so we took it slow and leisurely and had a better opportunity of viewing the country through which we rode. The road is much cut up and in many places is just like meal but in the spots, where the bridle path is diverged a very little from the main road, the riding is beautiful. Nearly the whole length of the road, over which we passed, is lined on both sides with shady trees and shrubbery and part of it passes through a pine forest. In many places the branches of the trees join each other over head and form a screen from the sun at all hours of the day. It is delightful to ride through these natural arbors at any time and particularly so on a warm day like this. When about 4 or 5 miles from camp we came upon a country church + grave yard. There was one large vault and many tombs. Nearly all of the stones were inscribed with the name of the church and the same of the vaults. There are six families of this name in the immediate vicinity and all of them own large plantations. The church was used only for the worship of the "Whites" and its religious denomination was Methodist Episcopal. I learned all this from an old Negro slave who passed by just as we demounted. I asked him what religion he believed in and he said Methodist. He said he did not think the Episcopal church was religious like the Methodist. He thought it was a queer kind of Church, he did not quite understand it, he thought the minister in that church preached more about how to till the land and raise the crops and tell the planters how to make money. I think the poor nigger was not far from right. The side door of the church was opened so I entered and as I did so I instinctively took off my hat for I felt as though I was in the near presence of God and a strong spell seemed to pervade the little church. On the pulpit laid a large gilt edge bible and in the choir was a small organ. I went upstairs to see it and found it was opened and ready for the fingers of some skilled one to touch its pure white keys; but when I put my hand to the bellows handle I found it had been disconnected from the pipes and would omit no sound.

The gilt edge bible + organ are things that I did not expect to find in an out of the way place like this. I tore 2 feathers from a fan that I found in the church and I send them home as a memento of my ride. About a mile farther on the road we came upon another much larger but less picturesque looking church – Methodist – and devoted to the use of the slaves on the plantations. After passing a glance at the large brick church and its surrounding we paid a short visit to a small negro settlement. In many instances two families are crowded into a small house and everything would look dirty and squallid. I think the slaves fared better when they were under their masters than they do at present when they have no one to look after them. There are any quantity of "South Carolina Cabbage" out a mile or two from camp. They do not grow more than 20 feet high and instead of having branches at the top as other trees do they have a kind of cabbage head of long pointed leaves that all grow out from the same trunk. This is the celebrated "Palmetto tree".

The residences of the planters instead of being along the side of the road the same as in our country are away back in the fields out of sight of the road. A person could ride for miles and not see a house but let him turn off at any of the little shady bridle paths that seem to lead nowhere in particular + right into the thickest part of the woods in general and if he continues to follow it for a short distance it will invariably lead him to the door of some planters house.

[QM Clerk E. Cook]

Beaufort, S.C .Saturday April 11th 1863

Very warm This morning a tug boat took us to the dock at Hilton Head and we were transferred with our mess chest and the Horses to the Ferry boat that runs to Beaufort. She left the Pier about 3 o'clock and arrived at Beaufort about 5 o'clock. We got a team to carry up our things and about six oclock we again found ourselves in a tent at the Hd. Quarters of the 1st Brigade. Col. Davis has selected a most delightful spot for his head quarters. The tents are pitched under the branches of a small Grove of large and wide spreading live oak trees in what was formerly a public square or park (apparently). There are some very pretty residences in the town and the shrubbery and shade trees are truly delicious. An officer who visited Beaufort about 5 years ago says it was then one of the loveliest places in the south and was occupied by the wealthiest men in South Carolina. And even now in its present torn condition I can easily find cause to believe his assertion is true.

[QM Clerk E. Cook]

Follys Island S.C. April 28th 1863

Our cannon is at the head of the Island we can see the rebels Just across the stream from us {unknown words} + can holler over to them they have a large gun {unknown words} + exchange newspapers + coffee +c give them for tobacco I must write you a little description of this Island it is about 7 miles long + varys from a mile to a mile + a half in width there never was any more than one house on it + that is where the Genl has his head Quarters the land is worthless for cultivation except a small peice Just around the White house as it is called There are a great many palmeto + June trees + a few red cedar plenty of snakes I guess when this summer get a little more entranced we shall have rattle snakes copperheads + other poisonous snakes but I guess we shall be off from it before that time for the last week we have had the woods on fire on this Island but the fire had gone down pretty much

[Private A Lyth]

Beaufort, S. C. April 30th 1863

Everything as yet is quite in this quarter every day when the tide is out we go down to the beach an have a talk with the Rebels yesterday they sent over a boat to us something in the shape of the monitor today we have been shaping it over + puting a turret on of a quart cup with a hole through for a port hole + a cannon gun stuck through the hole then we put a flag on which has + eagle + coat of arms on + say the union for ever in large colored letters then we printed + addition which made it read The union forever Thats what the matter Fighting for no niggers. From where we talk across to the rebels we can see fort Sumter very plain can see the warehouses on Sullivan Island + the church stepels in Charleston city. Just across the river where we talk with the rebs there are 2 large guns mounted on a fortification + yesterday some one of the

187

boys hollered over + asked them what kind of wood those guns were made off when they told us to come over + we should find out.

The other day we killed a large poisonous snake he was some five feet in length and as thick as a persons wrist in the thickest part of him we tied a string to him and hung him up in a palmetto tree in emblem of the Southern Confederacy Yesterday there was quite a phenomena occur on this Island in the afternoon a black cloud was observed rising in the west and it rose until it came directly over the point of this Island + about 60 or 70 rods from where we are stationed when it began to desend rapidly in the shape of a waterspout but when it got very near to the ground it turned into a whirlwind then the waterspout burst into a mist + spray and began to ascend with greater rapidty than it came down then the whirlwind followed {missing words} and took the sand over a hundred feet high it crossed over on to the of Morris Island then worked off on to the ocean + carried the water a considerable distance into the air .

[QM Clerk E. Cook]

Folly Island, S.C. May 20th 1863

Geo. Clark + I took a walk this afternoon and by the courtesy of the "Signal Officer" were permitted to ascend the "Lookout" and take a peep through the Telescope. We saw Sentinels walking in the Ramparts of Sumter + boatsmen rowing in the river. We could also look down into Charleston. There are 2 Rebel camps about 3 miles from Co "H" and I could distinctly see the "rebs" walking through the streets of their camp ground.

The woods on the island used to be full of snakes but the underbrush has been burned out and the dead snakes are lying thick as peas. There are any quantity of fireflies in the woods which the boys find quite useful + convenient. They (the boys) are not allowed to impose themselves or have any fires so when they are on guard at night they catch a fire fly and put him in their hats and the fly will give light enough to show the time on the face of a watch.

There are also a great number of chammeleons in the woods. They look like a lizard but sometimes they are Green then yellow, brown and I dont know what other colors. Sharks are also quite numerous. Some of the soldiers killed one of the tiger sharks on the beach that weighed 380 pounds. It was left in a kind of basin when the tide went out. One of the boys, not knowing what it was, took hold of its tail *when* it immediately turned round and inflicted a serious bite on the arm or leg of this soldier.

[QM Clerk E. Cook]

Beaufort, S.C. June 10th 1863

A Negro Regt made a raid down here at Beaufort S.C. the started from Beaufort towards the interior of the state for the purpose of destroying a bridge they burnt houses took some cattle and destroyed a very great quantity of Rebel property but they did not succeed in destroying the bridge as they were attacked Just as they were about to commence the destrucktion and they made a hasty retreat not knowing how strong the force might be that was attacking them the returned with about 700 contrabands the next day they enlisted some 250 of them and had them drilling. I must close my letter with my love to you all give love to Sarah Ann and William and the children and let me know How the Youngster gets along

[Private A Lyth]

Folly Island, S. C. November 23rd 1863

The Arago will be in tomorrow and I expect a letter as usal to day I posted a couple of "New Souths" and another newspaper with a speach of Henry Ward Beacher's in I think the speach is worth reading although he is an abolitionist Speaking of Slavery after this war is over slavery in this country will be over for if the slaves are not freed by the government they will free theirselves because since this war broke out they have learnt what it is to be free where ever our armies have penetrated the slave states there the negro has picked up a little education and have learnt that they need not be slaves if they wish to be free Take it in this department for instance every negro you come across has an A.B.C. book primer or second reader even old men sixty or seventy years old and they always carry them about with them and when they can steal a few moments from their work the sit down and open their books. Now around this hospital there are some ten or 12 niggers employed to scrub the floors and every moment they can hide away from the boss the stick theirselves in some corner and get out their books. I have asked them a great many times what they would do if they had to be slaves again. they would say 'I run away. or they can't make me slave any more. Here there is a nigger school and quite a number of the young ink stands go there. the other day I was down town and a five year old ink stand was counting over a roll of 'green $ backs'. when I said to him thats good for nothing. ain't it say he here you want and he offered it to me but when I reached out my hand as it to take it his eyes give one roll and he commenced to laugh Yah Yah Yah I tot dey was good for noting. it would be imposible to makes slaves of these nigs again particularly those that have been in the army.

[QM Clerk E. Cook]

N. End Folly Island S.C. Dec 22nd 1863

I wish you could experience for a single days the lovely weather that is almost continuous in this latitude at this season of the year. It is not like our northern "Spring" although it approximates nearer to that season than it does to our "fall". I know of no term that will express the idea of the sensation associated with this weather so well as "Joyful". It is joyful weather. To be sure we occasionally have rains and cold days. Last Sunday morning the water in our basins froze ½ an inch thickness but such instances are very rare during the winter month.

[QM Clerk E. Cook]

Morris Island So Carolina March 24 1864

It is a long time since I received a letter from home so I have made up my mind to write and give you a good blowing up, so here goes. but I guess I had better wait until I get a letter and see what you have got to say for yourselves. We expect to get a mail tomorrow or next day and then if I don't get a letter from some of you you'll have to look out. The weather here for the past two day past has been very windy and stormy and rained in torrents. yesterday it did not rain but the wind blew a perfect hurricane and quite a number of the tent in the Regt were blown down and the sand drifted same as the snow does in old Buffalo on a windy day. if a poor cuss put his head out side of the tent he was sure to get his neck ears eye + hair filled with sand In the tent that I stop we have got quite a nice little stove which an officer of the 3rd New Hampshire found missing one day when we set it outside for to get his chimney fixed and all I could do yesterday was to go out and steal a few wash tubs boxes or anything in the shape of wood to keep a fire going and keep ourselves comfortable but today it is a very pleasent in fact – the sun shines pretty hot Day before yesterday one of the men belonging to our Co fell overboard out of one of the picket boats as they were coming in from the harbor he lost his gun which he had in his hand at the time. They soon hauled him back into the boat again. but he had to leave his shooting iron behind.

[Private A Lyth]

Gloucester Point Va April 20th 1864

We the 100th Regt arrived here yesterday morning after having a most beautifull passage we left Hilton Head on the 16't. after having had quite a little muss there with the negro soldiers the night before we embarked one of the negro patrol attempted to take one of our boys that was making a little noise well the boys did not like to be hauled up by negros so they rescued him from the guard then a whole company of niggers came with loaded fire arms and the boys commenced throwing broken bottles brick bats and what ever they could pick up and leveled two or three and severely wounded half a dozen. then the niggers took aim and fired at our boys and wounded one then the boys made a rally for their muskets which were in a building but the officers locked the doors and stood with drawn swords beating the boys off. The negros left then and I tell you if they had not there would have been great slaughter for the boys were determined to have their guns and there was two Regts of us besides the rest of the white troops on the island even the Artillery boys who were ordered out with their peices to quell the riot turned on our side and swore they would spike their cannon before they would fire at us. Our Major then went to the provost Marshall and told him if he did not put on white troops to patrol the town he would not be answerable for what the Regt did. the Provo Marshall then put on white patrols and then the boys cheered them and then the boys kept everything quite and peaceable.

[Private A. Lyth]

Gloucester Point Va. April 23/64

Here I am at dear old Gloucester again. I would as soon {next 7 lines are illegible} {unknown word} {unknown word} after dark. We remained at Hilton Head two days & one night. While there some of our boys got drunk and raised a disturbance so that the authorities ordered out a company of negro soldiers to disperse our boys & drive them to their quarters. This only made matters worse & our boys instead of going to their quarters only defied the negroes until they fired on us & wounded one man so that he lost his leg.

Wednesday Evening

The affair would not have ended here if the officer in command at Hilton Head had not immediately ordered the negro companies back to their quarters and sent in their place a company of white soldiers.

[2nd Lt. E. Cook]

Gloucester Point Va April 25th 1864

I received your kind and welcome letter dated April 3rd and I was very sorry to hear that Emma and Willie were sick but I hope they are well by this time I guess you have heard before this of our Regt having left Morris Island and I tell you the boys of the 100th Regt were mighty glad to leave that desolate island were we have lost so many of our comrades. You will probaly have heard of the fuss our Regt had with the negros at Hilton Head so I will not mention it We left Hilton Head on the evening of the 15th on board of the steamer "Arago" but we did not know where we were going and I tell you the boys were mighty glad on the morning of the 19th when we tumbled out of our bunks and went on deck and found our steamer plowing the waters of the York river bound for Gloucester

Point the place where I first joined the glorious 100th Regt and where we passed so many pleasant weeks some 15 months ago. The secesh on this point were very pleased to see the 100th Regt back for they say that there has not been a Regt here since we left that treated them or paid them so well for eatables as the 100th. And I belive them for the other day when 2 or 3 of my chums and myself were at the house of an old widow lady taking her our washing a couple of soldiers of another Regt came along and commenced to tear down her chicken pen for to make themselves bunks of but we made them stop and talked a little to them 'till we made them ashamed of theirselves. I think this campaign is going to end the war either one way or the other. If our side wins – then the south is no more but if the South wins – the North must give up the struggle.

[Private A Lyth]

Bermuda Hundred, Va. Sunday June 12th 1864

This morning I went in company with Bell Mason & Ken VanHusen a short distance up the James River, and had a most delicious bath in its fresh waters. On our way we stopped several times at the foot of some of the many cherry trees that shade the roads & paths through the rich plantations, and had our fill of their delicious fruit. The whole country instead of having orchards as we do with, plant their fruit trees by the rodeside & bridle paths and wherever you go you will be sure to ride beneath the branches of cherry, apple, peach, pear & mulberry trees.

[2nd Lt. E. Cook]

Petersburg, Va.Sunday June 19th 1864

Nothing further has been accomplished as yet. The pontoon bridge across the James river has been taken up. Our lines (The Potomac Army) are advanced on one flank to within ½ mile of Petersburg. No news from our immediate front. An officer in a "<u>nigger calvery</u>" regiment and a {unknown word} got into a quarrel yesterday & the {unknown word} shot the Lieut. in the head and some of the officers men retalliated by shooting the {unknown word} who died today. The Lieut. is still living and is expected to recover. The ball entered near the ear and came out of his mouth.

How do the people North feel about the Petersburg affair. Everybody here is down on the niggers. Our loss was very heavy but a large portion of it was caused by the white troops firing into the retreating niggers. We had Petersburg in our power that day if the nigs had not been seized with a kind of unusual panic or if we had followed up our success, in taking the first line, by an immediate charge on the remaining line. The rebel force was very small in compassion to our own as it is proved that only 1 corps was in Petersburg.

[2nd Lt. E. Cook]

Deep Bottom, Va. Thursday Sept. 29/64

After a very fatiguing march last night through woods and over bad roads, crossing the Appomattox & then the James river on pontoons we found ourselves at 2 ½ oclock this A.M. halted at Deep Bottom. This does not look much like going to North Carolina. We stacked arms and laid down in our places with orders to fall in again at 4 oclock and continue our march.

A little after the appointed time we were under arms and moving forward towards the enemy's works. Just as we entered the woods we were surprised by a sudden and continuous rattle of musketry on the left. Our regiment which was reduced by straggling to less than half its proper number yes! less than 100 men was deployed as skirmishers on the extreme right. We advanced slowly, cautiously but surely until we came out in front of the rebs forts. We were not opposed as we expected {unknown word} and it was fortunate for us for we were in a perilous position skirmishing through a wood where they could have raked us with artillery if they had known of our approach & chosen to do so. We afterwards fell back to a position on the road. Here we rec'd a few shell from Jonny but they did us no damage. Soon the cheers on the left announced to us the fact that the storming party (Negroes) had been successful in their charge and carried the enemy's position. Then the order came to forward and we forwarded driving the enemy before us for 4 or 5 miles where he made a stand having been reinforced from the city of Richmond. We could not dislodge him by a direct attack so our division moved to the right up the Darbytown road to within 3 miles or less of Richmond while the 2^d Division charged their line, but did not succeed in taking the works. We then fell back about 3 miles where we turned the last line of the rebel works taken by us and entrenched ourselves.

[2nd Lt. E. Cook]

Before Richmond Va. Jany 14th 1865

I have just returned from a trip down the {unknown word} River to start off our regiment. They left fort Monroe and I suppose they are now in old Buffalo. I saw the old settlement of Jamestown the home of Capt. John Smith + Pocahontas. I send you enclosed a sprig of willow which I wish you to plant. I send home some relics which I wish have preserved. You would walk down to his house on Niagara Street and get them of him. There are three plants the smallest one was cut from the old Churchyard + all the rest + write soon

[2nd Lt. E Cook]

Richmond, Va. May 9th 1865

I went to St. Pauls Church in Richmond last Sabbath. I heard some fine music + singing but the preaching did not amount to much. The minister talked so much like a nigger that I could not understand more than half what he said. When I come home for good would you like to have me bring my nigger along with me to do chores + cooking. He is a splendid cook + a good chamber maid. Can make delicious buckwheat cakes out of wheat flour + water and improvise a mellow feather bed out of rails + oak leaves. Can milk a horse, drive a cow, feed canary birds tend the pigs, build tent houses split kindling wood and make himself generally useful besides eating all of his own rations and not leave any of his comrades' to waste + spoil. If you think such a specimen of negroality would be of service to you I will bring him along with me.

[2nd Lt. E Cook]

EDWARD COOK:
THOUGHTS ON POLITICS AND STRATEGY

Ed: Civil War soldiers were consumed with highly charged and partisan debates. They craved news from their newspapers and discussed the issues in camp. Patriotic and ideological issues had, in part, prompted them to enlist. They followed the activities of the Copperheads or Peace Democrats who opposed the war. The Copperheads became more vocal and active when the war was going badly from the Union side from the summer of 1862 to the summer of 1863. In the 1864 election, the Peace Democrats called for an armistice and peace negotiations and nominated General McClellen to run against President Lincoln. Lincoln stood for an unconditional victory in the war whereas McClellan advocated peace short of victory

Camp at Gloucester Point Va. Nov. 1862

You ask what we think of Lincoln's proclamation. We think more of getting through with the war than we do of all the rash proclamations of our President. We think with Europe that Lincoln had better get the nigger before he sets them free. This war is nothing more than a nigger war. The nigger down here is better than a soldier. Day before yesterday a soldier was confined in a dungeon because he whipped a nigger for driving over his foot.

It is a common saying among the soldiers that a man might as well strike an officer as to strike a nigger. We are willing to fight for our flag, our country + our Constitution but we are not willing to spill our blood for the lazy and ungrateful nigger.

Camp at Gloucester Point Va. Nov. 4th 1862

I wish I could be present to cast in my vote. I am almost inclined to believe that it would be in favor of Wordsworth although I know that the whole Southern Confederacy is not worth the precious Union blood that has already been spilled in the vain endeavor to retain it. And when we think of the vast amount that yet must flow we are ready to say let them go to the ruin they so wildly seek, but give us <u>peace</u>.

The curse of God shall yet rest upon the souls of those who have been the prime movers in this shameful rebellion and unholy war. I believe we are but little nearer the End than we were a year ago. I have not now the slightest hope of seeing my friends at home until my regiment is discharged after having served out the full term of years for which they were mustered into the service. Things of a certainty do not look near as promising as they did 2 months ago. How must it discourage the poor soldier when he learns that a place which is impregnable when garisoned by 10,000 men, has been surrendered, without a struggle, although at the time of the surrender it was defended by upwards of 11,000.

Again he is informed that an officer, when questioned as to the reason why he did not "bag" a rebel army when he had an opportunity, replied that "That is not the game the game is to maneuvre around until both armies are tired out and both sides desirous of peace to then receive the Confederate States into the Union with slavery" This is the "Game" our high Officers + Officials are playing upon the people.

Which is best? Shall we elect "Peace" parties to fill our high offices, those who openly declare themselves in favor of peace on any honorable grounds, or shall we submit to the miserable farce which is now being played off upon us, and finally find one compelled to make peace upon such terms as the "Rebs" see fit to force upon us! We have force enough to come down on the Enemy like an avalanche and crush him in an instant but we do not do it and why? Simply because that is not the "game". We have thousands of soldiers who are anxious to return to their homes and would fight like hell hounds if they could be brought into any action that they knew would be decisive, but this cannot be, and why? because such is not the "game". No! the poor soldier must remain in his camp, suffering from all camp diseases, too hot in summer + too cold in winter, with abundance of nauseating food to eat and sickening beverages to drink, no friend to comfort him if he feels despondent + unwell and no care taken of him if disease lays her pityless hand upon him; while his officers are playing at their unholy "game". Never will I advise a friend of mine to enlist until I see some signs of a disposition on the part of our "Starred" + "double Starred" strap wearers to put an end to the ruinous "game". Wait! Be drafted! Be anything but don't enlist!

The soldiers are willing and anxious to fight but we have no Generals or if we have those who are both able, and true to the Union they are kept in the background with small commands and not allowed to do anything towards bringing this war to a speedy close. But things will not go on so always, and even now I see that the public journals are taking the matter in hand and bringing the offenders before the public and inquiring into the wherefore of certain acts of some of our high officers. I hope the time is not far away when some kind of a change will be made in our army affairs enabling us to go ahead in the work overpowering + defeating our merciless foe.

I wish you would write to me as soon as the results of todays election are made known and tell me which party is victorious. For my own part it is but little I care which party is defeated.

Ed: Edward's tone is very negative and morale is obviously low in the camps around the Point. The 100th spent a half a year inactive and bored.

Camp at Gloucester Point, Va.Thursday Nov. 6th 1862

You ask me what I think about Jeff Davis arming the slaves. I do not think he dare do it and if he had the belief that it would aid his cause to arm the slaves, he has not got the arms to do it with unless he takes them from his white soldiers. From all that I have seen of the negro slaves I judge them to be a very cowardly people and I would be far less afraid to meet a regiment of armed slave than I would to meet the same number of slave women armed + in line, for of the two I think the negress is more courageous + manly than the negro. I do not dream, neither does any man in the regiment dream that any trouble is to be anticipated from the Southern Confederacy arming the slave population.

It appears for a certainty that Seymore is elected although we have not had all the returns. the very fact of the democrats carrying the day is that all the Republicans are in the army I know that by the very fact that there are 76 able men in our company and about 65 of them are voters and there are all Republicans excepting some 6 or 7 and it is the same throughout the camp and the camps of the other Regiments that I have been in you will the men useing various expresions against the democrats There are 12 men in our tent and they are all democrats but one but he is not a voter not being 18 year old.

Ed: The South did not start to seriously consider this option until late in 1864 and never reached a consensus as to how to compensate the slave owners or the slaves for their service.

Hilton Head, S.C. Saturday Jany 31st 1863

We are now in the pestilential state of South Carolina – the viper from which has eminated the rank poison of secession that now has been distilled into the veins of every state in the once lovely South. In the state of the "Palmetto Flag" that has led many brave and true hearts to a base and ignominious death in the unholy cause of rebellion. In the state of the "Palmetto Tree" that now warms over the grave of noble souls now hushed in the silent sleep of death.

St Helena Island, S.C. Sunday Feby 22[d] 1863
Washingtons Birthday Anniversary.

Raining in the morning, very pleasant in the afternoon. I hope the next anniversary of this day may find me witnessing the celebration of it in the beautiful street of my own loved home but I am very much afraid my hope will not be realized for I do not think this war will find an end in one year. I am glad to see the government changing its plans and tactics. I am in hopes that they are tired of finding their efforts their money and the precious lives of the poor soldiers in the vain attempt to take the Godforsaken city of Richmond. I hope the scene of war now is to be removed from the unlucky state of Virginia and shifted to the South + West where our arms have always been successful and where we may yet hope to meet and conquor our traitorous enemy. I believe the only true way to end this war successfully for ourselves and in the short speedy and lasting manner to attack, take + keep all the seaport towns and then move up from all points and cut off the enemies supplies and he will be obliged to yield. I think it is useless to try + take Richmond for even if we take it from the North the loss of life in the struggle will never be repay'd by the good we will gain or the advantage we will derive from the victory. If we take Richmond the enemy has command of the railroads to Petersburg and can speedily transfer all their men + stores to that place and fortify it fully as strong as Richmond or Fredericksburg now is. This is their policy in this war and the only way in which they can hold their own and if our government keeps on in the blind course which they seem to have been persevering for the last year and a half I am fearful that it will prove most ruinous to our cause and fatal to our success.

St Helena Island, S.C. Thursday March 5th 1863

Each day of delay adds strength to the enemy and weakens our forces in more ways than one. I trust my suspicions are not true but I am fearful that our next engagement will be a Fredericksburg repeated. There is not the least news as to when we are going to move. The quartermasters commenced to put rations aboard of their respective boats last week but their operations were suspected at the close of the first days week and now we are in a quandary.

St. Helena Island, S.C. Wednesday April 1863

Very cold I reckon the new congress meets today. We soldiers are building great air castles on the expected doings of the new democratic congress. Some are expecting congress to order home the troops some expect the declaration of a dishonorable peace and may expect an armistice during which time we can have a furlough to go home, but I expect things to go on as they have heretofore slowly and ineffectually.

Beaufort S.C. April 16th 1863

The report here is that we are to take Charleston if we sink every "Monitor" and kill half our men in the attempt. There is so much feeling in the north in regard to this expedition that it seems it is actually necessary to the sustainment of our cause Charleston should float the stars + stripes before any other movement of our armies takes place. The papers at the north and the northern people have a very inaccurate idea of our military strength in this department. It is confidently stated that we have 30,000 men to cooperate with the naval force and more expected, whereas, we have at no time been able to bring forward more than 16,000 and today as one whole brigade has left this point for New Bern S.C. we can not show for active operations above 12,000 to 15,000 men including niggers, cavalry, artillery + infantry. Nor have I heard of any reinforcements that were expected here. In fact there is no point whence we can draw more troops unless we take them from the Dept. of Virginia for Genl Foster is hemmed in by the enemy in North Carolina + Hunter was obliged to send a whole brigade from the forces here to relieve Foster of the difficulty in which he has very foolishly placed himself. I do not see for my part what becomes of all the soldiers. It has always been the cry since the war broke out "More men" more men" "reinforcements, reinforcement" And the general who really needs them can seldom or never obtain them. But they can be kept in large bodies doing nothing, accomplishing nothing where they are not needed at all or where a small force and light artillery would answer the purpose just as well. But we are going to Charleston with our little handful of 12 or 15 thousand men and we are going to trust to God and the righteousness of our cause for the complete and perfect fulfillment of the hard task which is alloted to us to perform. And I believe that God will bring us out conquerors for I trust that He is on our side. The issue now seems to be <u>freedom</u> or <u>slavery</u> and can it be that God will favor the cause of slavery? I do not believe it. From the very first outbreak I thought that this war would result in the abolition of slavery, and I then believed that God permitted it only for that purpose and I am now more fully and firmly convinced of it than ever before and I can not come to any other conclusion than that this is <u>God</u>'s war and He is on the side of freedom.

Ed: Note how a war that had initially begun to "restore the Union" had now morphed in Edward's thoughts into a war "to end slavery."

Beaufort, S.C. Friday April 24th 1863

Very warm this A.M. very windy this P.M. I saw a paper from the north to day and it gives a very gloomy account of the conditions of our affairs. The "Cut-off" at Vicksburg is a failure + our army of the West is acting on the defensive. Rosencranz is in danger of being surrounded + cut off. Genl Foster is surrounded and if not relieved he will have to surrender. The attack on Charleston is a failure. The Copperhead sentiment at the north is fearfully increasing. Treasonable remarks against our President + Cabinet are common in the daily journals and altogether it seems as though our cause to day look more gloomy than did that of the rebels a year ago.

Thursday afternoon

I think if I can get there I shall stand a good chance of obtaining a commission in one of the Negro Regiments as this place. As I write two companies of Negro Soldiers are marching across the park and it is a fact that they <u>march</u> <u>better</u> than the White Soldiers. Whether they do so from pride or on account of the natural capacity which possess of keeping time + step I cannot say; but whatever may be the cause the fact is true. Everybody around here says they are going to make good soldiers + I believe it is true.

[QM Clerk E. Cook]

N. End Folly Island Nov. 3rd 1863

I suppose you are having a very busy time up North in old York State today.

It is election day but us poor soldiers who are out here doing duties for our country are not allowed the priviledge of saying what men shall have a hand in propelling the ponderous wheels of government. If we could be allowed the priviledge of voting where you think would the poison copperheads stand? What would become of their party? But I believe there are enough true hearted patriots still left in New York State to carry the election against all the odds that vile treason can bring against it. The soldier longs for peace once more with a longing far greater than his friends at home for he knows how to appreciate the value of the blessing of peace but he does not want a peace disgraceful to himself + to the country for which he has periled his life. Peace still looks a long way off but still we do not want to return to our homes until we can do so with proud and thankful hearts that need not feel ashamed of the cause + country for which[ ] they have been fighting.

[QM Clerk E. Cook]

Ed: Soldiers were able to vote in national elections but not the local elections.

Hilton Head, S.C. Sunday April 10th 1864

I almost think that if I was sure that I would have to stay my 3 years out that I would reenlist and go home but I have some slight hope of being discharged before that time. Nearly everybody in the army seems to think that this war will have been used up by this spring & fall campaign.

I am in hopes that it will, not only for my own sake but for the sake of our country and all who are interested in her best welfare. It seems though too much blood has been spilled and to much money spent & wasted already on this rebellion and I think that our Government is henceforth going to push the war to its speedy close. I think we have fooled and played with the rebs about as much as we can afford and it is now about time to wake snakes and call the lizards up, or else cave in and acknowledge ourselves whipped. There is no reason in the world why our government should not whip Secession and drives it to its vile den & utterly demolish the whole scheme & structure. I think this if the feeling of General Grant and I hope he will continue to feel so until his purpose is accomplished and the war is ended and we are once more allowed to return to our homes and the bosoms of our families.

Ed: Now Edward has decided that secession is evil. An interesting change of thought!

On Board the "Thomas A. Morgan May 5ᵗʰ 1864

I have only an opportunity to let you know that I am well. I am now on board of the "Thos. A. Morgan" en route for "Fortress Monroe" & from there to "Bermuda Hundred" on the James River. I am still in the Q.M. Dept. but do not know how long I will remain in it. You can direct your letters to the "100ᵗʰ Regt., 10ᵗʰ Army Corps, Washington D.C." and I will get them all right. It has been a long time since I heard from you. Are the folks all well? We have heard of Gen. Grants successes. I cannot as yet call them victories. Time & the end of this campaign will decide that.

I think this campaign is going to end the war either one way or the other. If our side wins – then the south is no more but if the South wins – the North must give up the struggle.

The campaign has opened most gloriously, and if Grant has the same ability to meet and overcome unexpected reverses that he has to plan the first opening of the campaign, then our victory is certain and you may expect me home by next Spring. Our cause is most evidently in God's hands and he is on the side right & liberty. We cannot fail.

I don't give Grant praise for I feel that it is Gods goodness & power manifested through him that our present successes are owing to.

Ed: Edward was aware of General Grant's successful campaigns. He was hopeful for the coming of the spring campaign in Virginia. In fact, Grant's and Lee's armies were engaged in the Battle of the Wilderness.

On Board the Thomas A. Morgan June 7th 1864 Tuesday

We are very anxious to hear from Grant. There is a rumor that he is coming down this way and intends to make an assault on Richmond from this direction. I presume it can be done but it will only be by a terrible loss on our side. I believe we have about 70 pieces of cannon in the short space of 5 miles and we consider our position almost impregnable, but the rebs have even more cannon than we have and whenever we assault their works we can only take them by walking over our own dead. But I consider Grant a great strategist, and as strategy seems to have been his most powerful & successful ally in this campaign we are in hopes that if he comes here he will call into action the same power and give us victory without a loss great enough to dampen the joy & gladness which the news of a victory always produces.

Ed: Edward and his fellow troops were trapped in Bermuda Hundred, and Grant was engaged with Lee at the Battle of Cold Harbor.

Bermuda Hundred, Va. Wednesday June 14th 1864

A large number of 100 days men have arrived this week. Grants army is crossing the James River on a pontoon bridge about 6 miles below us and are marching towards Petersburg tonight. Genl. Grants Hd. Qrs. are at City Point just across the Appomattox. He was on this side to day and I had a very good sight of him. He is very plain and unassuming and attracts no notice. He came from City Point to this place in a little tug while Gen. Butler has for his private use the largest & fastest river steamer in the Department. He wore no sword or other outward trapping except his buttons and plain shoulder straps. His pants were tucked inside of a pair of long dusty boots and his whole attire looked dirty & travel stained. His shoulders are very broad, and from his habit of carrying his head slightly inclined forward and looking downward he has the appearance of being a little round shouldered. He walks with a long slow stride and slightly emphasizes his left foot step. I associated with his appearance the idea or similee of a huge ponderous Iron roller (on a very slightly inclined plane) which though hard to start yet when once fairly underway by its momentum carries everything before it and is almost impossible to stop.

Have you any fears for the result of the war? I have not. With such men as our army contains to fight for us and with such a cause as ours to fight for, we must succeed – there is no such word as fail. I still have every confidence in Grant and trust that my confidence may never appear to have been misplaced.

The raid up North has excited no particular interest in the army, and if it had been for the great scare which it has produced at home, and the great sensation which it has caused among the "newspaper dailies" I should not even have deigned to mention it. It is all over now and the rebs have got back with whole skins and unbroken organization just as I bet they would when I first heard of the raid. Nobody wanted to <u>check</u> their depredations or catch <u>them</u> when they offered our people a good opportunity to cut them off and use them up. One of the screws in the machinery of our government has been loose a long time and I am forced to believe the thread is worn off and it can never be tightened up again.

Ed: This is a marvelous description of General Grant and is true to photographs and other descriptions of him.

Bermuda Hundred, Va. August 4th 1864

I think Grant is going to give up the hope of whipping the rebs at Petersburg for the present. I cannot imagine what will be his next move but I believe he will leave only troops enough to hold the works and withdraw the main portion of his army to some other point. He has failed in this attempt but it was not from any fault in the plan (which seems to have been a good one and promised complete and prefect success to our army, and a most terrible & telling and decisive blow to the cause of seceshion. Man proposes & God disproves. A short delay of an hour, of a single hour, or the unaccountable panic that seized the niggers, lost us a battle, which if it had been gained, by us, would have proved to be the most important and decisive one of the campaign either in this department or any other. But we have failed and must submit for it is the will of God, and He doth all things well. It will only prolong the war for an additional length of time, but perhaps each delay will only serve to make our peace more lasting & complete when it does come.

I am getting tired of the service and if the war continues another year & I do not get out of it honorably at the expiration of that time I think I shall be in favor of Peace on any terms.

Petersburg, Va. September 3^d 1864

There is not 1/10 part as much shooting today as there was when we first came to this vicinity. Scarcely a shot is fired along the whole line during the day and not near as many at night as there used to be. Once in a while if we explore {unknown word} too much and too long they will send us a couple of bullets as reminder of our proper positions. The rebs are very anxious about the Chicago Convention. They want Seymour or Fillmore nominated. They think that McClellan is somewhat to be feared as being too much of a war democrat. But the nominations are now made and we are anxious to hear what the newspapers say about it. There has been no exchange of papers on the line today but perhaps there will be before night. There is a rumor that Sherman has Atlanta and, if it is true, I think very likely the rebs will allow no communication between the pickets for a day or two. There were no particulars rec'd of affair but the general impression seems to be that Hood has evacuated and is coming up to assist Lee in retaking the Weldon road. I fear for Grant but trust he is prepared.

I would like to see a peace but I don't wish to see such a peace that in a few years we shall have to fight it over again. I don't wish to see a dishonorable peace. What will our once glorious country be worth if we acknowledge the right of any state to withdraw herself from the union whenever any measure is adopted in the general congress, for the general good, that does not suit the wishes of any one state. Why our country would not be worth living in and I should be ashamed to own it and should want to live in Canada or South America or some other place where they had a government worthy of respect. I don't know what to think of McC's nomination. The idea of nominating a War Democrat on a peace platform is to me very ludicrous. And then what a platform. It is so very ambiguous that almost any party could nominate a candidate on it and then he the candidate could put any contrivetion on its meaning that he saw fit. If the war faction of the democratic party can succeed in keeping the name of McC before their faction and hiding from their supporters the principles of the platform and if the heads of the peace faction can succeed in keeping before their supporters the platform and hiding the candidate they may unitedly elect their McClellan but if the eyes of two factions can be opened to see this sharp political intriguering for the reins of government and the handling of hundreds of millions of money then good bye to their pretty achieve & success to old Abe. I have every hope that if Abe is reelected he will push this war to speedy end and let us have an opportunity to see our homes again.

Petersburg, Va. Friday Sept. 27th 1864

When you write again I wish to know all about how you are getting along with your studies and how you like the institution and its associations. Have you formed any acquaintance with Capt. Walbridge's sister or sisters. Whenever you want any money for books or clothes or tuition just let me know and I will get it for you if possible only you must pay attention to your studies and not let dress or other such influences draw your attention from its proper direction. Feel above the low minded, the bad dispositioned and the haughty-aired persons who will surround you; and do not let their taunts & slurs or sneering looks and insulting acts deter you from pushing straight forward and showing your own vast superiority over such dispositions by your excellence in deportment, character & studies. Learn too to love your country – learn its plans, its principles, its design, its laws, its government, the foundation on which it stands, the material of which it is built and then you will not have to learn to love it for such knowledge of such a country can only conduce to love – a love almost divine and second only to our love for Him who has given us life & being.

Let our young girls acquire such a love and let it grow with them, and then when they have become mothers and a new generation is born, let them instill it into the hearts of their sons and daughters, and what power on earth think you would be strong enough to wrest our country from its people. Union is strength, but the great power of a country to sustain herself against the machinations of traitors at home & enemies abroad lies in the "Amor Patria" of her people. Love your country!

Petersburg, Va. Oct. 25ᵗʰ 1864

When it [trenches] is finished a few men can hold it against a vastly superior force and thus enable Grant to remove the bulk of his army to some other point either to assail the enemy's position and force an entrance into the City or to take and hold another position towards the completion of his vast encircling chain of forts and breastworks. The works goes forward almost imperceptibly, but like a vast moving body its momentum cannot be resisted. It carries everything before it. Grant does not make a move until he is ready to make it. His army lies apparently inactive for a time, everything seems to indicate that the campaign is closed, and men and officers begin to build their winter operations, but all the time Grant is not asleep - he is cautiously and silently working in some unexpected quarter – adding weight to the vast mass that he intends to move, concentrating everything towards the complete success of his plan and when everything is ready, when a move is least expected and where it is least anticipated, he puts the mass in motion and it rolls on and on and over every obstacle until the design is accomplished and the plan carried out completely & effectually in all its points. This is Grant. He is now apparently inactive, engaged merely in {unknown word} up defensive work, but in reality working out beneath this calm exterior a plan of stupendeous proportions – a mighty storm is brewing + soon it will reach its proper temperature and then it burst over our enemy and overwhelm them in its onward flood working ruin in their army and destruction to their hopes. This is my conviction and my prayer is that I may not be swallowed up in the flood but live through it all to raise my voice in thanks to Him who giveth victory to the righteous and causeth desolation to swallow up the wicked.

Petersburg, Va. November 8th 1864

I think if the Jonnies let us alone that Gen. Grant will be satisfied to let them alone until the next spring campaign. Well this is Election Day. I tremble almost for the result. We are all fearing a fight at the north between the Unionists, and Copperheads. If there is fight I pray that father may take no part in it. Let him not compromise himself in any way. He does not know the horrors and terrors & trials and humiliations of a soldier's life and I pray God that he may never learn them.

I think nothing would ever tempt me to enter the Army again unless it was the imminent peril of my country. There is not wealth enough in the whole world to induce me to bind myself for another three years but then what is wealth compared to the salvation of one's own native land. Tell father not to enter the service on any account or to take any part in the deathly struggle that seems to be now threatening our homes at the North. I will answer for our family and surely one is enough where there are only two. I will do my duty – I have done it thus far and been well spoken of and I hope I may continue to do it well and nobly, but let one suffice from our family.

Petersburg, Va. November 10th 1864

All here is now on the {unknown word} to hear the returns from the elections of day before yesterday. I want you to write me all the news about how the election went and how it was carried on in City of Buffalo. Were there many fights and riots?

It is election day but us poor soldiers who are out here doing duties for our country are not allowed the priviledge of saying what men shall have a hand in propelling the ponderous wheels of government. If we could be allowed the priviledge of voting where you think would the poison copperheads stand? What would become of their party? But I believe there are enough true hearted patriots still left in New York State to carry the election against all the odds that vile treason can bring against it. The soldier longs for peace once more with a longing far greater than his friends at home for he knows how to appreciate the value of the blessing of peace but he does not want a peace disgraceful to himself + to the country for which he has periled his life. Peace still looks a long way off but still we do not want to return to our homes until we can do so with proud and thankful hearts that need not feel ashamed of the cause + country for which[ ] they have been fighting.

Ed: Again, Edward appeared to be talking about the inability to vote in state and local elections, not the Presidential election.

Petersburg, Va. December 2nd 1864

When I wrote you last I expected to be in a fight before this time and indeed we are still expecting it daily and I think it cannot be long delayed. The troops are all going into winter quarters but they have had no orders to do so and therefore they cannot blame anybody but themselves if they have to break up again and move. I thought at one time that Grant would remove from here all the troops that were not actually needed to hold this position and open a winters campaign farther south, but I have come to the conclusion the General's going to fight it out in this line of it {unknown words

Very many of the incidents and associations of a soldiers life are very pleasant and I think if it were not for the horrors & hardships of campaigning very few would ever leave it after once entering it especially if they hold any position above that of high private. I believe that no firmer friendship can exist between man and man than that which each soldier feels for his comrades. There seems to be an influence similar to that of secret organizations which binds one to another with an inseverable tie.

I must say Good Night and pleasant dreams, beneath {unknown word} branches and beside {unknown word} streams mayst thou in sleep appear to rest. And this I pray may emblematic be of life's bright close when having sailed the stormy sea, you sleep to wake among the blest.

Petersburg, Va. Jany 27th 1865

I think you are about right in regard to the class of young men left at home. I don't think it would be possible for me to remain at home in active while my country was pouring out her life blood in a terrible struggle for freedom and existence. It is the duty of every man to come forward at his country call and offer his arms and his life if need be for her salvation and support. I have never regretted that I joined my country's cause and if I live to get through this how I shall bless God that I was permitted to lend my fickle aid to the cause of liberty and union.

Petersburg, Va. March 11th 1865

We were reviewed by Genl Grant this last Sunday. He was accompanied by a large staff & numerous ladies. Our division at a review last week was reported to be the best in the army of the James and that probably is the reason why Gen. Grant came over to see us as he did not review any troops on this side but our division (the 1st Div. 24th A.C.) We did look splendid & no mistake and marched like clockwork I tried hard to steal a look at the ladies who were seated in ambulances but the dust was blowing toward them and they were compelled to keep their veils down I was extremely sorry of course at this heavy disappointment but I bore it like a hero. Genl Grant is of a very ordinary appearance so much as that the presence of ladies attracted all attention from him. Of course up north where you have lots of ladies & few Lieutenant Generals the case would be just the reverse.

I think this review is precursory to a move indeed an order was circulated yesterday saying that as this army was liable to move at any moment no more.

Appomattox, Va. April 16th 1865

I wrote you two letters since the charge on fort Gregg and today I received a letter from Laura. This is the first mail that has come through since we took Petersburg just two weeks ago today. Laura's letter was written on the 2d of April and perhaps at the same hour that I was in the hottest of the fight. In her letter she wonders what I am doing but she little dreams what scenes were at that time being enacted around me. Thank God I lived through that awful battle one of the most desperate of the war. We fought at the parapets of the fort until not more than twenty of the garrison was left alive and then we fought inside the fort. Such a desperate resistence is seldom met with in the history of any war.

I received {UNKNOWN WORD} Anthony's letter but shall not answer it until we go to Richmond or some other place to stay. Our men were starving for a few days but they managed to get rations through at last and today a train of wagon came in from Lynchberg with lots of Bacon Flour + smoking tobacco all of which were issued out to the officers + men free gratis. And now there is a good feeling manifest everywhere.

Nothing like {UNKNOWN WORD} to eat to make a soldier feel good. The war is virtually at an end and I hope soon to be with you again. The army was shocked today at a telegram from the north stating that Lincoln + Seward had been assassinated. If the news is true (and everybody here believes it is) all that we want is to be let loose and we will go through the parties who instigated such a deed with a vengeance that rivers of blood only will wash out. Thousands will swear war to the death under the black flag if they can be allowed to avenge the cowardly deed.

My God must our country become another France. Can not the lives of our Presidents be safe in the Capital of our country?

God will avenge such work.

[E. Cook]

EDWARD COOK: THOUGHTS ON RELIGION

Ed: Traditional religion supported the Civil War soldiers with ministers initially encouraging them to answer the call of their nation. Chaplains, being from home areas of the companies, encouraged the soldiers to remember their religious upbringings and behave accordingly. Their sermons talked about the righteousness of the cause with God being on their side. Death or suffering had meaning since it was in the Lord's cause. In their letters, soldiers repeatedly asked their families to pray for them.

Camp at Gloucester Point, Va. November 4th, 1862

I hope that I am prepared to die at any moment and feel that I shall but go to meet my friends in heaven. Such a hope is the only source of comfort which the soldier has to bear him up through every hour of danger and temptation. I hope that I shall always live so that when my sands of life have reached an end, my friends may feel that I but sleep to rise again at the last day and live an everlasting life of love and joy in heaven at the throne of God.

I am glad to know that there are prayers offered up for me. I should dread above all things to be a soldier and be without a hope based upon the Lord. It gives me confidence when fever + disease are daily visable around me; and when any danger is to be faced or any difficulty to be overcome it gives me courage and nurses my spirit to the ready performance of my duty. Not for a world would I be without my hope of future life in the world to come. Christ made the dying bed of poor Stowell a couch of peace + happiness. When I asked him, a day or two before he went to Yorktown, how he got along, he said, "Oh! Cook the knowledge of Christ does me more good that the medicine and all Else besides." "I went" said he "out in the field today and had a sweet + happy time in prayer to God and I feel better." He said more + I know that he had a firm hope established in the Lord.

I was in hopes that I should be able to write a letter to you today but we had no sooner returned from our target practice than we were ordered to get ready for Brigade drill at 1 oclock. Brigade Drill on Sunday – who ever heard of such a thing? No wonder our [ ] do not conquer when such work as this is going on. It seems to me like sacriledge thus to profane the Sabbath when there is no occasion for it. They might give the soldier one day in the week to devote to his own uses + purposes for I am sure he does enough for the government during week days to be entitled to the use of the Sabbath. But we are soldiers + are sworn to obey our superiors so we must not murmur or complain. When we got to our tents we immediately went to work, cleaned our guns, blacked our shoes + brushed our clothes and got ready just in time to turn out as the call was beat on the drum.

I was busy for 2 or 3 hours engaged in drawing the rations for our company and afterwards issuing them to the members. It is a tedious job and not a very desirable one for Sunday but soldiers are slaves or worse than slaves and must do as they are ordered. I might almost say there is no Sabbath in the Army so little respect is paid to the day. If during the week we are ordered to clean up during the whole forenoon in expectation of a Brigade drill 3 hours long in the afternoon you will hear the boys remarking to each other "It seems to me just like Sunday; don't it to you?

I am very sorry for I think that we will never see again as pleasant a camp as this we now have. As soon as I finish this letter I am going to pack my knapsack with such things as I want to take with me so as to be ready for a start at any time the order comes. I had a happy time last night from 8 to 12 while I was sentinel. The time passed by very swiftly and did not seem more than 2 hours. I was thinking of my house and holding sweet yet silent intercourse with My Lord + Savior while others were buried in their Slumbers.

Camp at Gloucester Point, Va. Saturday November 29th 1862

We were on picket today. I had a very pleasant time reading my testament aloud to those that were on post with me and copying a letter that I had written to [ ] the day before but which was blotted so that I was ashamed to send it + so copied it over on picket. We passed the night quietly + comfortably. I stood guard only 2 ½ hours during the night but I did not sleep an hour. We were on the centre, the same line we occupied last time. When we returned from picket and went out to discharge our pieces we found our boys that were left in camp had put up a nice new target. I was the first one that shot and I plumbed the target quite nicely. After firing our pieces we were allowed about half an hour to get ourselves ready for inspection + review. We had not time to pack our knapsacks properly and when the Colonel came to our company and saw how the knapsacks were packed he said "Oh hell! I don't want to inspect that company" and passed us by without more than a passing glance. Inspection over we were given about a quarter of an hour to rest ourselves, eat our dinner and then turn out for Brigade drill. Brigadier General Naglee drilled us for about 3 hours. We went through a great number of movements and did them up just as well as they are generally performed. But this is great Sunday work is it not? I must not stop to moralize however for if I do I shall never finish this letter.

Camp at Gloucester Point, Va. Monday, November 24th 1862

We amused our selves this evening with playing a game we call proverbs and find it very entertaining and perhaps a little instructional as it is a kind of mental discipline. It is played like this: one of the company steps outside the tent and while he is away the rest of the company chose a proverb, either religious or otherwise, and assign the words of the proverb in their proper order to the different members of the company as they sit in a circle around the stove. For instance we take the proverb "Wisdom is better than Riches" a proverb of 5 words: - the 1ˢᵗ word is given to the 1ˢᵗ man of the circle: the 2ᵈ word to the 2ᵈ man + so on. The person outside is then called in and steps up to the 1ˢᵗ man of the circle + asks him a question, and the answer to the question must contain the 1ˢᵗ word of the proverb. He then goes to the second man + asks him some question and the answer to the question must contain the 2ᵈ word of the proverb + the answer to the 3ᵈ question must contain the 3ᵈ word of the proverb + so on; and from all the answers the man must guess the proverb which is often very difficult + requires much memory to recollect all the answers. As we have voted that neither the questions nor the answers shall contain any thing that is not immoral we enjoy the game very much.

Camp at Gloucester Point, Va. Sunday December 28ᵗʰ 1862

I bought some fresh bread + molassas cakes and stole a good drink of cider out of the hole in a cider barrel and went on board again. Quite a spree for Sunday was it not? But I suppose that not half of the men knew that it was Sunday

Many of the boys remained outside by the fire when they were off duty but I went inside + laid down + had 2 good naps. I can assure you I thought of home many times during the day + wished I was safely returned again. I read my Testament in the afternoon as I laid out on the bank of the sound basking in the delicious rays of a January Sun. I fear if I had been in Buffalo my little testament would have been unnoticed in the usual hurry and excitement of the day. I hope and trust that before another year is ended this unnatural war will have closed and we all be returned to our homes in safety and security under the old stars + stripes.

Carolina City, N.C. January 14th1863

My Captain told me today that the order had come from Head Quarters to detail me as Clerk in the Q.M. Dept. so the thing is now fixed and determined upon. I have to thank Mr. Stowits in part for putting in a good word for me at the right opportunity but above all I am thankful to God for I feel + have felt that it is the answer of a gracious God to the earnest applications of a loving mother + prayerful relatives. You have prayed for my safe return and I trust that the same good being who has thus far kept me from sickness and disease will still continue to afford me his divine protection and finally grant that I may return to you in good bodily health + spiritual condition. Pray on, pray ever, remembering that "whatsoever ye ask in faith, believing it shall be given unto you.

There are a great many of the old Central schoolboys in the army scattered around in different parts of the Country. Joyous indeed will be the time when the war is ended and we all can meet again in our own loved city and grasp each other's hand in cordial friendship and upon the same or equal footings. There we shall not know each other by the rank we hold in military life, but again, as before the war broke out, "The Mind shall be the measure of the man" and by this only can we justly claim a rank above the level of mankind.

I do not know as yet whether we are going to disembark at this point or whether they intend to land us further up the river or take us further down the coast and disembark us in the vicinity of Savannah. All is doubt and uncertainty, and perhaps it is well that it is so for the soldiers' sake. He knows not whether he is going to a place of safety or to meet his dreadful death but only hopes that the next night may bring him as safe and soft a bed as that on which he slept the night before. The soldier is, in the judgment of the world, the lowest of all low classes that earn their bread by the sweat of their brow. His friends at home forget and forsake him, but absence chills their recollection and his occupation cools their love, + they soon entirely cease to think of that which is so distasteful to their mind and unpleasant to their feelings (I speak not of <u>Relatives</u> but of those who once have called us <u>friend</u>) but the soldier has two friends – <u>God</u> + <u>uncertainty</u> – that will never desert him though all else may forget him.

On Board a Steamship Sunday Feby 1st 1863

Another bright and holy Sabbath, but no sweet chimes to greet our ears or deep toned bells to send their joyous notes across the wave to where our vessel lies. 'Twill be a novelty to us when first again we have the church bells pealing forth their solemn call to morning worship. It is now more than 4 month since I have been in a church or heard the sound of a church bell.

I fear I am forming bad habits down here for although I have read 8 or 10 chapters in my testament this morning yet the greater part of the day was devoted to novel reading. The time hands heavy on our hands aboard this transport, but as soon as we land I shall have no time to spare for such light, idle and unbeneficial reading.

St. Helena Island, S.C. Sunday Feby 8th 1863

This morning I read 8 or 10 chapters in my dear little testament and in the evening I employed my time in thinking of my parents + relatives at the fireside at home.

St. Helena Island, S.C. Sunday Feby 15th 1863

Another Lovely Sabbath greets the soldier at his camp on <u>Land</u> and right glad are we to be allowed to spend it in our camp instead of being on the water put up in a foul unhealthy ship. This Sabbath is a doubly dear one for we have heard from – <u>Home</u> for the first time since Christmas.

St. Helena Island, S.C. February 16th 1863

This morning I listened to a sermon preached by the Chaplain of the 104th Penn. Vols. It was not very eloquent but was to the point and purpose. He urged upon the soldiers the necessity of being prepared at any moment to meet their maker. Two of the men were baptized previous to the sermon by sprinkling which shows that he labors with some effect.

Beaufort, S.C. Sunday March 15th 1863

Very warm. This morning I attended a meeting at the 104th P. Vols. Two converts were babtized by sprinkling. Our Chaplain has not preached once since he came to us. At the close of the meeting and after the Benediction was pronounced they struck up a song and then while singing went through an odd form of hand shaking – keeping time in the shakes to the cadence of the song. In the evening as I heard the bells pealing out their joyous imitation I could not resist the appeal and again I went to meeting but to another and a larger church. This time I was a little late and as all the seats downstairs were full I had to go up gallery. The congregation were all males with the exception of 4 or 5 females (officers' wives I presume) It seemed like old times to be seated in this church and I could almost fancy I was back in B again (As I am writing

I hear the slow and regular beating of the muffled drum. Another soldier is going to his last long home. They carry one or more past here every day) Pardon this digression but that slow and solemn music which has just struck up recalls sad thoughts and I could not help mentioning it. The music, the ambulance bearing the pine coffin covered by the American flag, the sad procession following the corpse to its grave, remind me but too fearfully that my time may not be far distant. We know not the day nor the hour. Heavenly Father, grant that in our blessed redeemer I may ever be prepared for death when thou shall call me!

Instead of preaching this evening they had a prayer meeting and well indeed did I enjoy it. The hand of Jesus is at work in this town and many conversions are being made. The meeting is lead by a regularly ordained minister, but is sustained by the soldiers. It is a soldiers meeting. They are going to hold meetings every evening during the coming week so that I shall have other opportunities of attending if we remain here. The church is as large I think as the Baptists church in B and is painted and adorned inside very tastefully

Beaufort, S.C. Sunday April 12th 1863

When I had finished my letter to Mr. Lyman I went to church. It is only a few rods from where we are encamped. The congregation was black and the persuasion I think is Methodist. The preacher was a white man and preached a very good sermon. There were many of the negro soldiers and some few white soldiers present but any quantity of negro wenches of all colors.

Now for a description of my ride. The day was very warm in fact most uncomfortably so and so we could not ride very fast for fear of injuring the horses so we took it slow and leisurely and had a better opportunity of viewing the country through which we rode. The road is much cut up and in many places is just like meal but in the spots, where the bridle path is diverged a very little from the main road, the riding is beautiful. Nearly the whole length of the road, over which we passed, is lined on both sides with shady trees and shrubbery and part of it passes through a pine forest. In many places the branches of the trees join each other over head and form a screen from the sun at all hours of the day. It is delightful to ride through these natural arbors at any time and particularly so on a warm day like this. When about 4 or 5 miles from camp we came upon a country church + grave yard. There was one large vault and many tombs. Nearly all of the stones were inscribed with the name of the church and the same of the vaults. There are six families of this name in the immediate vicinity and all of them own large plantations. The church was used only for the worship of the "Whites" and its religious denomination was Methodist Episcopal. I learned all this from an old Negro slave who passed by just as we demounted. I asked him what religion he believed in and he said Methodist. He said he did not think the Episcopal church was religious like the Methodist. He thought it was a queer kind of Church He did not quite understand it. He thought the minister in that church preached more about how to till the land and raise the crops and tell the planters how to make money. I think the poor nigger was not far from right. The side door of the church was opened so I entered and as I did so I instinctively took off my hat for I felt as though I was in the near presence of God and a strong spell seemed to pervade the little church. On the pulpit laid a large gilt edge bible and in the choir was a small organ. I went upstairs to see it and found it was opened and ready for the fingers of some skilled one to touch its pure white keys; but when I put my hand to the bellows handle I found it had been disconnected from the pipes and would omit no sound.

The gilt edge bible + organ are things that I did not expect to find in an out of the way place like this. I tore 2 feathers from a fan that I found in the church and I send them home as a memento of my ride. About a mile farther on the road we came upon another much larger but less picturesque looking church – Methodist – and devoted to the use of the slaves on the plantations. After passing a glance at the large brick church and its surrounding we paid a short visit to a small negro settlement.

Beaufort, S.C. Monday April 13th 1863

I went to prayer meeting again this evening. I tell you it is delicious to be allowed again to sit and listen to the singing and bow to the prayers that are offered up and hear the words of exhultation. It reminds me of the days when I first held a hope of everlasting life through our redeemers blood and again how fully do I realize that there is no real happiness save in Jesus Christ

Beaufort, S.C. Tuesday April 14th 1863

This evening it rained quite hard and as it was dreary at the tent I thought I would go to the prayer meeting again. I went and was repaid so well that I think I shall go again tomorrow. Every evening there are several persons use to request the prayers of their comrades in their behalf. We have been very busy today drawing + issuing camp equipage to the regiments.

Beaufort, S.C. April 16th, 1863

But we are going to Charleston with our little handful of 12 or 15 thousand men and we are going to trust to God and the righteousness of our cause for the complete and perfect fulfillment of the hard task which is alloted to us to perform. And I believe that God will bring us out conquerors for I trust that He is on our side. The issue now seems to be <u>freedom</u> or <u>slavery</u> and can it be that God will favor the cause of slavery? I do not believe it. From the very first outbreak I thought that this war would result in the abolition of slavery, and I then believed that God permitted it only for that purpose and I am now more fully and firmly convinced of it than ever before and I cannot come to any other conclusion than that this is <u>God</u>'s war and He is on the side of freedom.

I have been to prayer meeting every evening this week and I do not regret the time that I spend going there. Even if I were not a professed Christian I should rejoice at the work of salvation which is going here among the soldiers. It has been said that a soldier cannot be a Christian but one evening spent in this town at the soldiers prayer meeting will give the lie to every and all such assertions and prove direct that a Soldier can be a Christian. It would do the heart of many Christians good to come down here and remain about two weeks to see the good work that is going on in this department both among the soldiers and the once neglected slave.

I want to go to church this evening so I can write no more and as this is the last day of the month I think I will conclude this and commence anew tomorrow on the next letter

Morris Island, S.C .September 22nd 1863

I believe the fate of Charleston and rebellion is signed & sealed by the Great Hand whose power moves the universe. Time will work it out. This is not the day of miracles, God in these later years does not perform great works in an hour or a day, but brings them on in the natural way, in a way that the little mind of man can understand and his reason comprehend.

Morris Island, S.C. December 25th 1863 Christmas Night

This Christmas has been a very quiet, but not a sad one. I have not passed it in a <u>merry mood</u> neither have I felt down hearted or dispirited, but it has seemed to me very like a Sabbath day because we have done no business in the office and everything has passed off so very quietly since morning

Mother I have read the sermon of Rev. Mr. Smith that you sent to me, and was delighted with it. I have passed it around for others to read, and they all like it. I have also read & passed around the speech of Hon. E.W. Gantts formerly General in the Rebel Service.

My fire is going down & I will catch cold if I don't end my writing and go to bed so a "Merry Christmas" to all & to all a Good Night

Folly Island, S.C. February 3rd 1864

I often think that I can date my real <u>existence</u> from the time of my return. I believe the time of my return will be the happiest hours of my life and from that day I shall begin to <u>live</u> for I will know how to appreciate and enjoy the comforts + luxuries which this world contains. How often I have repeated the familiar words "There is no place like home" but now I feel the full force of the six little words as I never understood them before. There <u>is</u> no place like home for the heart is there, the thoughts are there, the affections are there, everything that makes life loveable is bound up in the associations connected with that little word 'Home'. I shall be there one of these days – I hope. But if I never am permitted that happiness, then pray to the Being above that I may meet you all as an unbroken & undivided family in that world of endlessness, when, meeting once, we shall never again be disconnected, but dwell on in heavenly love and pure spiritual enjoyment in the presence of our sainted Savior and all the host of bright robed-ones before the throne of that God whose love is infinite.

Morris Island, S.C Tuesday March 15th 1864

As you will perceive by the heading of this letter I am again with my company. I presume you will feel a little disappointed when you learn that I have rejoined my regiment; but it is from no wish of mine that I am here. I was ordered to return and orders are imperative. I look upon any unavoidable occurrence as a decree of an overruling Providence and feeling this I must say that I am as contented & happy in one place as in another; and it is my wish that you will not murmur or feel sad at any change that may take place in my situation or affairs for you must remember as you have often told me that God is present everywhere, and always takes care of his children wherever they are. My only hope is that I am one of his children and I desire your {unknown word} prayers that I may be such and that I may have faith in his promises for then I need have no fear & you need have no fear for me, for whatever may befall me I shall be sure of a mansion in heaven.

Bermuda Hundred, Va. June 7th 1864

And now I have the pleasure of informing you and all the rest of my friends that unexpectedly and unasked I have received a commission as 2nd Lieut. in the 100th N.Y. Vols. I shall return to my regiment tomorrow and try to perform my duty to my country and to my friends. I trust that neither may ever have cause to blush for my conduct on the field. Pray for me that I may always be blessed with courage to stand up to my duty to God, to my country and to my fellow man. I do not fear to face the enemy, but on account of my comparative ignorance of military matters I should have preferred to be with my company as sergeant.

Bermuda Hundred, Va. Monday June 13th 1864

Give my love to all and all pray for me. Pray that I may never act the part of the coward, that I may always be where duty calls me, and that I may always do my duty to the honor of myself & my friends & to the Glory of God. Pray that if in this war it is God's will that I should fall, you may have courage to bear the affliction and faith to look forward to another life where I may meet you all in the presence of our Maker in the new Jerusalem. Pray that I may live and die a Christian & have a home in Glory.

Bermuda Hundred, Va. Wednesday June 14th, 1864

But God only can penetrate the hearts of men and understand the mysteries that there lie hidden. The noblest work that God ever made is man & the noblest man is the soldier. He (the soldier) may make rash vows and use idle words, he may swear that he will not fight, but let the drum beat "to arms" and the bugle sound to "charge" and his officer say "Come boys!" and every man, but the coward at heart, forgets in a moment all his idle threats, and with his bayonet at a charge rushes on to meet his unknown fate. God have pity on the soldier for no one else will pity him. God have mercy on the soldier, for no one else will show him mercy. God pardon him his sins and forgive his transgressions for he is thrown into the midst of great temptations and he knows not what he does; for Jesus' sake forgive-amen.

Petersburg, Va. Friday Sept. 27th 1864

I received three papers from home to night. The last time I wrote to you
we were on the point of marching. We broke up camp that same night
and marched to the rear a distance of 2 miles or so. We were relieved by
the 2^d Corps. We are encamped in a field between two woods. We are
out of range of bullets and out of line of shells. The rest of our Corps is
encamped in the same field. We are altogether again the camp of one
regiment joining right on to that of another for the distance of nearly a
mile. Oh! it seems so good to be once more out of range where we can
sleep above ground and not have to live in holes and have {unknown
word} and proofs and earthworks built above and around us. I never
experienced such a perfect feeling of relief as the first day we pitched
our camp in this position. In our old camp we could not step out of our
tents without hearing a bullet go ping or pish or burr, over our heads
& then chug as it struck the ground. Our men are feeling as merry as
crickets & happy as birds. The reversion of feeling experienced for us
all on account of the sudden and unexpected change from a position of
constant danger to one of perfect safety is almost miraculous. I cannot
describe it but I can realize it and one must need be placed in the same
situations to rightly understand it. It was not fear, that in our other
camp, kept down our spirits and destroyed our natural flow animation.
It could not be fear for we never for a moment hesitate to go from tent
to tent or lounge about in the company tents and talk and transact
business even when the bullets were flying the thickest. What was it
then? It certainly was something – a constant knowledge of our danger
and knowledge that at any moment we might be called to face our
Maker, and give an account of our stewardship. There certainly is such
a change in the feelings of the men that they seem like a different set of
individuals. I only hope that we may continue in our present camp for
some length of time but I fear not.

Petersburg, Va. Thursday Oct. 6th 1864

Your letters always do me good for they are full of Christian faith and holiness. My trust is in the Lord. Without him I should be weak indeed. I have a hope that if God sees fit to deliver my body unto death during this war my soul shall live to find a home & {missing word} in heaven. It adds much to my present happiness to know that my friends pray for me, and that they have strength & faith to put their trust in God and permit Him to shape the course of events and {unknown word} to submit unto Him all the ways of life and all the future of our friends. Still continue to think and pray for me for I need a mothers prayers. Temptations are many & powerful and it needs the strength & faith of a true Christian to withstand them. I dare hardly think of the many sins that I commit but I pray God in that all powerful name "Christ Jesus our Redeemer" to forgive my sins and strengthen me against the hour of temptation. If truly good works and the obedience of the commandments could make us whole and give us the everlasting life where would our salvation be and who among the Sons of Men could hope to find mercy at the {unknown word} of God. But may the Great {unknown word}! be forever praised – He has opened unto us a way whereby we may be saved even through the blood of his own dear precious Son. And we though sinners vile as earth may hope for {unknown word} at His throne for sinners fallen from their birth, his precious blood will full atone. His precious blood His sacred blood – each drop is worth a thousand lives – T'was spilled for all – the bad the good & for every soul that seeks & strives. Great God be praised that he has given to ev'ry man that hateth sin a way of entrance in heaven by which the good may enter in.

Thou precious One, thou sainted One
To Thee give we our holiest love
Thou suffered for the sins of men
Prepared for them a home above

Peterburg, Va. Monday, October 31ˢᵗ 1864

The next morning the rebs advanced & drove in our Cavalry Pickets so about noon we received orders to fall in under arms and advanced again. Arriving in dangerous proximity to the enemy's bullets skirmishes were thrown out, the troops formed line of battle in their rear and when everything was ready the Cavalry charged across a field & the skirmishes advanced along the whole line. The Johnnies did not stand at all but skeddadled into the works. We held the position until evening when we retired and left the Cavalry occupying their old position. None of our regt. were hurt. God's own hand seems to be over us to protect us from all harm and shield us from all danger. I feel more thankful and prayerful than I can tell you and as God knows my heart I attribute my preservation thus far to faithful prayer & divine providence.

Before Richmond, Va. Jany 23ʳᵈ 1865

I am sorry you worried so much about me during the long interval that I did not write but I think I am making up lately for the delay and hope to be able to do better in future.

Tell ma she must not cry when she thinks of me for I would rather that she would joy to think that I am in the army of the right fighting for a good cause and in the hope of a speedy and glorious victory. This war is soon going to end and I hope to see you all again in the full blush of health and prosperity. Matters are now looking more brightly than ever and God is smiling on our cause and promising by the success which he is giving us to lead us to happy close and a more perfect reunion in which the accursed institute of slavery shall have no part or foothold.

235

EDWARD COOK: THOUGHTS ON DEATH

Ed: Civil War soldiers, being products of the Victorian age, viewed death as a part of the natural order of things. Death was a release from medical maladies and was an opportunity for a better life. Death and dying were favorite topics in Victorian literature. The body was cleaned and laid out in a formal manner in the home. After viewing, the body was gently lowered into the ground. While soldiers accepted the possibility of death, they adopted a certain degree of fatalism regarding death in war. The battle line tactics delivered shot at the enemy lines without aiming for individuals. Bullets fell on the just and unjust alike. This fatalism spilled into interest in fortune telling, knowing that fate determined the time of one's death. However, many soldiers did carry pocket Bibles or New Testaments and attended religious services and evangelical revivals. Their fatalism or their religious faith helped soldiers overcome their fear of death and prepare for battle. Either it was their destiny to die or it was God's will. In either case, there was nothing that they could do about it.

The soldiers knew that regiments could lose over one third of their numbers over the course of a three year enlistment. Indeed, they could lose that number in a single battle. As the war progressed, the soldiers became more callous about death. The treatment of the dead, however, did horrify them. Regardless of the side that they were on, they deserved respect and recognition of their valor, patriotism, and moral worth. To see hands and faces of the dead who had been hastily buried reminded the soldiers of the enemy's savagery and their own mortality. Soldiers repeatedly asked their families to pray for them, and the devoutly religious reminded their families of the certainty of a heavenly reunion.

Camp at Gloucester Point, Va. Tuesday December 2nd 1862

The order was to have the regiment in line at 3 ½ oclock but for some reason or other it did not form until 5 oclock so that we buried the soldier by moonlight. It was a solemn sight that long funeral procession and produced a feeling vastly deeper than that occasioned by the sight of a funeral at home. None of the regt had guns except the escort detailed to fire the salute over the grave of the buried soldier. We first marched to the hospital and the regiment was there drawn up in line and the escort received the body which was borne to the grave on 2 muskets and carried by 4 soldiers. The coffin was of plain neat pine and the funeral services were of course Episcopalian for the Rev. Mr. [ ] officiated. The deep sad tone of the muffled drum, the sight of the escort with their arms reversed and the coffin draped in the stars + stripes as it was borne along by us as we filed off towards the grave, the slow, short step of the regiment and the silent ranks where not a word was spoken or a whisper breathed from the time the body was received until it was lowered into the silent grave; all served to produce a deep and lasting impression upon my mind. Arrived at the grave the regt was drawn up in line again and facing the grave looking towards the west. The sun had set and the moon was looking coldly down upon the solemn scene. The services were read in a [ ] and impressive tone, and as is the case with all episcopalian services was most beautiful and especially striking at such an hour as this. Behind the grave and in the west was a narrow strip of crimson light extending along the horizon for about 20 degrees while all around this little opening was a mass of dense, dark + dismal looking clouds, and when the salute was fired over the grave it seemed as though it was to waft the spirit of the dead from this drear world, through the bright window in the west to the heaven of love beyond. It is the first funeral that we have been called upon to attend since we came here although several have died out of our regt at the Yorktown Hospital.

We came down here to fight + any day we may be cut down by the bullet or the sword. This may be my last letter but I hope not. If I am

killed in battle I have the happy knowledge that you will not mourn
for me for you will feel that I am not dead but only sleeping. not dead
but only gone before. Mourn not for me if I am killed; weep not a tear,
then smile and feel that to a home I've gone where lives not sin or guile.
My peace with my dear Savior now is made and I am free to part in
peace with friends + life whene'er the time shall be. Then mourn not
for a single hour but spend an hour in prayer beseeching that through
Christ dear Lord we'll meet together there. Farewell if this should be
my last. Adieu if I should write again.

Off Port Royal, S.C. Saturday Jany 31st 1863

All is doubt and uncertainty, and perhaps it is well that it is so for the
soldiers' sake. He knows not whether he is going to a place of safety or
to meet his dreadful death but only hopes that the next night may bring
him as safe and soft a bed as that on which he slept the night before.
The soldier is, in the judgement of the world, the lowest of all low classes
that earn their bread by the sweat of their brow. His friends at home
forget and forsake him, but absence chills their recollection and his
occupation cools their love, + they soon entirely cease to think of that
which is so distasteful to their mind and unpleasant to their feelings (I
speak not of Relatives but of those who once have called us friend) but
the soldier has two friends – God + uncertainty – that will never desert
him though all else may forget him.

Beaufort, S.C. Sunday April 12th 1863

Pardon this digression but that slow and solemn music which has just
struck up recalls sad thoughts and I could not help mentioning it. The

music, the ambulance bearing the pine coffin covered by the American flag, the sad procession following the corpse to its grave, remind me but too fearfully that my time may not be far distant. We know not the day nor the hour. Heavenly Father grant that in our blessed redeemer I may ever be prepared for death when thou shall call me!

Bermuda Hundred, Va.. Thursday afternoon May 4th 1864

I shall have been in Uncle Sam's employ 8 months and have never yet been in a battle while many other poor fellows have measured their length on the cold damp ground for the last time and now sleep in death.

Bermuda Hundred, Va. April 5th 1864

We have had a very pleasant day after the rain & storm of yesterday. Many of the bodies of our poor soldiers who were killed in the charge on fort Wagner were disentombed by the rain & tide yesterday but were reburied today by some of the boys of the 3rd R.I. Artillery. I enquired of one of the party if the rebs buried our dead deep enough he replied that the bodies were buried deep enough but every wind that blows is constantly shifting the sand, making hills of the hollows & hollows of the hills, and a little rain completes the work & reveals the partly decayed bodies of our poor boys. Such is war.

Give my love to all the folks and tell them all to pray for me, that I may do my duty manfully, suffer any pain patiently, and if I die that I may die hopeful of life here after, where I can meet you all, where there will be no more parting, no more pain, and where sin and death cannot enter. I do not dread a battle field except for your sakes. Life is sweet to me only that I may someday add happiness to the lives of those who have done so much for me. And whenever I think of death, I remember only the sorrow that such an event causes in the fond loving hearts around the home circle. If I could be assured that you, all of you, could look on death only as a temporary parting, and all feel that there was no need of mourning & sorrow, for soon we all would meet again around our saviours throne, I could go back to my regiment with a far lighter heart for a heavy burden would be lifted from my thoughts. Try and feel this way and then if it is my lot to be a sacrifice to this struggle for freedom the blow will not fall so heavily on you, for you will know & feel & realise that your Edward is not dead but only sleeping, only gone before.

Bermuda Hundred, Va. August 14th 1864

The 2d Corps embarked at City Point yesterday and then dropped down the river a short distance until night, when they steamed up, and about 10 or 12 oclock, they all sailed past Bermuda 100 in sight of an our office. I sat up until very late watching them pass. It was a pretty sight but it was saddened by the thought that before the same hour next morning many of them will have {unknown word} their last journey and fought their last battle. Yet all are unconscious of their fate, and many are passing their last hours on earth in sweet untroubled sleep, on board the boat that carries them toward their graves. There is no reliable report from the scene of operations, but we have heard quite heavy firing in the direction of the troops that would indicate some severe fighting. I feel as though I ought now to be with my regiment, yet I cannot but think that it is through a kind providence that I have been kept were I am and I have no inclination to rush into danger when duty does not call me. Tonight is the anniversary of George Clark's death at the charge of Fort Wagner

Before Richmond, Va October 25th 1864

The position that we now hold is being made very strong. We have a continuous line of breast works, and good ones too, from the right of the line to the left and in front of each brigade they are building redoubts to contain from three guns upwards. This will be one of the strongest positions in the whole cordon that Grant is throwing around Richmond and Petersburg. When it is finished a few men can hold it against a vastly superior force and thus enable Grant to remove the bulk of his army to some other point either to assail the enemy's position and force an entrance into the City or to take and hold another position towards the completion of his vast encircling chain of forts and breastworks. The works goes forward almost imperceptibly, but like a vast moving body its momentum cannot be resisted. It carries everything before it. Grant does not make a move until he is ready to make it. His army lies apparently inactive for a time, everything seems to indicate that the campaign is closed, and men and officers begin to build their winter operations, but all the time Grant is not asleep - he is cautiously and silently working in some unexpected quarter – adding weight to the vast mass that he intends to move, concentrating everything towards the complete success of his plan and when everything is ready, when a move is least expected and where it is least anticipated, he puts the mass in motion and it rolls on and on and over every obstacle until the design is accomplished and the plan carried out completely & effectually in all its points. This is Grant. He is now apparently inactive, engaged merely in {unknown word} up defensive work, but in reality working out beneath this calm exterior a plan of stupendeous proportions – a mighty storm is brewing + soon it will reach its proper temperature and then it burst over our enemy and overwhelm them in its onward flood working ruin in their army and destruction to their hopes. This is my conviction and my prayer is that I may not be swallowed up in the flood but live through it all to raise my voice in thanks to Him who giveth victory to the righteous and causeth desolation to swallow up the wicked.

Before Richmond, Va. November 20th 1864

You spoke in your letter of the funeral of Genl Bidwell. When I think of the pomp displayed at home over the body of one who has died in his country's service of how he is laid in state – how the flags are lowered at half mourning and droop as though they were intelligent and understood that they were mourning over the last remains of one who had poured out his last drop of hearts blood in their defence and to their glory and honor – how the people come to take a last look of him on earth and then follow, sad and mournful, the hearse that bears him to his last resting place. And then contrast all this respect, and honor, pomp & display with the contempt and sneers and abuse and ignominy that is cast upon the soldier who still lives to peril his life yet again & again for those who remain at home to dispise and shun him in society if he returns and to breath out treason & curses on his deeds if he remains, I feel as though a nation of such people were scarcely worth fighting for because they can never attain nobility of mind sufficiently to appreciate the blessings of a good home and the value of a country instituted & based on free & democratic principles and organizations. The proper escort to a soldier's funeral is a fife & drum, and his mourners are his comrades, his shroud is his uniform and his blanket is his coffin. I rejoice that the result of the late election has shown us that all do not think that we are fighting for a vain, useless and unworthy cause. There are many still left who are proud to take a soldier by the hand and tell him "Welcome to our hearth stone" Thousands still left who are not ashamed to receive and assist the poor fellows who have become maimed & disfigured for life in the struggle to build up a name and a sure foundation on right principles for this country the best that had a name and recognition

Before Richmond, Va. Jany 28/65

What a strange philosophy is death. None can foretell his coming and none can divine his shape – he cometh in his power to the strong man and like a whirlwind cutteth him down, he {unknown word} his step from the presence of the invalid who lyeth at the brink of the grave and straightaway the man is restored to health and strength. O death! how strange thou art how multiplied thy {unknown word}; war, accident, disease thy agents are, from whom no man escapes. How much then it behooves us all they messengers to meet – to be prepared when summoned hence by agents strong and fleet – to stand before our Savior's throne and offer to his love the record of our worldly deeds and claim a life above. Sweet thought that when the good shall die their souls will live again no perfect happiness in heaven where Christ & glory reign.

Appomattox, Va. April 16th 1865

I wrote you two letters since the charge on fort Gregg and today I received a letter from Laura. This is the first mail that has come through since we took Petersburg just two weeks ago today. Laura's letter was written on the 2d of April and perhaps at the same hour that I was in the hottest of the fight. In her letter she wonders what I am doing but she little dreams what scenes were at that time being enacted around me. Thank God I lived through that awful battle one of the most desperate of the war. We fought at the parapets of the fort until not more than twenty of the garrison was left alive and then we fought inside the fort. Such a desperate resistence is seldom met with in the history of any war. I received Anthony's letter but shall not answer it until we go to Richmond or some other place to stay. Our men were starving for a few days but they managed to get rations through at last and today a train of wagon came in from Lynchberg with lots of Bacon Flour + smoking tobacco all of which were issued out to the officers + men free gratis. And now there is a good feeling manifest everywhere. Nothing like food to eat to make a soldier feel good. The war is virtually at an end and I hope soon to be with you again. The army was shocked today at a telegram from the north stating that Lincoln + Seward had been assassinated. If the news is true (and everybody here believes it is) all that we want is to be let loose and we will go through the parties who instigated such a deed with a vengeance that rivers of blood only will wash out. Thousands will swear war to the death under the black flag if they can be allowed to avenge the cowardly deed. My God must our country become another France. Can not the lives of our Presidents be safe in the Capital of our country? God will avenge such work

ALFRED LYTH: THOUGHTS ON
ANDERSONVILLE AND FLORENCE PRISONS

Ed: The Hill-Dix Accord governed the exchange of prisoners until the spring of 1864. A prisoner exchange was in effect from the start of the war. However, in April, 1864, the South began to make a distinction between black and white troops, Viewing blacks as contraband rather than prisoners of war, they returned them to their former masters, sold them, or sometimes executed them. Based upon the South's distinction between black and white troops in captivity, General Grant ordered an end to the prisoner exchanges. From a military standpoint, Grant's order also reduced the manpower capability of the South. However, his decision had a disastrous effect on the prison camps both in the North and South. The worst camp was in Andersonville, Georgia. Built to hold 10,000 prisoners, its population swelled to 33,000 by August, 1864. The prisoners were without shelter, had limited rations, and experienced foul drinking and bathing water. Thirteen thousand prisoners died at Andersonville.

[Bermuda Hundred May *16, 1864]*

"Many of the Regiment were taken prisoners, not having a chance to leave the rifle pits before the rebel line was upon them, and were sent on to Richmond. When captured, I was taken with several others to the stump lot, and guarded by a couple of Rebs, one of who soon started to gather plunder and trophies, the remaining soldier's attention being occupied in watching the field in the distance and the success of his comrade. Embracing a favorable opportunity, I darted behind a stump nearby, and taking advantage of circumstances made good [my] escape to a piece of woods to the right and rear of the open field in which the Regiment was at the opening of the fight. In running across a corner of the field to gain the wood, a bullet struck the cap off [my] head, a loss very much regretted at

245

the time – the head-gear being a very fine cap, presented to [me] by Lieut Jas. H. French a few days before. While hurrying through the woods [I] came across a soldier severely wounded, being shot through the arm and the bullet penetrating his side. The wounded soldier was Corp. Stark, Company A of the 100th. He begged so hard for help and we stopped to bind his arm with a handkerchief to stop the flow of blood. Then, urging him to follow, we started again to find a place of safety. At the edge of the woods to our left, we came to an opening descending to what appeared to be the bed of a creek, the banks overgrown with underbrush. Upon the slope on the opposite side of the creek were stretched, as far as the eye could reach a line of infantry wearing the Union blue. On the crest of the hill above, their infantry and field guns were planted, showing that out troops had formed a new line of battle, or reserves were preparing to meet the foe. On reaching the creek, which proved to be dry, musketry firing from our left and rear was quite rapid, and glancing in that direction, a line of rebel infantry was seen advancing. The Union line opened up with volley after volley, and the cannon above sending their greetings in rapid succession, the confederates withdrew. During a lull in fighting, a number of Union soldiers, including several from the 100th, lying low in the bed of the creek, ran for the lines, passing on to the rear making inquiries for a field hospital. Being directed to a small grove on the Weldon Railroad, we found a large number of wounded congregated in the vicinity indicated, some severely, others more or less injured. No surgeons or commissioned officers being there, no one with authority to direct affairs, we were at a loss what to do next. A soldier passing said the field hospital was now located at the junction, a mile further on the railroad. Assuming to direct affairs, we ordered the worst cases to be placed upon two flat cars, conveniently at hand; all who were able lending a willing aid to push them along. About 120 or 30 crippled and wounded started down the track at the junction. Half a mile from the starting point had been gained. A soldier walking in front of the moving cars on the lookout cries out a warning, "Rebel cavalry ahead, boys!" Immediately several ran out to the front of the cars to ascertain, and coming to the conclusion it is a false alarm , that the horsemen in the distance are Unionists, we proceed, but only, in a few moments, to be hailed by mounted rebels on the banks of the railroad cut above us, to throw down our arms and surrender. Many instinctively turning to the rear for a chance to run, we find a troop of Confederate cavalry coming down the track. Hemmed in on all sides, with no possible chance to escape, the only course was to cast aside the weapons we possessed and submit to the inevitable.

The flat cars containing the severely wounded were continued moving along the track in the direction for Petersburg, Va., the others are directed to march on behind the cars. Proceeding in this manner nearly a mile, a halt was ordered. Soon, however, those on foot were directed to fall in, and proceed towards the city. Our wounded on the cars, it was said, would be given surgical and necessary assistance at once, or sent to hospitals.

Many wounded, other than those mentioned, requesting the same consideration were refused, being told they would be taken care of in the city. Reaching Petersburg at night-fall, weary and tired – in fact, completely exhausted – we were crowded into the city jail, a stone structure similar to many others in southern cities, used to confine criminals. Entering the portals the detachment we were marched into one room, soon realizing that there, we must remain at least for the night. No rations were issued, most everyone being provided, having well-filled haversacks.

That night, in Petersburg jail, its horrors, its suffering, the agony, groans, shrieks, moans of sick and wounded men, crowded so thick together that there was not room for all to lie down upon the floor, in one corner of which there were two buckets for use to answer nature's calls, many suffering from diarrhea."[12]

[Petersburg, Va. May 17, 1864]

"Some of the worst among the sick and wounded were sent to a hospital; all were taken to an adjoining room and searched for valuables, knives and money; their name, rank, Company and regiment recorded, being told that all taken from us was entered on the register to our credit, and would be returned to us when released Some of the worst among the sick and wounded were sent to a hospital; all were taken to an adjoining room and searched for valuables, knives and money; their name, rank, Company and regiment recorded, being told that all taken from us was entered on the register to our credit, and would be returned to us when released. During the search those who were suspected of trying to conceal anything, were stripped naked and every particle of clothing thoroughly inspected; under the arms, in the hair, shoes and stockings, or where suspicion might dictate that a stray greenback was allowed.

That day several embraced the opportunity to pencil short letters to the dear ones at home, trusting that they would reach them and relieve their anxiety regarding our fate. Then follows another night in jail, to some the suffering worse than the previous night. The next day we were transferred from the jail to more commodious quarters in a tobacco warehouse nearby. Suffering from the wound in my foot and diarrhea for several days following, I was too ill to note passing events."[13]

[Petersburg, Va. May 27, 1864]

"At the end of the week we were glad to get orders to be ready to move, any kind of change being agreeable. In the early morning we were marched to a train of box freight cars, in which we were all crowded like so many sheep – not enough room for all to lie down at once. Thus the journey of seven days and nights, from Petersburg, Va. to Andersonville,

Ga. began. During that time we were only out of those closely packed cars one night, and during the removal from one train to another."[14]

[Andersonville, Ga. June 1, 1864]

" . . . On the first day of June the train arrived at Andersonville. Leaving the railroad station, fifteen hundred prisoners from Richmond and Petersburg were marched to the headquarters of the commandant of the prison, Capt. Wirtz. Our names, rank, Company and Regiment taken, and a search for valuables was commenced but soon abandoned, all having been searched at Richmond or Petersburg. While standing in the ranks a very heavy shower of rain poured down upon us, and being in the front rank we stepped to the rear that a comrade might receive part protection from the rain by sharing our piece of oil cloth blanket. . . . Our names being taken we were marched into the prison camp, or stockade as it was called. The walls were formed of large hewn pine logs, planted in the ground, side by side, about twenty feet high above ground and enclosing a square of about twelve to fourteen acres. Passing through the gate men from every state were gathered about the entrance anxious to see if any of the new-comers were from their regiments or were acquaintances. The sight there spreads out before our eyes was horrible beyond description – hundreds, and it seemed to us thousands of men appeared to us as if they were walking skeletons arisen from the grave. Many almost naked, with what was once a shirt and pants to cover their nakedness; pants tattered and pieces torn from the legs to patch the seats; shirts ragged and all covered with filth and vermin; hair, long and unkempt; eyes, sullen and lusterless; men with swollen limbs and raw sores on their bodies, was a spectacle to strike us with terror, and almost freeze the blood in our veins. . . . There cannot be a worse hell than this. Standing and viewing the strange and horrible sight, a familiar tap upon the shoulder causes us to look aside. We are greeted by comrade Chas. R. Moss of Co. H, who informs us that James Pixley, Thomas Russell and Albert Tombers are there with many others of the Regiment captured in the trenches on the 16th of May, and taken to Richmond, having arrived at Andersonville two days before. No shelter whatever was provided for prisoners by the prison authorities. Drenched and wet by the afternoon rain, late at night, we lay down, wet and weary, sharing our piece of blanket with a comrade. Early the following morning, rising heartsick and nearly discouraged at the prospect before us, our daily routine of prison existence begins.

On the first of June, when we entered the stockade, it contained about 10,000 prisoners. Recollect, all those were collected in a space of about thirteen or fourteen acres, out of which space, taken of by the dead line and the swamp and creek running through the center, was to be deducted. The dead line was a line of demarcation all around inside the enclosure, and located twenty feet from the stockade, and was composed of posts three feet high, ten feet apart, on top of which was nailed a light board railing. To pass beyond this line was instantaneous death. The sentinels were posted on platforms arranged inside the stockade at regular intervals, having strict orders to shoot anyone trespassing over this line, without warning. It was said that guards killing a Yankee were always rewarded with a furlough for thirty days. The swamp in the prison was a horrible place. Along the edge of all the sink arrangements of the prison were located, and through this swamp ran a stream supplying the prison with water. At the edge of the swamp in the slime, mud, and filth, maggots by the millions were constantly crawling, and thousands of these maggots, with wings, were dropping on the sores of men lying asleep and exposed, and stinging them like gadflies. On the left side of the prison and close to the railing of the dead line there was a road across the swamp. At this point the water was deemed to be pure, the creek here entering the stockade and passing on through the swamp. Those wanting water would go to this point, and reach as far up the stream as they could to get water as pure as possible. It was here that many a poor fellow reaching beyond the dead line a little too far was shot, which at one time was almost of daily occurrence."[15]

Private Alfred Lyth Diary

June 1, 1864: Rain

June 2, 1864: Heavy rain shower; wet all night

June 3, 1864: Hot sun in the morning; arrival of more prisoners; showers.

June 4, 1864: Prisoners from Sherman's army; rain all day; cleared upon the evening; lay in wet clothing all night. Two escaped prisoners turned back into stockade, and compelled to wear ball and chain six days.

June 5, 1864: Rain in showers; rumors of an exchange.

June 6, 1864: Hot in the morning; rain in the afternoon; cleared up in the evening.

June 7, 1864: Early in the morning cloudy; tremendously hot at noon; very heavy rain storm in the afternoon. Comrade James Pixley very ill.

Letter from Private A. Lyth to his Father and Mother

Prison for Federal Troops
Andersonville Georgia
June 10th 1864

Dear Father + Mother

After I was taken prisoner to Petersburg I wrote you a few lines to let you know that I was well as thank the Lord I am at present. Since I last wrote they have fetched us all here to Georgia where most all the prisoners are now located our prison is a large camp surrounded with stocades Our Regt lost very heavy the day I was taken there is between 120 + 120 of us here as prisoners there is 12 of our Co here and Jim Pixley is one of them he wishes you would let his folks know that he is well We both try and intend to keep up good courage and hope for the best and that we may not have long to remain here the weather is very hot you can write me a few lines if you chose enclosed you will find a confederate stamp which if you write you can use if you write

Address
Alfred Lyth
Prisoner of War Andersonville, Georgia

Via Flag of Truce boat and do not seal the letter Give my respects to all the neighbors I send my love to you all

From Your Loving Son
Alfred Lyth

Private Alfred Lyth Diary

June 8, 1864: More prisoners arrive, and report Grant closing around Richmond. Rain after sunset.

June 9, 1864: Lay in pool of water all night.

June 10, 1864: Scorching hot part of the day; rain in the afternoon, Tombers helps carry out the body of a dead comrade.

June 11, 1864: Rain again. James Pixley very sick.

June 12, 1864: More rain; rations one-half pint of sour rice; one ounce and a half of meat which the maggots are contending for.

June 13, 1864: Cold, raw day; rain in showers; rations one-third pint of rice, three ounces of coarse meal; rumors of parole and exchange.

June 14, 1864: Rain most all night; no wood today; Pixley much better.

June 17, 1864: Commenced to rain at 3 o'clock A. M. ; heavy showers all day; Three men from our detachment who went outside for wood with a rebel guard, when in the woods, tied the guard to a tree, and taking his gun, started for "God's country.

June 18, 1864: One of the men recaptured, placed in stocks all night; blood hounds hunting for others; showers in the afternoon; arrival of prisoners from Sherman's army.

June 19, 1864: A well being dug caved in last night; a poor fellow lying near slipped in and was smothered; guard on post 14 near our quarters, fired at a crazy prisoner who had wandered across the dead line; failed to hit him, but badly wounded others lying nearby; more prisoners from Grant & Butler

Letter from Private T. Maharg to Private A. Lyth's Father

Camp 100th N.Y. Vol
Bermuda Hundred
June 19th/64

Dear Sir

I rec. your letter for information yesterday in regard to Alfred being missing but as I am not in the company + therefore not in the fight I am a fraid I will not be able to satisfy you but I will tell you what the boys of the company sayes They told me that he got off the battle field all wright + was crossing the Rail Road when they seen a car loaded with our wounded coming down the track + Alfred went to help push it so as to get it out of the way as the rebs was chacing them up but they faild in geting it out of the way + we think that Alfred was taken with it. He was taken on the 16th of May he had nothing with him but his haversack + cantene but the Ordely will take care of his knapsack as long as we stay hear now if you would like to have his things sent home. Mr Lyth I have just been over + seen the Ordely + he said that there was an order from the Col. to look over all the knapsacks belonging to the wounded + missing + if there was anything in them that was worth anything to take it out + burn the rest for after the 16th of May we did not know how soon we would have to leave + we could not carry them, he told me he thought that some of the boys had some trinkets belonging to Alfred + as soon as they get in off picket I will hunt them up + see what they are, + tell you. We have had two or three Battles cince but have not retaken the ground where they fought when Alfred was taken but I hope we will before long. The Lt. did not want him to go with them this day they left camp as he was company clirk + his place was in camp but he would go for he had never seen a fight + he thought if he stayed back the boys would think he was afrade + I guess you know that he was a boy that would not have that said of him.

Mr Lyth you must not worry yourself to much about him for I am pretty shure that he is only a prisoner + that is not so bad as it might be we are having boys come back allmost every day that was taken at the charge of Wagner they have been gone almost a year + they look fresh + good so you see there is a good sight for Alfred to get back all wright.

From Your Humble Friend Thos Maharg

Ed: This must have been a difficult letter for Thomas to write.

Private Alfred Lyth Diary

June 20, 1864: Joseph Achuff, one of the men that escaped on the 17th, came into the stockade, having been in the stocks for thirty-six hours; he says when they tied the guard to a tree, he separated from the others and started off alone, and in his own way search for liberty; soon he heard the deep voice of the blood hounds, and he took to the swamp, thinking they could not track him there. In a short time, however, the hounds and their yelling owner were upon him. He turned at bay with his back against a tree, and a dry limb in his hand. His only clothing was a ragged shirt, pants, shoes and cap; five dogs attacked him; his stick broke, and for ten minutes he fought the hounds with his fists; the owner orging them to fiendish and hellish work with yells; when at last overpowered, he was torn and bit until the brutish owner was satisfied. He called the dogs off, catching one by the hind legs and tearing him off with part of his pants and some flesh following. When brought back, Wirtz ordered him put in the stocks, exposed to the hot sun and rain. Bloodly, wounded, sore as he was, he was compelled to suffer, and when Wirz was appealed to during his torture, he swore at him and told him to shut up or he would blow his damned brains out.

June 21, 1864: Very hot morning; afternoon, rain; a man leaning on the dead line wasfired at, but not hit; another is wounded, however, and not expected to live.

June 22, 1864: Very hot; average deaths in stockades about sixty a day; many go out to hospital and die there; first day this month no rain fell.

June 23, 1864: Very hot; rebs filling up tunnel discovered; two ounces of fresh beef to-day.

June 27, 1864: Scorching; sand almost hot enough to cook rations; about five hundred more prisoners arrive, among them some of the 100th New York, taken at the charge upon Fort Wagner.

June 29, 1864: There is a gang of rowdies organized in the prison, who plunder prisoners, especially new arrivals on their first night in prison, and take from them money, watches, blankets, and any property they may have been fortunate enough to keep from the rebels, frequently knives were used to enforce their demands. One night they surrounded some men belonging to our regiment, searched them and took a watch from one. A police force was organized among ourselves to arrest the raiders, as they were called, and a great many arrested were thus made. The rebel authorities gave permission to us to arrest raiders, and those known to be guilty were captured. Twenty-four were sent to be held for trial by a jury, which, being selected from among the new comers, they were tried on July 1, and six of the number, being found guilty of murder, were sentenced to be hanged. The balance were turned into the stockade and made to run a gauntlet of enraged sufferers, ranged in two lines, with clubs ready to mete out such punishment as they could by striking them as they passed through the lines. Many were fearfully punished, some escaped lightly and two or three, it is said were killed... Digging out through tunnels was frequently attempted, and had it not been for the many contemptible traitors in our midst who, for some favor or an extra ration, would betray any attempt to escape, many would have gotten away. These sneaks and traitors were generally traced to the raider gang.

[Andersonville, Ga. July 1, 1864]

"The prison pen is enlarged at the north end and an addition of some ten acres being added and stockades were erected, the partition between the old and the new part was allowed to be torn down by the prisoners, which was a godsend in the shape of fuel to cook rations. Our little family, by industry, secured a good supply. It would be curious if among so many prisoners there were not at all times many brains concocting schemes for freedom. Digging out through tunnels was frequently attempted, and had it not been for the many contemptible traitors in our midst who, for some favor or an extra ration, would betray any attempt to escape, many would have got away. These sneaks and traitors were generally traced to the raider gangs."[16]

Private Alfred Lyth's Diary

July 14, 1864: An alarm among the Rebs. Wirtz has discovered another tunnel; All sentry platforms overlooking the stockade are filled with soldiers, each having forty rounds of ammunition. Three or four hundred march into the stockade and take position inside the dead line where the tunnel is located, ready for action if necessary. A gang of slaves, with teams, are set to work filling up the tunnel, and Wirz had several men arrested, suspected of being connected with the project. They are to be placed in the stocks and rations reduced to two ounces of corn bread per day Oh! I hope that I may live to see the day when this fiend, Wirtz, will swing.

August 7, 1864 The rebel Quartermaster informs the detachments that Winder has received orders to parole all prisoners and send them to Federal lines as soon as transportation could be procured. On the 9th of August heavy rains washed away the earth supporting the stockade in four places. Double lines of troops are placed before the openings, the guns manned and three shells fired over the stockade as a warning. This action is greeted with laughter on our part, and I believe many were anxiously praying that firing amongst us would begin in earnest. The many determined faces and set lips foretold the fire that lay slumbering ready to break forth. Lumber is sent into the prisons to build shelters dispelling all ideas of exchange.

August 31, 1864: It is just two years ago to-day since I enlisted for three years; where shall I be when that third year has expired? None can tell;

perhaps in the grave yard near here, where Union soldiers are going at a rate of eight per day.

Letter from Private A. Lyth to Private T. Maharg

Camp Sumter, Andersonville
Sept. 3rd, 1864

Dear Friend Tom

I send you these few lines to let you know that Jim Pixley and myself are in good health, also that Tom Russell is doing well. When we first came to this prison there was about 130 of the Regt but 15 of them have died since. There was 12 from our Co. mainly T. Russell, C.R. Moss, C. Fone, A. P. Cushman, T. B. Reynolds, W. Bishop, A. Tomes and myself and Jim. We are also doing well except W. Phillips who is in the hospital with thescurvy. We oft wish we were with you and the old Salt Junk again. Give my best respects to all the boys. Sergt. Maj. Jones is well. Jim sends his regards to you all.

From your old friend,
Alfred Lyth

[Andersonville, Ga September, 6, 1864]

"There is a great ecstatic thrill pervading the whole camp. Eighteen detachments were ordered to be ready to move at a moment's notice. At last! At last! This last rumor really looked as if it would really amount to something. Some said, "We have been lied to so often and believe there is no truth in the rumor." However, the next morning a line of men from the hospital were seen moving towards the railroad station, and five detachments go out to the cars, and we really now believe they are off for our lines and "God's country." [17]

Private Alfred Lyth Diary

Sept 6, 1864: Eighteen detachments were ordered to be ready to move at a moment's notice. At last! At last!

September 12, 1864: When my regiment got orders to go to the cars, I am unable to accompany them. [swollen and inflamed foot] Comrades J. Pixley and Al Tombers urged me to make the effort and undertook to lead me, but it was of no use.

September 14, 1864: All who left the stockade the day previous returned, the train bearing them having run off the track; several were killed and about forty were wounded. One of Company B, of the 100th, was killed and two badly wounded.

September 15, 1864: All the sick that could walk to the station were told to get ready. I determined to make one grand, determined effort. Having reserved our tent saplings, I got some men to make me a couple of rough crutches. By this aid I got through the gate past the guard, where I sank to the ground completely exhausted and unable to maintain an upright position any longer. Determined not to give up, however, seated on the ground, the lame foot elevated in the air, I propelled myself to the cars, crab fashion, and being assisted into an old baggage car by comrades my spirits soared to the skies, and the happy, blissful contemplation of being homeward bound, seemed to fill the world with sweetness, and for the time being made me forgetful of pain and hunger.

[Florence, Ga September 16, 1864]

"The train which bore us from Andersonville arrived at Macon, Ga., early in the morning of the 16th of September, and reached Augusta the same afternoon, where we changed cars for Charleston, S.C. Late in the evening, the train stopped at a place called Lawrenceville, and it dawns upon us that we are not going to Charleston to be exchanged, but are going to some other prison. On the afternoon of the 18th we are ordered off the cars a few miles above Florence, S. C. and commanded to get in line to march to another stockade, two or three miles away. Oh! The agony of that keen disappointment! Can these fiends of rebels have hearts at all, to deceive suffering, dying men in the systematic manner! Many of our poor fellows lay down beside the railroad track and died. All that could walk were taken to the stockade. Those unable were told to get there as best they could, no means of transportation at hand. My wound was very painful. I, however, began the slow crab-like process toward the prison, in the hope of receiving some attention for my wound, and something to eat. It rained during the night, the weak and sick being scattered all along en route from the railroad to prison, the whole line being covered with dead; the poor fellows, becoming exhausted, stopped and died, many expiring on the spot where they were lifted off the cars.

The 20th was a dull, heavy day and showery; the sick and wounded are gathered together under some trees outside the prison, which is a stockade similar in construction to the one at Andersonville. My foot is now in a very bad condition, gangrene getting in its work in fine style, the suffering from pain being intense, and that dread affliction, scurvy, is causing my gums to swell and bleed. The collection of sick and wounded under the trees is classed as being in the hospital, and rations for the time being are far better than at Andersonville – rice, sweet potatoes and corn bread- but having no means of cooking, it is eaten raw. No medicine for the sick and bandages for the wounded for several days.

E.V. Austin, a Massachusetts soldier, on the 23rd cooked some food for me. Otherwise, in my helpless condition, I would have to go hungry. On the same day, a farmer brought in some milk and biscuit. I received one biscuit and one gill of milk, having begged it to make a poultice for my foot, but I was so hungry that I divided with my foot, eating one-half and using the other for poultice. Up to the 26th, no medical treatment whatever had been received and rations were cut down to so small an allowance that there was not even enough to sustain life, many actually dying for want of food.

September 27th will ever be a day to be remembered. Having suffered such intense pain during the past week, and acting on the advice of a rebel doctor, I consented to submit to an amputation of the foot; in fact several days previously I had myself requested the operation and then backed out. This day, however, several operations were to take place, and the surgeon in charge, with several young men, medical students, was on hand to assist in the operations. I was laid on a couch of pine boughs, covered with an old blanket, awaiting my turn. A young man named Dr. Clark, who was a hospital steward in our navy when taken prisoner, and under parole as an assistant in the hospital department, happened to be passing where I lay. Noticing my forlorn and dejected condition, he stopped, asked a few questions and examined the foot, then gazing upon the prostrate and helpless figure before him he shook his head in a sympathetic manner, at the same time muttering his thoughts, which were not intended for my ears. I caught part of his words – "Poor boy! Poor boy! I believe I could save that foot."

Ah, how the blood thrilled through my veins as I caught those joyous words that to me meant life.

"Dr. Clark," I cried, "you shall have the chance."

"Too late," he replied, and passed on. Soon my turn came for the operation. I said to the doctor, "I have changed my mind and will not have the operation performed."

"Tut, Tut, young man," replied the Chief Surgeon,

"There is no use; it must come off; there is no other help for you.

Besides, I understand you have requested this yourself." Rising to a sitting posture, I said "Doctor, I have changed my mind. If you cut that foot off, you will have to kill me first. I might as well die fighting for life as in any other way, because if you cut the foot off I will die anyhow."

The young fellows gathered about the couch on each side, grasped hold of my arms and laid me down, one having hold of each arm and one of each leg. I began a desperate struggle, and wrenching one of my arms loose and swinging it blindly with all the force possible, I struck the doctor in charge a terrific blow in the face, drawing blood. Two of the students immediately grasped clubs and were about to strike when the good old fellow who had received the blow stopped them saying: "Well, that boy's got some spunk left; we'll attend to his case later on," and passed on. It might be said here that I never heard of a single amputation either at Andersonville or Florence that did not prove fatal.

The next day Dr. Clark burnt the gangrene from the wound with a blue powder, and, as I was afterwards informed, it took six men to hold me while the burning process was under way, and that I was raving all night; however the following day when the wound was washed, it presented a very good appearance, fleshy parts looking red, the ligaments and bone being rather dark or black looking, the foot a little swollen. The results of the treatment gave me considerable relief from pain and an opportunity to get a little sleep at night, although it was very cold. The rations for several days were one and one half hard tack and four spoonfuls of molasses for 24 hours."[18]

[Florence, Ga November, 1864]

"In November the nights became so cold that many could not sleep, and they would walk up and down the path ways trying to keep warm; towards morning, becoming exhausted, they would lie down on the ground almost anywhere and die. There was plenty of wood outside near the prison, but none was allowed for fires, only one small stick for each 100 men to cook with. In the hospital corner we were furnished plenty of wood and fires were lighted and kept burning during cold nights. The fire over which I was accustomed to crouch nightly was located near a railing dividing the hospital from the prison, and rebel guards paced their beats along the line of the railings to prevent prisoners of the stockade coming into the hospital section. During several severe cold mornings, just about dawn, a poor little fellow would come crawling near the line watching an opportunity when both guards' backs were turned, to snuggle through and lie by the fire until the sun arose, with a favorable opportunity for flanking out occurred. He was bare footed, bare headed, having only a pair of ragged pants and part of a flannel shirt in the shape of clothing or covering for his body. One morning, coming rather late, there were five, including myself, waiting, expecting his visit, and as was our custom, ready to help him get past the guard by going to the ends of their beats and attracting their attention, while others were ready to cover the little fellow with a piece of blanket as soon as he dodged under the rail. But alas! "The red-headed devil" of a lieutenant, having come in early and walking nearby saw the boy get to the fire. He rushed up and grasped him by the hair of his head and the seat of his pants, raised him as easily as a feather and kicked him in the stomach, beat him, then carried him and threw him over the railing, jumped after him, dragged him away quite a distance and left him to die. The five comrades at the fire sat down together after witnessing this brutal fiendish act, talked the matter over, and each took a solemn oath, that if ever it should be their good fortune to live to be released, and they should meet that "red-headed devil", they would kill him on the spot."[19]

[Florence, Ga November 4, 1864]

"One of the incidents of our prison experience at Florence should not pass without notice, and that is the interest the Rebels seemed to manifest regarding the coming presidential election at the North. McClellan was their universal favorite and they built high hopes on his success. "If McClellan is elected," they would say, "we shall have peace in a short time." On election day a quantity of white and black beans were sent into camp to be used for ballots, and all were given a chance to deposit a bean in a bag hung upon the stockade inside of the dead line, and a detachment marched up to the bag, each man being given both a white and a black bean, and allowed to vote which he chose, the white beans representing McClellan, the black ones President Lincoln. The result chagrined the Johnny Rebs very much, the Lincoln votes being considerably in the majority, many democrats voting with republicans for Lincoln."[20]

[Florence, Ga December, 1864]

"The latter part of November, we were told that we were going to be paroled, that an exchange had been agreed upon and we should soon all be sent home. As usual, a few were sanguine to believe; the majority shook their heads and muttered "another rebel hoax.

"On December 4, however, a number from the hospital were taken out and told to sign a parole. It seemed like a pleasant dream, and many expressions of joy were manifested; still it was impossible to remove all doubts from the mind. The day following we marched down and boarded a train for Charleston. The train rolled away amid cheering by ourselves. A happier lot of men never started on a journey. We were going home; that was enough to make us bright, happy and cheerful.

"On the 6th we were marched through the streets of Charleston to the wharf where two steamers were moored. One was the flag of trace boat, containing Rebel officers, the other a large flat deck streamer of transport for the prisoners. On board the steamer, we began to feel like free men again, breathing the pure air coming in from the sea – those dirty, ragged, disease-racked skeleton frames seemed to drink in the inspiration of freedom and joy.

". . . the trip through the harbor of Charleston, passing closely the tumble down walls of old Sumter; after I took part in that long siege on Coles, Folly and Morris islands, (had much interest to me) as one who had been . . . helping to batter down the defenses he now was passing. Reaching the outer harbor towards our fleet, the transports of the Union were waiting to receive us. From the rigging we descry the stars and stripe. To cheer? An attempt was made. Overpowering joy was too much; we could not cheer. It was a touching sight to see upturned faces, gazing upon that flag so dear to their hearts. Passing from the Rebel boat to the deck of the transport New York, it seemed like our cup of happiness was full.

"On Board, we stripped off all of the wretched garments and threw them overboard, gladly witnessing them float away, lice and all. Conveniences for a thorough wash were provided, and though the water was cold we were glad to be clean once more. We were then given a full suit of Uncle Sam's blue, with underclothing, shoes – in fact a full "rig-out". On board the New York we received our first meal of army food. Ah, boys; never again do I expect to partake of such a feast. Salt beef, hard tack and coffee; a pint of hot coffee! . . . We sang, we danced, and every man was full of happiness and contentment. Thus ended our prison life, only to be recalled in our dreams and imagination, or when in after years the seeds of disease there planted in the system would ever be reminders of our terrible experience."[21]

Letter from Private A. Lyth to his Brother

Annapolis Md. Feby 6th 1865

Dear Brother

I take my pen in hand to write you a few lines to let you know how I am getting along here well for the last few days I have been on the lookout for a letter from you and I hope I will get one before this reaches you and I want you to be very punctual in answering my letters you receive.

The most of my time so far I have spent in reading novels but I get tired of the nonsense and wish I was with my Regt then I think of the nice little songs that the "minie balls" sing and the very unpleasant noise of shells bursting also how I would look with but one leg and then I come to the conclusion I am better off here. though to tell the truth I should like to have a chance to pay the rebels for a few of those pints of corn meal that they were so kind to give me while I was pay a visit to "Dixie's Sunny Land" last summer.

The weather here is very pleasant we have light frosts at night but warm pleasant days, there was a few inches of snow on the ground when I first arrived here but that has all disappeared Tom Maharg has got charge of a cook house where they cook for over 400 men so of course Jim [Pixley] and myself suit ourselves as to what we eat in the shape of grub and Tom says if there is an exchange likely to come of soon he will have us detailed in his cooking establishment if we wish it and I have no doubt but we will accept the offer.

I wish you would write as soon as convenient and send me cousin William's directions as I have forgot them and I wish you would send me a Buffalo paper occasionally also a few postage stamps as they are very hard to procure here

In my next letter I can tell you how I come out on my furlough but I think now I shall very likely get my ration money however I cannot tell for certain. Let me know how father is getting along at the oil well I must close now, hoping these few lines will find you all enjoying good health as it leaves me at present thank God.

Give my best respects to Lewis and his sisters also to Jim [Pixley]. My love to you all

Your Affect Brother
Alfred Lyth

Letter from Private A. Lyth to his Brother

Richmond Va April 15th/65

Dear Brother

Before this reaches you I shall be with my Regt We left City Point yesterday afternoon and came up the James river on a steam boat Just below this city the river has been blockaded in 8 or 9 different places. In coming through one place where our men had just opened it large enough for a boat to pass through our steamer struck and nearly capsized and in the excitement 15 men jumped over board and got a shore when the boat righted again and got through they were left behind and had to walk to the city. we landed after sunset and marched through the city to Head Quarters and we went through the part that was burnt down which is about 30 of the finest squares in the city in marching through the streets the boys sung a lot of patriotic song such as 'rally round the flag boys' 'Red White + blue' John Browns Body +c Our Regt is somewhere outside this city part of our Brigade is doing provost duty in the city and they tell us just before Lee surrendered our Regt was in a fight and lost heavily. My headquarters are now in a tobacco wharehouse on Franklin Street I will close now with my love to you all

Alfred

I have sent a Richmond paper

Ed: Alfred rejoined his unit after recovering in Annapolis, MD.

EDWARD COOK AND GEORGE BARNUM:
THOUGHTS ON HOMECOMING

Ed: The Civil War soldiers who enlisted to serve their country in the early 1860s were generally young and unskilled. They were patriotic and enthusiastic about the potential of personal glory on the battlefield. They embodied the spirit of adventure and felt that the war would be a short one. They wanted to enlist early so that they would not miss the experience of a battle. Coming from a culture of independence and democracy, they found the transition from citizen to soldier was a difficult one. Their leaders, usually only a few years older than the recruits themselves, were inexperienced as well in regimentation, discipline, and strategy.

For most soldiers, their letters and journals sent home provided an ongoing and frequent record of their military service and observations. The understanding of the southern region of the country was greatly advanced for both the writers and readers of these letters. Since travel away from the regiment was greatly restricted, the soldiers compared themselves to slaves without the freedom to roam where they wished. Nevertheless, during the course of three years of experience serving in several areas of the South, they were able to describe a region unlike their own with fertile soil, insects, and heat. It was apparent to them that the South had a different economy, topography, and work ethic from what they were used to in the North. They talked with citizens, slaves, and former slaves. They saw plantations and Negro huts. They described poor roads, small villages without public buildings, and houses with chimneys on the outside. Yet, they also wrote of wonderful landscapes, brilliant sunsets and sunrises, unusual fish and shells, fruit trees, beautiful harbors, and sails. They called the soldiers of the Confederacy rebels or secessionists and felt that the South was and should remain a part of the nation. They overcame initial cultural and personal prejudices and learned to respect the blacks as they saw them progress to soldiering and acquit themselves well on the battlefield.

269

Many of the soldiers experienced the ultimate test of the battlefield but mostly endured long stretches of inactivity, boredom, and difficult conditions. They struggled with inadequate and inconsistent food, sickness in the camps, and the humiliation of lice. They felt that their families didn't understand how difficult was the role of a soldier and were insensitive to the criticism from the "boys" of poor strategies used by their commanders with the resulting inability to achieve decisive wins. The men also worried about changes in themselves over the course of their service. They had endured much and hoped that they would "fit in" when they returned home. Their families had the same concerns. The soldiers had been isolated from civilian life for three years. They compared themselves to those men at home who had not served in the Union Army. Would they be welcomed home?

Carolina City, N.C. January 14th 1863

My Captain told me today that the order had come from Head Quarters to detail me as Clerk in the Q.M. Dept. so the thing is now fixed and determined upon. I have to thank Mr. Stowits in part for putting in a good word for me at the right opportunity but above all I am thankful to God for I feel + have felt that it is the answer of a gracious God to the earnest applications of a loving mother + prayerful relatives. You have prayed for my safe return and I trust that the same good being who has thus far kept me from sickness and disease will still continue to afford me his divine protection and finally grant that I may return to you in good bodily health + spiritual condition. Pray on, pray ever, remembering that "whatsoever ye ask in faith, believing it shall be given unto you.

There are a great many of the old Central schoolboys in the army scattered around in different parts of the Country. Joyous indeed will be the time when the war is ended and we all can meet again in our own loved city and grasp each others hand in cordial friendship and upon the same or equal footings. There we shall not know each other by the rank we hold in military life, but again, as before the war broke out, "The Mind shall be the measure of the man" and by this only can we justly claim a rank above the level of mankind.

Folly Island, S.C. Sept. 10th 1863

I have about an inch of candle left after having finished my work this evening and its light shall be devoted to your use. More than a year has now passed since I joined the volunteers. It does not seem so long does it? But when I think of the many things that have transpired in that short space of time then it seems as though I had been a long time away from my dear old home a very long while. One think, within that time 2 or 3 of my girls have got married and I don't know how many more are contemplating the same act so that by the time I return there will be none of them left for me. But never mind "Ed" + I have got a plan of our own. And I will it to you if you won't tell anybody. I have got a country girl picked out that none of you know anything about and when I return Ed + I are going to marry her – perhaps – and take father's land warrant and go out and locate it and turn cozy old farmers in short order. Will you come out and visit us once in a while? I would tell you the girls name but I do not know it myself although I know that there is such a girl.

N. End Folly Island, S.C .Oct. 21th 1863

I have given up drinking tea + coffee since we have been getting in water from the sanitary commission. I bless the sanitary commission and thousands of other soldiers bless them for this great and almost inestimable luxury which they furnish us free gratis. I wish the newspapers would speak of what good the commission is doing and of the opinion that the soldiers entertain towards it for it would encourage the patrons of the commission to greater efforts, and make them happy to know that the soldier received and appreciated the good things that are sent to him and learns that his wants and wishes are not forgotten by those at home

Our batteries have again opened on Sumter and have already succeeded in knocking down the sea wall. There is a heavy smoke hanging over Charleston. But whether it is from shells thrown from our batteries or from fire caused by other means I do not know. We expect every night to hear that our men have stormed Sumter. The firing today is very rapid and heavy and chases away all thoughts of lonliness and fatigue. I had rather hear the firing of cannon and the bursting of shell than the song of the sweetest singer or the chords of the grandest organ. You have no idea of the lonliness that pervades our feelings on the days when there is no firing. It makes us feel sad and almost homesick, but as soon as the cannon begin to roar and the echoes pick up the sound and carry it from wood to cloud & from cloud to wood again, our hearts bound within us and chase away each gloomy thought and drown each homesick sigh. It is our music, and its melody is sweeter to our ears and more touching to our souls than the voice of the lute or the notes of the harp.

Folly Island, S.C. Jany 28th 1864

I was much pleased to receive a letter from you about a week or {unknown word} ago. It came just about to time that as moved our office to Gen. Vogdes head quarters and I was so busy that I did not have time to reply to it by the return steamer, so I will answer it now and have it in good time for the next steamer. I wish I could receive a letter from you much oftener than I do, but I suppose your time is fully occupied in daily duties and leaves you little leisure to dip the pen and write the lines. I think that the soldier will know how to value the services of a wife or mother when he returns to his home, for his experience down here is a lesson that will not soon be forgotten. He will know how to value her ceaseless industry and tireless energy. What better lesson can be taught him than the lesson of experience? The soldier has to cook, wash, mend clothes, darn stockings make {unknown word} + {unknown word} them, and in fact perform for himself all those little things which his wife or mother used to do for him & which we would never have learned to appreciate if he had not turned himself into a bold volunteer. {unknown word} anxious wives and loving mothers bless the day when your sons + husbands joined the army, for when they return to your pleasant homes and cherished society they will value your love and the blessings of home far more than they ever could if they had never been separated from them. An absence of 3 years from everything we hold most dear is a long time to look forward to, but how precious will be the hour when we are again permitted to join them. I think that the happiest day of my whole life – past + future – will be when I return to my home and find all there whom I have left. But if one should be among the missing whether sister, parent or my dear old grandmother I think the happiness should be destroyed. How many hours I have spent in thinking of my reunion with the loved ones at home? I almost fancy sometimes that I am on the point of meeting them, and my happiness is almost complete but alas the dreams of day do not last and my happiness is soon return.

Folly Island, S.C. February 3rd 1864

I assure you my dear sister that you do not look forward to my reunion with my relatives in Buffalo with more interest and anxiety than I do. I often think that I can date my real <u>existence</u> from the time of my return. I believe the time of my return will be the happiest hours of my life and from that day I shall begin to <u>live</u> for I will know how to appreciate and enjoy the comforts + luxuries which this world contains. How often I have repeated the familiar words "There is no place like home" but now I feel the full force of the six little words as I never understood them before. There <u>is</u> no place like home for the heart is there, the thoughts are there, the affections are there, everything that makes life loveable is bound up in the associations connected with that little word 'Home'. I shall be there one of these day – I hope. But if I never am permitted that happiness, then pray to the Being above that I may meet you all as an unbroken & undivided family in that world of endlessness, when, meeting once, we shall never again be disconnected, but dwell on in heavenly love and pure spiritual enjoyment in the presence of our sainted Savior and all the host of bright robed-ones before the throne of that God whose love is infinite.

Morris Island, S.C. April 4th 1864

This cruel war is almost over. I know it. – I feel it and we are coming home 300. Then lookout girls for we are like wild men & with our heads unshaven & unshorn are enough to {unknown word} to flight about. Eleven hundred & Eleventh-Eleven young ladies. I wish they would send some of our regiments back for a home guard; we would take care of the miserable traitorous Copperheads and put them where they would never bother this country again or any other country. Don't they want this war to end? If they don't we do and we are going to end it, if <u>He</u> will permit and surely He is on the side of the right, and end it so that it will stay ended and we will never again be bothered with the sentiments of nullification and secession.

Morris Island, S.C. April 10th 1864

Won't that be a happy time though when this war is ended and we go marching home? Wont our eyes light up with joy and our hearts kindle with gladness as we approach the city & hear the hills ringing & the guns firing and the people shouting because this cruel war is ended and we have reached our home cooking.

Bermuda Hundred, Va. Sunday April 24th 1864

I hope I shall live to march into Buffalo at some future day along with the Bloody Hundredth as everybody calls us.

1st Lt. George Barnum Personal Notes

"The pay master made his appearance before we left Richmond and soon after on August we left for Baltimore and were then transferred to a lot of cattle cars and taken to Albany, New York where we were mustered out.

The Board of Trade at Buffalo with other citizens had sent word that they were going to entertain us on our arrival at Buffalo. As I did not care to make a show of myself marching up the street of Buffalo, I left Albany a day ahead of the regiment and stood on the sidewalk and watched them pass".[22]

PART III

⌒✐⌒

ROLL CALL

Some of the "Boys"

100th Regiment, New York State Volunteers

"Taps have sounded. Lights are out. The soldier sleeps.

Company H

George Barnum- George Barnum died on August 2, 1936, in Duluth, Minnesota, at the age of ninety-two years. After the war, he moved to Duluth to help survey the land for the railroad. In 1894, he organized the Barnum Grain Company and remained as president of the firm until he died. He won fame for her benefactions to charity and welfare benefit organizations, especially for the benefit of orphaned children. The town of Barnum, Minnesota, was named in his honor. Never active in the Grand Army of the Republic, he always turned over his monthly Civil War pension check to the Children's Home. He would occasionally attend the Veterans Association reunion meetings of his old regiment in Buffalo.

George Clark- George Clark was never seen again after the assault of Fort Wagner on July 18, 1863, and was presumed lost.

Edward Cook- Edward Cook died in his home in Oakland, New York, on November 1, 1919, at the age of eighty-one years. He was a resident of Buffalo for many years, and he was engaged in the plumbing and heating business. He was treasurer of the Veterans Association for a number of years and was a regular attendant at the meetings until unable to do so. He was a gentleman of the old school and had countless friends.

Alfred Lyth- Alfred Lyth passed away on December 15, 1924, at the age of eighty-one years. In "civil" life, he was a member of the firm of John Lyth and Sons, a brick and tile business. He also became a director of several Buffalo banks. He was one of the most faithful, active, and dependable members of the Veterans Association from its inception until the day he died.

Thomas Maharg- Thomas Maharg died in his home on November 26, 1931, at the age of eighty-nine years. Returning to Buffalo at the close of the war, he went to work for his uncle Hugh Thompson who operated a soap factory at Chicago and Perry Streets. Entering the real estate business in the 1880s, he was successful almost from the beginning. He retired from active business shortly after building his James Street residence near Elmwood Avenue in 1895 and pursued his hobby of sailing on Lake Erie.

Thomas was an active participant in the Veterans Association, and he was the last Buffalo survivor of the 100th Regiment, New York Volunteers. His death reduced the number of the 100th Regiment survivors to less than a score. Accepting his role as the last man in a philosophical manner, Mr. Maharg had only one complaint in later years. "I can take care of my own affairs each day," he once told an interviewer, "but it is rather lonely to have nearly all your old friends gone. I feel sort of left behind."

Edwin Nichols- Edwin Nichols died in 1891. He had returned to Buffalo after the war but left by 1867 to become a farmer in Leland, Washington. He did not participate in the activities of the Veterans Association.

PART IV

⌒⁂⌒

EPILOGUE

The 100th Regiment, New York State Volunteers was mustered into service between September, 1861, and January, 1862, and mustered out of service on August 28, 1865. Of the 2,021 men that joined the 100th regiment, a total of 294 men died in service. In addition, 264 men were missing and 436 men were wounded. The total of dead, wounded, and missing soldiers amounted to 994 men or 49% of the total regiment![23]

When the men enlisted, they had no appreciation for rules or discipline. It was an army virtually without previous military experience. There were no training programs. It was led by officers similarly without experience and drawn from the ranks of military appointees. In addition, there was inadequate planning for camp sanitation, supplies, proper medical care, or food. Foraging for food and supplies was rampant. Unnecessary hardships such as woolen uniforms to be used in hot climates, lice, maggots in the food, and leaky tents prevailed. However, the youthful soldiers were high spirited and patriotic and developed their own activities of sports, songs, and religious services to occupy them on the camp ground. They were bound to each other by coming from the same area of the country, by fighting to preserve the union, and by sharing extraordinary comradeship and loyalty to their regiment. In short, the soldiers were for the large part ordinary human beings who were rendered extraordinary by their experience.

"In the *History of the One-Hundredth, New York State Volunteers,* the soldiers who authored this book chose to reflect upon the war and express their hope for the future of their young republic. It is fitting to close with their words as well.

"The task is done. The marches, battles and sieges in which the one Hundredth took a prominent and honorable part are recorded . . . . The battles have been refought. During the past year by night and by day, have we stood by the side of dead and wounded comrades, and felt, oh! how intensely, the great sacrifice of human life for the restoration of the Union.

"We have stood by the side of open graves on Morris Island, and before Richmond and Petersburg, with an acute anguish, as deeply felt in imagery, as when the gloom of the hour enthralled us. *Now* we hope to push the *fact* and *thought* far into the mists of memory, and come up as cheerfully as we may have to the consideration of the fruits and blessing of that great, grand and glorious struggle for the life and existence of the nation.

"In the whirl of the age, this great civil war has passed into the shadow-land of history. So recent, that the grass has barely grown over the graves of thousands of the fallen. As a soldier, we were taught to love our country more. The sky, the green earth, the blue waters, *all,* are dearer to us now, than when we had no this bitter lesson of sanguinary war. We were pleased to veil from memory most of the events that attend our thoughts; but they are ever present as the tuition for the practical lessen we have learned, to value the country beyond compare, and daily teach the children under our care to love it beyond words to express.

"The "*unmarked graves*" throughout all the South appeal to us: at Gettysburg, Fortress Monroe, Andersonville, and Morris Island, speaking in tones of thrilling import:-we died that you might live. Their bones are bleaching on the Isles, and along the streams, to be remembered as the sacrifice for the existence of the best and freest government the world has ever seen. Their forms are ever present, and their deeds are held in grateful remembrances. Our fates might have been reversed. They might have stood where we stand, while we would have been known only as they are known, in praise, in story and in song. Let us not think lightly, not undervalue the martyred dead, who have been sacrificed in a war to save and perpetuate the Union and every star in the "Dear Old Flag". Thank God, they are all there; and those of us, who have survived the crimsoned ordeal, will ever cherish this symbol of our national unity; knowing, that when kissed by the breezes of all lands, the nations will feel and know, that the flag is the emblem of unity and freedom, baptized in the blood of heroes, for its protection and perpetuity, while government lasts and the living millions are shadowed with its folds of stripes and stars.

"As a soldiery, we are not forgotten. In the battle and strife of material life, the soldier may feel that he is neglected, but reflection will speak to him the truth; that it cannot be, as long as memory lasts and government exists, and these waters of the lakes rest in their cradled basins, and the Niagara's current moves swiftly along to the cataract's verge, where rising mists an incense offered to the Giver of all blessings, of a nation's gratitude for the preservation of its unity, peace and power forever.

"To live the life of a soldier does not occur to the citizen but rarely in the course of a century, or in the life of a nation. As soldiers, we tried to do our duty; as citizens, we rejoice. Should foreign foes, or factious one at home, seek again the life of the nation in our day, and then the military culture acquired will serve us, as in the days of the rebellion.

"As a people may we know war no more. May neither our children nor our children's children every act its bloody drama; but in its growth, enterprise, power and vitality, may this youthful republic enjoy peace and freedom evermore.

Hosannas for a land redeemed
The bayonet sheathed, the cannons dumb;
Passed, as some horror, we have dreamed
The fiery meters that have streamed
Threat'ning within our homes to come.

Again, our Banner floats abroad,
Gone the one stain, that on it fell;
And battered by His chast'nigh rod,
With streaming eyes uplift to God,
We say: 'He doeth all things well'"[24]

NOTES

⁓

1. *Veterans Association, 100ᵗʰ Regiment-Proceedings of the Third Annual Reunion, July 18, 1887* (Buffalo, New York, 1892) pages 6-12.

2. George Barnum, Personal Notes, March 7, 1932, page 3.

3. Veterans Association, page 14.

4. Ibid., page 14

5. Ibid., page 15

6. Ibid., page 15

7. Ibid., page 15.

8. Diary of E. Nichols, *Veterans Association of the 100ᵗʰ Regiment, N. Y. State Volunteers – Proceedings of the Thirty-Seventh Annual Reunion held at Buffalo, New York on July 18, 1923*, pages 14-15.

9. Ibid., page 17-19.

10. Ibid., page 19.

11. Ibid., page 16.

12. *Veterans Association, 100th Regiment-Proceedings of the Third Annual Reunion, July 4, 1889* (Buffalo, New York, 1892) pages 21-24

13. *Ibid.*, pages 25-26.

14. *Ibid.*, page 28.

15. *Ibid.*, page 25-26.

16. *Ibid.*, pages 34-35

17. *Ibid.*, page 37.

18. *Ibid.*, pages 42-46.

19. *Ibid.*, pages 47-48.

20. *Ibid.*, page 46.

21. *Ibid.*, page 49-50.

22. Barnum, page 14.

23. Frederick Phisterer, *New York in the War of the Rebellion,* (Albany, New York: 3rd ed. (Albany, New York, J. B. Lyon Company, 1912).

24. George H. Stowits, *History of the One Hundredth Regiment of New York State Volunteers* (Buffalo, New York: Printing House of Matthews & Warren, 1870), pages 359-362.

BIBLIOGRAPHY

Books:

Bradshaw, Timothy E. Jr. *Battery Wagner.* Columbia, South Carolina: Palmetto Historical Works. 1993

Bryan, Charles F. Jr. and Lankford, Nelsen, ed. *Eye of the Storm.* New York, New York: The Free Press, 2000

Burton E. Milby. *The Siege of Charleston 1861-1865.* Columbia, South Carolina: University of South Carolina Press, 1970

Billings, John D. *Hard Tack and Coffee,* Old Saybrook, Connecticut, Konecky and Konecky, 1887

Cimbala, Paul A. and Miller, Randall M. , ed, *Union Soldiers and the Northern Home Front,* New York, New York, Fordham University Press, 2002

Horn, John. *The Petersburg Campaign June 1864 – April, 1865.* Conshohocken, Pennsylvania: Combined Publishing Company, 2000

King, W. C. and Derby, W. P. of the 27th Maine. *Camp-Fire Sketches and Battlefield Echoes* Springfield, Massachusetts, King, Richardson and Co, 1886

Lankford, Nelson. *Richmond Burning.* New York, New York: Penguin Books, 2002

Little, Henry F. W., *The 7ʰ New Hampshire Volunteers in the War of the Rebellion* Concord, New Hampshire, Ira. C. Evans, 1896

Longacre, Edward G. *Army of Amateurs.* Mechanicsburg, Pennsylvania: Stackpole Books, 1997

Marvel, William. *Andersonville, The Last Depot* Chapel Hill, North Carolina: The University of North Carolina Press, 1994

McPherson, James. M. *For Cause and Comrades*, New York, New York, Oxford University Press, 1997

Meer, Sarah, *Uncle Tom Mania: Slavery, Minstrelsy and Trans-Atlantic Culture in the 1850's*, Athens, Georgia, University of George Press, 2005

Phisterer, Frederick. *New York in the War of the Rebellion, 3ʳᵈ Ed.* Albany, New York: J. B. Lyon Company, 1912

Ray, Jean R. *The Diary of a Dead Man 1862-1864.* New York, New York: Eastern Acorn Press, 1981

Robertson, William Glenn. *Back Door to Richmond.* Baton Rouge, (Louisiana; Louisiana State University Press, 1987

Stowits, George H. *History of the One Hundredth Regiment of New York State Volunteers.* Buffalo, New York: Printing House of Matthews & Warren, 1870

Geoffrey C. Ward,.*The Civil War.* New York, New York: Alfred A. Knopf, Inc., 1990

Wheeler, Richard. *Voices of the Civil War.* New York, New York: Thomas Y. Cronell Company, 1976

Winik, Jay. *April, 1865, The Month that Saved America.* New York, New York: Harper Collins Publishing Co., 2001

Wise, Stephen R. *Gate of Hell.* Columbia, South Carolina: University of South Carolinas Press, 1994

Woodhead, Henry. *Voices of the Civil War.* Alexandria, Virginia: Time-Life Books, 1997

Periodicals, Diaries and other Publications:

Personal Notes, George Barnum, March 7, 1932

Diary, Alfred Lyth

Diary, Edwin Nichols

Index

CPSIA information can be obtained at www.ICGtesting.com
Printed in the USA
LVOW130958270912

300474LV00005B/85/P